SOY *of* COOKING

Easy-to-Make Vegetarian, Low-Fat, Fat-Free, and Antioxidant-Rich Gourmet Recipes

Marie Oser

JOHN WILEY & SONS, INC.

New York • Chichester • Weinheim • Brisbane • Singapore • Toronto

This book is printed on acid-free paper. ♾

Photography: John Strange Photography

Published by John Wiley & Sons, Inc.
Published simultaneously in Canada
Previously published by Chronimed Publishing

ISBN: 0-471-34705-1

Printed in the United States of America

10 9 8 7 6 5 4 3

Dedication

With much love and gratitude to my husband, Lanny, whose steadfast support of my work makes everything possible.

And our children, Kyra and Justin. They are my light and my inspiration.

Grateful acknowledgment to:

Everyone at Chronimed Publishing, especially David Wexler, who "really, really, really" wanted to do this book.

Jeff Braun, my editor, whose skillful eye, warm humor, and good nature made this project a joy to complete.

Tom McReynolds, a.k.a. "Tommy Tofu," a gifted writer and exceptional country music talent, for his valued input and ongoing support. While a great title is worth a thousand pictures, when I "hit a wall" looking for just the right segue, I know I can depend on Tom.

Ellen Tarantino, my personal assistant, who is always there for me, doing whatever is needed, without complaint. She is a jewel.

Mary Lisardi, my computer maven, and Pat Moore, my personal cheerleader, who have provided me with indispensable encouragement.

Judy Rae, Dale Hallcom, Mimi Clark, and Rosemary Campagna for valued recipe testing, tasting, and input.

The many nutrition professionals, food scientists, and biochemists who have shared research and lent their expertise to this work, among them:

Mark Messina, Ph.D., for his ongoing distinguished efforts in disseminating valuable information regarding the beneficial effects of including soyfoods in the diet. And Ginny Messina, R.D., M.P.H., whose considerate and thoughtful manner make speaking with her a pleasure.

The American Soybean Association, especially Susie Oberdahloff, for providing a wealth of data for my soy endeavor.

William Shurtleff of The Soyfoods Center, for information and advice that have contributed to this effort.

Scott Sanders, Ph.D., of Creative Food Consultants, and Russ Bianchi, Ph.D., of LSI Specialty Products, who are always generous with their time, and have allowed me free rein to pick their considerable brains.

Contents

Foreword

The soybean's tiny size belies the power within. For decades, white-coated investigators have teased this tiny legume apart seeking to explain its strength against cancer, heart disease, and day-to-day annoyances, like hot flashes. And they have found hundreds of natural compounds hidden in the soybean that drive cholesterol levels down, put hormones into balance, activate toxin-destroying enzymes, and work other wonders.

A second group of white-coated explorers are discovering the bean's magic in the kitchen. Just as carbon can turn into diamonds or pencil lead, the diverse manifestations of the soybean are no less remarkable. It is steamed in the pod as an appetizer and turned into tempeh to replace burgers or sausage. When transformed into tofu, it becomes the most versatile ingredient ever to find its way into the pantry. Soy also becomes hot dogs, sloppy joes, tacos, pizza topping, and spaghetti sauce.

Soy of Cooking is a treasury of recipes that are quick, easy, and wonderfully tasty. The heartiest meal remains low in fat, and none has even a speck of cholesterol.

Marie Oser has done a wonderful job in bringing together this extraordinary compilation. May you enjoy these delicious foods in the very best of health.

Neal D. Barnard, M.D.
President, Physicians Committee for Responsible Medicine, Washington, D.C.

Preface

Soyfoods are hot! Nutrient-rich soybeans are proving to be an important dietary staple. Recent findings show that substances found exclusively in soybeans can lower cholesterol and help prevent disease. Numerous studies attest to the role soyfoods can play in preventing many forms of cancer, heart disease, and osteoporosis, and in controlling diabetes. How can you take advantage of the unique properties of this wonderpod? If the only soyfood you know is tofu, then read on.

Adding soy to your diet has never been easier. There is a great variety of new and lighter soy products, which I have used to create these delectable dishes. Although widely available, some of these wonderful soyfoods may be unfamiliar to some cooks. Not to worry, though, just turn to the Soyfoods Pantry (page 17) to learn about both new and traditional soy products. While the majority of ingredients used in *Soy of Cooking* are found in supermarkets and health food stores across the country, the Quick Guide to Ingredients and the Resource Guide will help you locate products.

Soyfoods are delicious! The new meat analogues defy detection by even the most skeptical and can help to recreate your favorite traditional meals, healthfully. Lite silken tofu and soymilk lite are very low-fat and versatile ingredients that add richness and creaminess to dips, quiches, soups, sauces, cakes, and pies. When you are looking for something to "sink your teeth into," the flavorful, chewy texture of soy tempeh will surely fill the bill. Using easy, innovative techniques and marinades, you can change the texture of tofu to a richly flavored, meaty consistency. Soy flour and soy grits are used to boost the nutrition of baked goods while adding a pleasant nuttiness.

These are only a few of the many wonderful soyfoods I have used to create this collection. There are 31 tasty ingredients derived from soybeans listed in the Soyfoods Pantry, and this is only the beginning. You'll be amazed by the number of innovative soy products that continue to enter the market every day.

The new and lighter soyfoods offer the health conscious cook the ability to create exciting meals—delicious meals with many added health benefits; enticing meals without the high-fat and cholesterol-laden ingredients offered at virtually every meal by, as John Robbins refers to it, the Great American Food Machine. *Soy of Cooking* speaks to the role that soyfoods can play in replacing unhealthy foods. It is a cookbook that can help you move toward a well-balanced diet that is low in fat, high in fiber, rich in phytochemicals, and cholesterol free. All this is made easy because soyfoods, especially lower-fat ones, are now widely available.

Soyfoods play the starring role in *Soy of Cooking,* but there is a terrific supporting cast of hearty whole grains, luscious fruits, vegetables, and legumes, all rich in nutrients and phytochemicals. In fact, the recipes here contain no food products from animal sources—no meat, fish, eggs, or dairy products. They are completely vegetarian meals. You will find that your opportunity to reap the impressive health benefits of replacing animal products with soyfoods is enhanced exponentially by including the many other important plant foods in your diet.

I will show you how to create an enticing variety of delectably satisfying meals, from appetizer to dessert, while always keeping fat to a minimum. No recipe exceeds 5 grams of fat per serving. Indeed, they average about 3 grams of fat.

The extra good news is that these guiltless, low-fat dishes are as delectable as they are healthful. Family and friends will marvel at the diversity of flavors and presentations you can achieve using the ingredients and techniques outlined here for the health conscious cook. *Soy of Cooking* is more than a cookbook. It holds the key to what most enlightened physicians and nutritionists consider the optimal diet. Using this book daily will lead you to a more healthful lifestyle.

Soy of Cooking is your guidebook for expanding your culinary repertoire. The recipes are easy to follow and the recommended ingredients are wholesome and of high quality. Each recipe is a delicious opportunity to incorporate soyfoods into your diet. My hope is that these luscious gourmet dishes will inspire you to include this important staple in your diet. Join me and explore the amazing world of soy. Your heart will thank you for it!

Marie Oser

One more thought: Regarding the type of diet presented in *Soy of Cooking,* I am certainly not the first person to promote vegetarian-centered cuisine. However, if I have piqued your interest, I heartily recommend the books of John Robbins, president of the EarthSave Foundation (see Recommended Reading, page 249). Robbins' book, *Diet for a New America,* an international bestseller that was nominated for a Pulitzer Prize, has had a tremendous impact. First printed in 1987, it has changed the lives of many. My son Justin, now 16, read the book when he was 10 and has been vegetarian ever since. *May All Be Fed,* a more recent work from Robbins, is a beautifully written guide to eating and to understanding how our food choices affect our health and the planet. John Robbins' wisdom and compassion can also encourage you toward a more healthful lifestyle.

Introduction

Times are rapidly changing. Just look around. Veggie burgers are turning up on restaurant menus—not to mention supermarket shelves, next to the vegetarian hot dogs. And don't be surprised if the next time you ask someone what they are planning to make for dinner tonight, they say, "tempeh sloppy joes," "tofu stir-fry," or "vegetarian chili over rice."

Soy of Cooking is riding the crest of a wave—the movement toward a plant-based diet. A 1992 Yankelovich survey sponsored by *Vegetarian Times* magazine found that almost 7 percent of American adults are making an effort to eat less meat and identify themselves as vegetarians. That same year, the National Restaurant Association conducted a survey that found that 20 percent of restaurant-goers are looking for a meatless entrée when they eat out.

The movement toward a plant-based diet isn't just a fad—it's a permanent lifestyle shift. No wonder. Driving the shift is a mountain of scientific research linking plant-based diets with lower rates of coronary artery disease, several types of cancer, obesity, high blood pressure, and adult onset diabetes. Even severe atherosclerosis has been shown to be reversible in some cases, without the use of drugs or surgery, when a low-fat vegetarian diet is eaten.

The benefits of a plant-based diet are difficult to ignore. Foods of plant origin contain fiber, vitamins, minerals, and phytochemicals, substances that protect against disease. Soyfoods, for instance, have been determined to contain isoflavones, phytochemicals which may have cancer-fighting properties.

In contrast, animal products—meat, eggs, and high-fat dairy products—are devoid of fiber and contain saturated fat and cholesterol, substances that are disease-promoting in the amounts eaten by most people in Western countries. Animal products contribute greatly to the overabundance of protein and total fat in the diet, as well.

We are learning more about the complexities of nutrition and the links between diet and health every day. What now appears to be clear is that increasing the ratio of plant to animal products in your diet is a smart move. That means making fruits, vegetables, grains, and legumes (dried beans and peas) the foundation foods of your diet. It also means cutting way back on your consumption of foods of animal origin—all types of meat, eggs, and fatty dairy products.

In its 1993 position paper on vegetarian diets, The American Dietetic Association acknowledges that "vegetarian diets are healthful and nutritionally adequate when they are appropriately planned." In fact, foods of animal origin are not necessary at all for good health. Assuming that reasonable attention is paid to basic principles of nutrition (junk-food junkies, that caveat is meant for you), then a diet comprised of fruits, vegetables, grains and grain products, and legumes can provide you with all of the nutrition you need while helping you avoid the dietary excesses that characterize the typical Western diet.

If you do choose to eat animal products, however, they should be a minor part of your meals. If you eat them, think of meats, eggs, and dairy products as condiments or side-dishes—minor ingredients in a dish—rather than the focal point of the plate.

How does soy figure into the picture? Soyfoods can help ease the transition to a more plant-based diet. Soy products such as tempeh, tofu, soymilk, textured vegetable protein, and others make great substitutes for meat, eggs, and dairy products in traditional recipes. Need something fun to take to a summer cookout? Try veggie burgers and tofu hot dogs. They taste great. Have a hankering for quiche, scrambled eggs, or egg salad sandwiches? They can all be made with tofu instead of eggs—deliciously. Your favorite dip. Soups. Sauces. Casseroles. You name it. Almost all of your favorite recipes can be modified by using soy products in place of animal products.

Soy of Cooking will show you how delicious, nutritious, and versatile soy foods can be. By integrating low-fat soy foods into your daily diet and substituting them for animal products, you'll benefit two ways. You'll get the good qualities of soy, packed with vitamins, minerals, and phytochemicals. At the same time, you'll displace the biggest sources of fat, saturated fat, and cholesterol in your diet.

You may find that you have more variety in your diet, as well. Dishes made with soy products can be an introduction to cuisines of other cultures, many of which have vegetarian traditions. You'll discover a whole new world of dishes based not only on soy but on other legumes, grains, vegetables, and fruits. Some people think that when one reduces or eliminates meat, the diet becomes more limited. Most vegetarians, however, would say the opposite is true. When meals are based on foods of plant origin, the variety is nearly endless.

Enjoy the delicious, health-supporting recipes in *Soy of Cooking* and learn how to incorporate versatile soy foods into your meals. Above all, let *Soy of Cooking* help you take the first steps away from yesterday's "meat and potato" ways, to swap old traditions for new, and to make the transition to a healthful, satisfying plant-based diet.

Suzanne Havala, M.S., R.D., F.A.D.A.
Registered dietitian and author of Shopping for Health: A Nutritionist's Aisle-by-Aisle Guide to Smart, Low-Fat Choices at the Supermarket *and* Simple, Lowfat & Vegetarian

SOY *of* COOKING

Soyfood for Thought

How can you adopt a diet that will meet your nutritional needs and protect health? Is there a nutrition plan to prevent heart disease, lower the risk of cancer, even help you lose weight? Is there a practical and appealing approach to a more healthful eating style? These are just a few of the questions that have spurred scientists and physicians to investigate the plant kingdom in a quest for the optimal diet.

A number of prominent medical professionals recommend a diet based on four food groups that may surprise some readers. The food groups are grains, legumes, vegetables, and fruits. Neal Barnard, M.D., is president of Physicians Committee for Responsible Medicine (PCRM), in Washington, D.C., and a well known author. He cites overwhelming evidence that this approach to a more wholesome lifestyle can help prevent disease and promote health. He presents this powerful menu as an ideal prescription for lowering cholesterol, staying slim, preventing cancer, and maybe even slowing the effects of aging. In his latest book, Dr. Barnard's nutrition strategies are offered as a defense against the chemical assualts that are fundamental to the aging process. Though we have not yet discovered the "fountain of youth," it is the power of your food choices that will counteract the effects of aging. Make healthy food choices and you will aid the body in strengthening bones, cleaning arteries, dissolving fat, rejuvenating skin, and boosting the immune system.

The New England Journal of Medicine, The Journal of the American Medical Association, and many respected professional groups all link nutrition and lifestyle to health. They report that there are substances in vegetables, not only vitamins and minerals, which appear to have a protective effect against certain diseases, and that nutrition can play a vital role in the prevention, treatment, and cure of a variety of ailments.

MOVING FROM MEAT TO SOY

The counterpoint to the high-fat, fiber-barren American diet is a naturally low-fat, high-fiber, plant-based diet. Even the government endorses plant-based diets.

The latest Dietary Guidelines for Americans, released by the U.S. Department of Agriculture early in 1996, endorses vegetarian diets for the first time since it started issuing dietary guidelines in 1916. The guidelines are the official blueprint for school lunches and all other federal nutrition programs. The revised guidelines, championed by PCRM, won the support of top medical authorities, such as the famed pediatrician Benjamin Spock, M.D., Colin Campbell, Ph.D., of the China Health Study of Oxford and Cornell, and Henry Heimlich, M.D., who invented the lifesaving technique that has saved over 50,000 lives in the last 25 years. The Dietary Guidelines Advisory Committee endorsed the safety of vegetarian diets and pointed out that the failure to include vegetarian diets in the past was a serious oversight.

Dean Ornish, M.D., is another physician and author who makes a strong case for setting aside the traditional meat and potatoes approach to eating. Dr. Ornish's Preventive Medicine Research Institute has been enormously successful in reversing heart disease through its Life Choice Program. The program uses no cholesterol-lowering drugs or surgery; instead it focuses on a low-fat vegetarian diet, stress management, smoking cessation, moderate exercise, and emotional support. In the first randomized, controlled clinical study of its kind, the "Lifestyle Heart Trial" demonstrated that arteries that have become clogged with fatty deposits actually respond to lifestyle and dietary changes. Though the major focus of the research was on preventing and reversing heart disease, participants in the Ornish program lost an average of 22 pounds while eating abundantly. Dr. Ornish's program was a revolutionary approach that the medical establishment has recognized as both sensible and well founded.

A study published recently in the *Journal of the American College of Nutrition* showed that patients following a very low-fat, plant-based vegetarian diet (no eggs or dairy products), experienced a significant lowering of serum cholesterol and blood pressure in only 12 days. John McDougall, M.D., the study's principal investigator and medical director of The McDougall Program, conducted the study with colleagues at St. Helena's Hospital and Health Center in Deer Park, California. They examined 500 patients with high cholesterol who participated in an intensive 12-day live-in program focusing on dietary modification, moderate exercise, and stress management over six years, between 1986 and 1992. (The program's criteria for high cholesterol is any measurement over 200 mg/dl, and participants are encouraged to continue working toward a goal of 150 to 160 mg/dl when they finish the 12-day program.) Participants were fed a vegetarian diet that was 5 percent fat, 12 percent protein, and 83 percent carbohydrate.

The results were very encouraging. On average, participants in the short-term program reduced their total serum cholesterol by 11 percent and blood pressure by 6 percent. If they continued over many years to observe the dietary and lifestyle changes learned during the live-in program, this reduction would translate into a 22 to 33 percent decrease in risk of dying from coronary heart disease. While more comparative studies are needed regarding the effects of the plant-based, very-low-fat diet on triglycerides as well as total and HDL cholesterol, the researchers concluded that dietary and lifestyle changes prescribed by the McDougall Program are an effective way to lower total serum cholesterol and blood pressure.

It seems as though a new study is released every day that emphasizes the need to reassess the meat-centered diet that has been the gold standard most of this century. But how does one make the necessary changes in diet and lifestyle without sacrificing the flavor, texture, and protein in familiar dishes? Is there an easy way to make the transition? Enter the soybean.

THE HEALTH BENEFITS OF SOY PROTEIN

Soybeans are nutrient-rich legumes. And replacing animal protein with soy protein makes good sense. Soy protein is considered essentially equal in quality to animal protein, like that in meat, milk, and eggs, and is recognized by the U.S. government as a protein alternative equivalent to meat.

Typically, the average American diet contributes twice the amount of protein necessary—approximately 70 percent—from animal sources. In China, protein intake averages only about two-thirds of what it is in the West, and only about 10 percent of the total protein intake is from animal sources. Contrary to general impression, an abundance of quality protein is available in the plant kingdom. Furthermore, including a variety of wholesome grains, legumes, vegetables, and fruits in your daily diet will ensure well-balanced nutrition.

A vegetarian diet provides plenty of protein without any careful planning, provided it is drawn from a variety of foods. The concept of "protein complementing," requiring various food combinations at each meal to assure adequate protein, has been discarded, as dietitians have found that any varied diet of plant foods provides more than enough protein.

Soybeans are much more than an excellent source of high-quality protein. They are also rich in calcium, iron, zinc, and many of the B vitamins. A healthy diet is important for strong bones. Would you guess that green leafy vegetables provide a better source of calcium than milk? Well, they do because the calcium in vegetables such as kale is more easily absorbed. The calcium in soyfoods is also well absorbed by the body, and there is evidence that soy protein may ward off osteoporosis by improving calcium utilization. Some brands of tofu are excellent sources of calcium because they are coagulated with calcium salt. Depending on how it is processed, a half cup of tofu can provide between 80 and 435 milligrams of calcium.

CALCIUM IN SOYFOODS

Soyfood	Calcium
Soybeans, mature, 1/2 cup	80 mg.
Soybeans, green, 1/2 cup	130 mg.
Tempeh, 1/2 cup	77 mg.
Tofu, 1/2 cup	130 mg.
TVP, 1/2 cup prepared	85 mg.
Soymilk, 1 cup	80 mg.
Soymilk, fortified, 1 cup	250-300 mg.

REDUCING THE RISK OF CANCER AND MORE

Beyond the excellent nutritional quality of soyfoods, consider that an impressive amount of research has shown that substances found almost exclusively in soyfoods can have an impressive effect on our health. There is a class of non-nutritive components found only in plant foods called phytochemicals (which actually means plant chemicals). These phytochemicals have been investigated by the scientific community in recent years because of the beneficial way in which they can affect our health. Many plants contain plant estrogens or phytoestrogens, and soybeans contain high levels of a unique type of phytoestrogen called isoflavones. It is the isoflavones in soybeans that are credited with the role that soyfoods play in cancer prevention and reducing the risk of osteoporosis.

In the mid 1980s, studies began to suggest that an isoflavone in soybeans, genistein, could be an effective weapon against many types of cancer. A number of scientific studies conducted in China and Japan have shown that frequent consumers of tofu and soymilk have a lower cancer risk than those who rarely consume these foods.

Early in 1994, the first international symposium on the "Role of Soy in Preventing and Treating Chronic Diseases" was held in Phoenix, Arizona, and chaired by Mark Messina, Ph.D., a leading authority in the area of soyfoods and a former program director at the National Cancer Institute. Forty speakers presented papers with topics that included studying the effect of soyfoods in lowering blood cholesterol levels and reducing the effects of chemical carcinogens. Almost 30 other studies were also presented. The consensus at the conference was that if people consumed more soyfoods, they would reduce their risk of heart disease and some forms of cancer.

Some of the more intriguing studies dealt with the role of soyfoods in the reduction of bone mineral loss and minimizing some of the unpleasant effects of menopause. It seems that there is no Japanese phrase for "hot flashes," and that Japanese women who consume a traditional diet high in soy experience a mild menopause. Bones tend to be stronger in Asia and broken hips and spinal fractures are less common. Western women consume much more meat and four times as much fat as do women on traditional Asian rice-based diets, but they consume only one-fourth to one-half the fiber. Women who enter menopause on a low-fat vegetarian diet often breeze right through it, with mild or even nonexistent symptoms.

Researchers investigating the relationship between soyfood consumption and cancer prevention at the National Cancer Institute found that soyfoods are rich in anticarcinogens. It was reported that genistein, the main isoflavone found in soybeans, not only can inhibit cancer cell growth, it can also cause cancer cells to differentiate—that is, to go from cancer cells to normal cells, actually reversing the cancer process. In addition, researchers indicate that genistein inhibits angiogenesis, the growth of blood vessels that allows tumors to grow beyond a very small size.

In 1995 alone, more than 300 scientific papers were published attributing potent cancer-fighting characteristics to genistein. But how much isoflavone, particularly genistein, is needed each day to make a difference? That's difficult to say because cancer is affected by many factors. However, based on epidemiological studies, Mark and Ginny Messina (authors of *The Simple Soybean and Your Health*) recommend one serving of soyfoods a day—which provides approximately 25 to 40 milligrams of isoflavones—in order to reduce the risk of cancer.

Isoflavones, unlike vitamins, are not destroyed by conventional cooking methods. The following is the isoflavone content of selected foods:

SOYFOOD	ISOFLAVONE
Soymilk, 1 cup	40 mg.
Tofu, 1/2 cup	40 mg.
Tempeh, 1/2 cup	40 mg.
TVP, prepared, 1/2 cup	35 mg.
Miso, 1/2 cup	40 mg.
Soy flour, 1/2 cup	50 mg.
Soybeans, cooked, 1/2 cup	35 mg.
Soynuts, 1 oz.	40 mg.

Another interesting benefit of a soyfoods-based diet is its effect on glucose control. Recently, scientists have become interested in the role of soyfoods in controlling diabetes. A number of studies indicate that a healthful diet and exercise are the keys to managing diabetes. A diet that is abundant in complex carbohydrates and very low in fat is especially important. Soybeans have a low glycemic index, which is a measure of how much blood sugar rises when a particular food is consumed. Foods with a low glycemic index produce a smaller rise in blood glucose, which is helpful in controlling diabetes. Soybean's low glycemic index (lower than any other bean) may occur because soybeans are high in compounds called phytates and tannins. These substances slow the absorption of the starch in soybeans.

While weight loss is fundamental in treating type II diabetes, which does not require insulin, scientists have found that in both types of diabetes, soluble fiber can be helpful in glucose control by delaying the absorption of nutrients into the bloodstream. Soybeans and some soyfoods like tempeh, textured soy protein, and soy flour are rich in soluble fiber. To control blood sugar, many people plan their meals and snacks using the Exchange Lists for Meal Planning, developed and published by the American Dietetic Association and American Diabetes Association. Soyfoods can be included in this menu planning approach using the following exchanges:

SOYFOOD	EXCHANGE
Soybeans, 1/2 cup	1 protein
Tofu, 1/2 cup	1 protein
Tofu hot dog, 1	1 protein
Tempeh, 1/4 cup	1 protein
Roasted soynuts, 1/4 cup	1 protein
TVP, prepared, 1/4 cup	1 protein
Soy cheese, 1 oz.	1 protein, 1 fat
Low-fat soymilk, 1 cup	1 milk
Regular soymilk, 1 cup	1 milk, 1 fat

FIGHTING CHOLESTEROL

Heart disease is still the number one killer in this country, and no one disputes the fact that elevated cholesterol levels sharply increase the risk of heart disease and stroke. At the same time, an impressive amount of research has shown that eating soyfoods can dramatically lower cholesterol levels in the blood. Soy may prevent heart disease in many ways. Certainly, reducing blood cholesterol is an important factor, however, there are many other factors that affect the risk of heart disease. Though it is not yet clear that soy protein inhibits cholesterol oxidation (which occurs when cholesterol that has been exposed to oxygen undergoes structural changes and, as such, can damage the arteries), genistein has been shown, in test tubes, to inhibit the growth of cells that form the plaque that lines arteries. Genistein may also inhibit the formation of blood clots.

In August of 1995, the *New England Journal of Medicine* published a study by James Anderson, M.D., which concluded that adding soy protein to a low-fat diet appears to be one of the most potent cholesterol fighters. This study suggested that moderately high to high levels of cholesterol are significantly lowered by introducing soy protein into the diet. They found that an average of 47 grams of soy protein per day can decrease low-density lipoproteins (LDL)—the bad cholesterol—by 12.9 percent in just one month, while leaving the high-density lipoproteins (HDL)—the good cholesterol—alone. Most intriguing, they found that the higher the concentration of cholesterol in the blood the greater the power of soy to reduce it. At 300 milligrams per deciliter of blood, the cholesterol level plunged by 20 percent. Although these effects of soy are considered speculative, they indicate that eating soyfoods is a wise choice and may help protect against heart disease.

A Healthy Kitchen

Healthy meals and snacks start with healthy ingredients. In *Soy of Cooking,* you will find that added fat is kept to a minimum, and butter, shortening, and margarine are never used. Butter is unnecessary in my approach to gourmet food; it is very high in fat and cholesterol and is an animal product. Shortening and margarine are hardly health foods since they contain unwanted trans-fatty acids produced by the addition of an extra hydrogen atom. They are hydrogenated, like many oils, which are labeled as "partially hydrogenated." Hydrogenated oils should be avoided because several studies have suggested that the trans-fatty acids created in this process make them physically equivalent to animal fats. Unenlightened commercial bakers like to use hydrogenated oils because they extend shelf life. The baked goods found in this cookbook are heavenly without added fat.

OLIVE OIL

You will note that in those recipes that use oil, vegetable oil cooking spray and olive oil are listed. Pump action sprays made with canola oils are wonderful for lubricating baking pans, or anywhere a little oil is needed. Canola oil is very low in saturated fat and has a neutral flavor. Olive oil is largely monounsaturated fat and, as such, lowers the LDL (bad) cholesterol, and raises the HDL (good) cholesterol. Studies of the traditional Mediterranean diet conclude that regular olive oil consumption lowers arterial blood pressure and reduces the risk of stroke. Olive oil contains antioxidants that guard against free radical damage to cells—the type of damage that precipitates cancers and the unwanted effects of aging. This is not to say that you should increase the amount of fat in your diet. What is recommended here is to replace the unhealthy fats with monounsaturated fat, while reducing the overall amount of fat in the diet.

The olive oil I prefer to use is extra virgin olive oil. It is the finest grade, and therefore the most expensive, but it has a rich, full-bodied flavor and a lovely fruitiness. I feel the same way about using the best quality olive oil as I do about using a good quality wine in cooking. These ingredients impart a special flavor and a distinctive gourmet character to the finished dish. Some would say that it is a waste to use extra virgin olive oil for cooking, but even in small amounts it makes a difference. In addition, because it is used in small quantities, a bottle will last a long time. Virgin olive oil is somewhat similar to extra virgin in flavor, though it is slightly more acidic. It is less expensive than the higher grade and may be substituted with good results.

GARLIC

The most often combined ingredients in my kitchen are onions, olive oil, and garlic. It is a marriage made in heaven, not only because of the superior flavor, but because of their special protective qualities. Garlic is actually a member of the lily family and is closely related to the onion. When you cook with these gourmet treasures, you might well be getting more than just great flavor. The potential health aspects of fresh garlic and its cousins are an added incentive to the generous use of these aromatic ingredients.

While there has been much myth and magic surrounding garlic, the evidence about garlic is almost as stunning as the folklore. Potent compounds in garlic appear to retard heart disease, stroke, cancer, and a wide variety of infections. Garlic contains the amino acid allicin, which has antibiotic and bactericidal effects, according to scientists. This compound renders raw garlic more powerful than penicillin and tetracycline. Hundreds of studies confirm garlic as a broad spectrum antibiotic effective against a long list of microbes that spread disease. How much? A mere half clove of raw garlic a day can improve the blood clot dissolving activity that helps prevent heart attacks and strokes.

Interestingly, garlic is also good for dogs. I keep a jar of chopped garlic in the refrigerator for my beautiful black Labrador retriever, Colby. Adding a teaspoon to his food keeps fleas at bay. I think he likes the "gourmet" touch, too.

Garlic unleashes at least 100 sulphur-containing compounds, which are linked to its medicinal uses. "Undisturbed, the garlic bulb has limited medicinally active compounds," says Eric Block of the State University of New York at Albany, who is an authority on garlic's chemistry. "Cutting triggers the formation of a cascade of compounds that are quite reactive and participate in a complex sequence of chemical reactions." He adds, "Chopping, steaming, and food processing do miraculous things to garlic. Ultimately, an amazing array of chemical compounds are produced."

TOMATOES

Tomatoes are an excellent source of potassium, vitamin C, and fiber. Each tomato contains about 22 milligrams of vitamin C and 1 gram of fiber. Tomatoes also contain a carotene (carotenoids are pigments) that is different than other vegetables. It is called lycopene, the substance that gives tomatoes their distinctive red color. Lycopene has been shown to lower the risk of several forms of cancer, including cancers of the pancreas, cervix, and bladder. Most recently, a study published in the **Journal of the American Cancer Institute** indicated that lycopene intake was associated with a lowered risk of prostate cancer. Not only available in raw tomatoes, lycopene is present in processed products like tomato paste and tomato juice.

PEPPERS

Peppers are a most flavorful and frequently used ingredient in my kitchen. Bell peppers are very high in vitamin C and sweet peppers are a good source of beta carotene. Chilies are the spicy peppers used liberally in Mexican and South and Central American cuisine, among others. I have not often used whole chili peppers, such as jalapeños, in this collection; however, many times I will season the oil at the start of a sauté with crushed red pepper. This quick "hit" of added spice seems to become a bit milder with longer cooking. Capsaicin is the substance that gives hot peppers their heat and is very evident in the crushed pepper and cayenne used in my dishes. Capsaicin has been found to be an effective pain reliever, and can boost metabolism, causing the body to burn calories faster. Spicy foods have been known to clear up stuffiness, making a rather tasty nasal decongestant! Also thought to be useful in clearing arteries, capsaicin seems to prevent excessive stickiness that leads to blocked arteries.

CARROTS

Carrots are root-imentary in my repertoire. Making soup without colorful chunks of carrots is almost unthinkable, and what vegetable melange doesn't profit from the addition of its delightfully sweet flavor. Carrots are part of the unbelliferae family. Characterized by their lacy, feathery leaves, celery, fennel, dill, and parsley are all relatives of the carrot.

The health benefits of carrots have been touted for many years, and of all fruits and vegetables, carrots are the highest in beta carotene. Remember when you were told to eat your carrots for good eyesight? Well, their high level of beta carotene (one carrot contains 13,500 IU of beta carotene) makes carrots a powerful ally in the prevention of premature aging and cataracts. This is in addition to counteracting the oxidizing effects of free radical damage to cells in the body. Furthermore, this fiber-rich vegetable is high in a type of soluble fiber that has been shown to reduce cholesterol. The average carrot contains 2.3 grams of fiber, and researchers recommend eating two carrots a day to reduce cholesterol levels by as much as 20 percent. One carrot contains enough beta carotene to meet your total daily allowance requirement of vitamin A.

I'm fond of using what is commonly referred to as "baby carrots." True baby carrots are very young, slender carrots, generally sold in bunches. The baby carrots in my recipes are those that the industry calls "baby cut carrots." These are mature carrots that have been peeled, cut, and bagged. Mature carrots contain more beta carotene than the young variety, and should have a healthy reddish-orange color. It is interesting to note that cooking does not destroy beta carotene, and that the beta carotene in cooked vegetables is more easily assimilated in the body.

POTATOES

While once considered a lowly starch, potatoes are now recognized as a nutritious, beneficial vegetable to be included in every balanced diet. A 7-ounce baked potato has 5 grams of protein, 26 milligrams of vitamin C, 20 milligrams of calcium, an incredible 844 milligrams of potassium, and only 220 calories. Potatoes are also high in water-absorbing fiber that makes one feel more satisfied and less hungry. Not only great tasting, inexpensive, and nutritious, potatoes are virtually fat free. Sweet potatoes are nutritional powerhouses, bursting with beta carotene. A 6-ounce sweet potato contains 265 milligrams of potassium, and 26,082 IU of vitamin A, and only 136 calories.

Potatoes are an excellent source of complex carbohydrates, the body's best energy source. Complex carbohydrates are far superior to simple carbohydrates, like those found in sugars and refined products that tend to give a quick lift. Complex carbohydrate foods like potatoes deliver a slow release of energy, thereby keeping the blood sugar level steady longer. A high-carbohydrate meal can actually boost metabolism and speed the burning of calories—ideal for weight control.

CRUCIFEROUS VEGETABLES

Cruciferous vegetables such as cabbage, broccoli, cauliflower, and brussels sprouts are rich in the cancer-fighting chemical, sulforaphane. Researchers at Johns Hopkins

University and the National Cancer Institute have found that sulforaphane appears to protect against some forms of cancer, particularly of the colon, stomach, and rectum.

Broccoli, because it is a dark green vegetable, is also an excellent source of beta carotene. A good source of fiber, this tasty vegetable also contains a considerable amount of vitamin C, potassium, folic acid, calcium, and selenium. In addition to sulforaphane, snowy white cauliflower is also high in B vitamins, vitamin C, and fiber and is a source of essential minerals like calcium, potassium, and phosphorus. Brussels sprouts look like tiny cabbages and, as the name implies, are native to Belgium. They contain the most fiber of all vegetables—7 1/2 grams per cup. Rich in antioxidants, they are every bit as high in vitamin C as citrus fruits and are a source of vitamin E and beta carotene.

The Soyfoods Pantry

Which country produces the largest crop of soybeans in the world? Is it one of the Asian countries, which are well known for their use of soybeans? After all, the Chinese have been using soybeans in a myriad of foods that have sustained them in robust health for over 5,000 years. And in Japan, tofu and miso are an integral part of the daily diet. Asia might well be a logical answer, given the history of the soybean; however, if you chose anywhere in Asia, you are mistaken. The United States is by far the largest producer of soybeans in the world; 29 states grow soybeans on more than 62 million acres of soil.

How do Americans treat this nutritional treasure growing in their own backyard? They use soybeans as the basis of cattle and hog feed. Animals destined for the slaughterhouse actually enjoy a healthier diet than people in this country. Despite the American penchant for traditional meat-based diets and a generally cavalier attitude toward those concerned with achieving sound health through a wholesome diet, consumer interest in the many new healthy food products made from soybeans is quite high. Soy is truly the magic bean, with the ability to play a part in any course, any meal, any time of the day!

The following is a summary of the variety of soyfoods that play important roles in many of the delightful recipes in this collection. Use this book as your guide. In no time you will count these versatile soyfoods among the essentials on your shopping list. No need to change your diet! Clever use of ingredients like creamy lite silken tofu, hearty tempeh, and the many ingenious soy-based meat analogues will allow you to recreate your favorite dishes with a much healthier bottom line. Bon appétit!

Baked Tofu—A delicious form of precooked and ready-to-eat tofu that can be sliced and added to salads and sandwiches right from the package. Available in three varieties from The Soy Deli: Savory Baked Tofu, Five-Spice Baked Tofu, and Hickory Smoked Tofu, each having a flavor reminiscent of smoked meat or roast duck. Tree of Life also makes a baked and savory baked tofu. These versatile ingredients are quick, high-protein additions to stir-fry and baked dishes and are available at health food stores nationwide.

Barley Miso, Country Barley Miso—Reddish brown in color, with a chunky texture and rich flavor. This flavor of miso is strongly preferred by the American macrobiotic community. Mellow barley miso is similar in color to mellow white miso, but not as creamy.

Bragg Liquid Aminos—A mineral-rich liquid seasoning derived from soybeans. Though not fermented, this tasty flavoring is used in the same way as soy sauce, and it contains many of the essential amino acids. Available in health food stores nationwide from Live Food Products.

Dressings made with soy—There are some terrific salad dressings on the market that are made using tofu, miso, or shoyu. My favorites are sold under the brand names Nasoya and Simply Delicious. They are available in health food stores nationwide.

Firm Nigari Tofu—A very firmly pressed tofu with a dense texture that is somewhat lower in fat (3 grams per 4 ounces) and vacuum-packed. Vacuum-packed tofu will keep unopened in the refrigerator for up to 2 months. Once opened it should be used in a few days. Made from organic soybeans and sold under The Soy Deli brand name, this tofu has a subtle sweetness and handles well because of its firm texture.

Gimme Lean—This wholesome meat alternative is available in sausage and ground beef style, and sold in the refrigerator or freezer section of most health food and specialty stores. This easy-to-use product is exceedingly authentic in flavor, texture, and appearance, and holds together well when making patties or "meat" balls. Made by Lightlife Company, with a combination of textured soy protein and wheat gluten.

Green Vegetable Soybeans, in the pod (Edamamé)—These green or immature soybeans are harvested at about 80 percent maturity. They are available, usually frozen, in health food stores, Asian markets, and some supermarkets. They are quite flavorful, with none of the stronger "beany" taste associated with mature beans, and they make a nutritious snack or a delicious addition to an appetizer buffet.

Hatcho Miso—This richly flavored miso is a dark cocoa brown with slight overtones of chocolate. Hatcho means "eighth street" and takes its name from this location in Okazaki, Japan (near Nagoya).

Lean Links Italian—This is a low-fat vegetarian sausage link product from Lightlife that duplicates the taste and texture of Italian sausage. Available at health food stores and specialty stores nationwide.

Lite Silken Tofu—A very low-fat tofu (1 gram of fat per 3 ounces), lite silken tofu has a rich-tasting, smooth texture and a custard-like consistency. It is widely available in aseptic packages in supermarkets and health food stores nationwide as Mori Nu Silken Tofu Lite. Because of its award-winning packaging, this is the only tofu that can be eaten right from the box. It is a time-saving ingredient for dips, spreads, and dressings, because it does not need to be precooked. Its creamy versatility makes it an excellent substitute for eggs and dairy products in baked goods and cream sauces.

As this book neared completion, Mori Nu announced it was changing the package size of lite silken tofu. For this reason, recipes were rewritten to reflect volume rather than weight. The original package size (10.5 ounces) equals 1 1/4 cups of lite silken tofu; half the original package size equals 1/2 cup plus 2 tablespoons.

Mellow White Miso—Pale beige color with a subtle, sweet fragrance, this highly versatile miso has a rich, creamy texture. This rich-tasting miso has many applications in soy-centered cuisine.

Miso—This savory, fermented soybean paste has a consistency somewhat like peanut butter, and may be aged for several years. A mainstay of Japanese cuisine for centuries, miso is a living natural food, rich in enzymes and beneficial bacteria. Miso is easily digested and highly nutritious, and adds depth of flavor to soups, sauces, marinades, dips, salad dressings, and main dishes. Available in health food stores and Japanese markets, miso should be kept refrigerated.

Nayonaise—The brand name for the tofu-based mayonnaise I always use in place of traditionally prepared mayonnaise. Made by Nasoya, this tasty, wholesome alternative contains no eggs and therefore no cholesterol, and is also much lower in fat.

Ready Ground Tofu—This ready-to-use meat analogue can be used in many dishes or added to a colorful vegetable mélange for texture. Its loose consistency makes it perfect for sloppy joes, tacos, pot pies, etc. However, it does not hold together for patties or "meat ball" type applications. Made by Tree of Life, it is available in three styles (original, hot and spicy, and savory garlic) at health food stores nationwide.

Shoyu—A naturally brewed, high-quality soy sauce. Processed in the traditional Japanese method, it is aged 2 to 3 years without coloring, additives, or preservatives. Shoyu is true soy sauce and is available in Asian markets and health food stores.

Smoked Tofu—Smokehouse-style tofu that has the texture and flavor of smoked cheese. This exciting product can be used as a spread or sliced and tossed into a salad. It's available from at least two manufacturers, each in two styles: Tree of Life makes hot and spicy, and original, and Wildwood Natural Foods makes garlic teriyaki and mild Szechuan. All are delicious and available at health food stores.

Soy Boy Ravioli—Prepared, frozen ravioli stuffed with tasty fillings, all made with organic tofu. These low-fat products are available in three flavors: ravioli (plain pasta with a ricotta-like filling), ravioli rosa (tomato pasta with roasted pepper filling), and ravioli verde (spinach pasta with garden herb filling). These products are made by Northern Soy, Inc. and can be found in health food stores.

Soy Flour—A finely ground flour made from soybeans that is very high in protein (35 percent—twice that of wheat flour) and low in carbohydrates. Generally mixed with other flours, especially in baking, as it contains no gluten. Soy flour may also be used to bind sauces and replace eggs in baked goods. Soy flour is available in 1 1/2 pound packages from Arrowhead Mills, in health food stores across the country.

Soy Grits—Whole soybeans, lightly toasted then cracked into small pieces. They are great for boosting nutrition while adding texture and consistency to baked goods. I have added soy grits to bread crumbs when breading or making a crusty gratin. Cooked soy grits can be used in many recipes in place of whole cooked soybeans. They cook a good deal faster than whole beans (less than 15 minutes without presoaking) and are somewhat lower in fat than whole soybeans. Soy grits are to be added to recipes uncooked, unless otherwise specified. (Fearn Soya Granules are soy grits and are available in health food stores nationwide.)

Soy Sauce—A generic term for the dark salty sauce made by fermenting boiled soybeans and roasted wheat or barley. Most soy sauce sold in the United States is artificially colored and processed from defatted soybean meal and wheat mixed with chemicals.

Soybeans, whole—This delicious legume is available as a dry bean, which needs to be presoaked and cooked for 3 hours. Once precooked, soybeans are a delicious ingredient ready to be used in many recipes. Arrowhead Mills organic soybeans are sold in 1-pound packages in health food stores nationwide.

Soymilk—A nondairy product made by pressing ground, cooked soybeans. Higher in protein than cow's milk, soymilk is cholesterol free and low in fat and sodium. It can replace cow's milk in any recipe.

Soymilk Lite—An organic, 1 percent fat soymilk that is sold under the name Westsoy Lite Nondairy Soy Beverage and made by Westbrae Natural Foods. Widely available in supermarkets and health food stores across the country, this is the soymilk of choice in my kitchen. Aseptically packaged, this soy beverage has a long shelf life and needn't be refrigerated until opened. It has a clean, wholesome taste—not "beany" like some soymilks—and is a versatile ingredient in baked goods and cream sauces.

Soynuts—These roasted, crunchy snacks are similar to peanuts and can be found in many grocery stores. See page 60 for a quick and easy way to make homemade soynuts that are fresher and tastier than the store-bought variety.

Tamari—A natural soy sauce made only with soybeans. Tamari is similar to shoyu. Its mellow flavor is slightly stronger than shoyu. You will find tamari in health food stores and Asian markets. Imported tamari is far superior to the domestic variety and is well worth the higher price, as its darker, richer flavor will go farther. For this reason I prefer the imported variety, which I have used in formulating these recipes. Tree of Life tamari is made with organic soybeans and is found in health stores nationwide.

Tempeh—Fermented from whole soybeans, tempeh is an easily digestible, live cultured food. It has a chewy texture and a distinctive nutty flavor, contains more protein than tofu, and is the best known source of vitamin B12 for vegans (strict vegetarians). Because tempeh is made from the whole bean, it is richer in flavor and nutrients than tofu. Tempeh can be found in the refrigerator or freezer section of health food stores as tempeh burgers or as the cultured soyfood ingredient used in many recipes in this collection. Tempeh is available under the brand names, Pacific Tempeh, Lightlife, and Soy Power, among others.

Textured Vegetable Protein (TVP)—TVP is made from defatted soy flour. Once rehydrated, TVP is a very credible low-fat meat substitute and an excellent soyfood to introduce your family to the goodness of soy. It is trademarked by the Archer Daniels Midland Corp., and available in ground beef, chicken chunk, or steak strip styles, among others. (The recipes in this collection use only the unflavored variety.) Because dry TVP has such a low fat content, it has a long shelf life. A wide selection of this extremely economical, high-protein food source is available through the Harvest Direct Catalog or The Mail Order Catalog (see Resource Guide, page 245). TVP is sold in health food stores, generally in the flavored ground beef style.

Tofu—Soybean curd made from coagulating soy milk with nigari (seaweed) or calcium chloride in much the same way cheese is made from milk. High in protein, low in saturated fats, and cholesterol free, tofu's blandness and ability to absorb flavors make it a very versatile ingredient.

Tofu Mayonnaise—(see Nayonaise)

Tofu Wieners—A wholesome alternative to traditional hot dogs, these are very authentic in taste and appearance. Available in health food stores nationwide, they are sold under the brand names, Yves Veggie Wieners, Not Dogs by Northern Soy, and Smart Dogs, made by Lightlife.

Yves Veggie Canadian Bacon—This is a very authentic meat analogue; very close to Canadian bacon or ham in appearance and taste. It is made with soy protein and wheat gluten and can be enjoyed right out of the package. Used in sandwiches and salads, it is also a delicious ingredient in stir-fry and baked dishes, adding protein and carbohydrates, but very little fat.

Yves Veggie Pepperoni—Another authentic meat analog from Yves, it's terrific in sandwiches and colorful salads. Yves also makes a vegetarian deli slices (bologna).

A Quick Guide to Ingredients

The ingredients in *Soy of Cooking* are easy to use and generally available in health food stores and supermarkets. However, some ingredients may be unfamiliar to some cooks. Here is a brief description of those ingredients. For more information, including manufacturers of soyfoods and other products, check the Resource Guide (page 245).

Agar Flakes (Kanten or Agar Agar)—This vegetable gel, derived from seaweed, is colorless, odorless, tasteless, and calorie free. It has been used for over 1,000 years. Agar is also available as bars; however, recipes in this collection use agar flakes.

Applesauce—In recipes that call for applesauce as a fat replacer, you should use unsweetened applesauce. It is widely available in supermarkets and health food stores.

Arrowroot—This powder can replace tapioca flour or cornstarch where a thickening paste is required.

Baking Powder—Nonaluminum, double-acting baking powder is available nationwide at health food stores and many supermarkets. Rumford, Featherweight, and Cellu baking powder are all nonaluminum.

Balsamic Vinegar—Slightly sweet and fragrant with a distinctive depth of flavor, genuine balsamic vinegar is aged at least 6 years and produced in the Modena area of Italy.

Basmati Rice—An aromatic, long-grain rice, scented with a faint nutlike flavor and aroma. Many cooks consider this high-quality rice to be the world's finest. The recipes here calling for basmati rice use white basmati. It is also available in brown basmati rice varieties, which take longer to cook. Check package for cooking directions.

Couscous—Found in Middle Eastern cuisine, these tiny grains of pasta are made from milled wheat. Sold in this country presteamed, couscous needs only to be added to boiling water or broth, stirred, removed from heat, and set aside for 5 minutes to absorb the liquid.

Date Pieces (sometimes called Date Nuggets)—These are chopped dates that are rolled in oat flour rather than sugar. They are available in health food stores and specialty stores.

Egg Replacer Powder—EnerG Egg Replacer is a dry product made from tapioca starch and leavenings. A most effective ingredient in baked goods, it is sold in health food stores, and is also available through the EnerG catalog (see Resource Guide). Recipes in this collection that use egg replacer were created with this product.

Florida Crystals—This is an unbleached and minimally processed sugar, which is light in color and finely granulated. It can be substituted on a 1:1 basis for refined white sugar.

Fruitsource—A wholesome sweetener made from grapes and grains. Though available at natural food stores in both liquid and granulated forms, I have used only the liquid Fruitsource for the recipes found in *Soy of Cooking*. Fruitsource also acts as a fat replacer in baked goods, because it is a source of pectins. Fruitsource is widely used in commercial baking under the name Fruitrim.

Garbanzo Beans—I have used low-sodium garbanzo beans, available from Eden Foods, in these recipes with great results. They are flavored with kombu and contain no added salt. Available at health food stores and some supermarkets nationwide.

Gingerroot—A knobby root with an aromatic, spicy ginger flavor. Fresh gingerroot is peeled and grated before adding to the recipes in this collection. Gingerroot is found in supermarkets and grocery stores across the country.

Granulated Garlic—Textured into grains like sugar, this form of garlic is far superior to garlic powder in flavor and aroma. Available at health food stores.

Jasmine Rice—Distinctly fragrant rice that is at the center of Thai cuisine.

Kombu—A dark green deep-sea vegetable harvested in cold northern waters. Kombu is used to tenderize dry beans and tempeh as they cook and as a flavor enhancer in soup stocks.

Mashed Potato Flakes—I use Barbara's Mashed Potatoes, made from whole, unpeeled Idaho potatoes and distributed by Barbara's Bakery.

Mirin—Lower in alcohol than Japanese saké, mirin is a sweet, rice wine that tenderizes and enhances sautées.

Nutmeats—A number of my recipes, particularly baked goods, use nuts for added crunch and flavor. Nuts are a good source of protein (almonds have 30 grams of protein per cup), but are also high in fat. I have found that 1/3 cup of nuts will add just the right crunch and impart plenty of flavor. Plus, my recipes are so low in fat, you can afford a bit of "nutty indulgence."

Nutritional Yeast—Available in health food stores, these delicious flakes are very high in protein and B vitamins. Not to be confused with brewer's yeast, which has a characteristically bitter taste, nutritional yeast adds a rich, cheese-like flavor and creaminess. It is also an effective thickening agent in dairy-free cream sauces and soups.

Oat Bran—A fiber rich bran derived from oats that adds a distinctive hearty flavor to baked goods. Available at health food and specialty stores.

Oil Cooking Spray—A pump action, nonaerosol canola oil product used to oil baking pans or wherever reduced fat is desired, such as sautées. Pam and Wesson make pump-action oil sprays, which are available in supermarkets and health food stores nationwide.

Onion Soup Mix—I always use Mayacamas brand, which is made with natural ingredients (including soy protein) and contains no preservatives. It is available nationwide at health food stores and supermarkets.

Orange Blossom Water—The distilled essence of orange blossoms used to perfume sweets in eastern Mediterranean cuisine. It is used sparingly, and will fill your home with its fragrance.

Orzo—A light and delicious rice shaped pasta that is perfect in soups or as an innovative ingredient for the creative cook. Widely available.

Phyllo Pastry—These paper-thin leaves of dough are available in the freezer section of most supermarkets.

Prune Purée—Puréed prunes are a very effective fat replacer in baked goods. Prepared prune purée is available in supermarkets across the country and can be found with the Kosher foods or in the baking aisle. Brand names include Solo, Lekvar, Baker, and Sokol. See Techniques for a simple recipe for homemade prune purée.

Rose Water—The distilled essence of rose petals, used to perfume sweets in eastern Mediterranean cuisine. Like orange blossom water, it is used sparingly, and will fill your home with its fragrance. Folklore says the soothing flavor of rose water will put you in a happy mood.

Sea Salt—Salt derived from evaporated sea water, which retains some natural trace minerals and contains no additives.

Semolina Flour—Semolina is a coarse-textured flour ground from durum wheat. Pastas made with semolina flour are higher in protein and have a firm texture. I use Semolina Flour Mix by Arrowhead Mills, a blend of organic semolina flour and organic kamut flour, to make all my pastas.

Shallots—Used extensively in French cuisine, this mild member of the onion family combines the flavor of onion and garlic.

Shiitake Mushrooms—Available both fresh and dried, these distinctive mushrooms are used in stir-fries, soups, and salads.

Soba Noodles—Sold in health food stores, specialty stores, and Asian markets, this dried pasta is traditionally made from buckwheat.

Sucanat—A granulated form of unrefined cane sugar; made from cane juice. Sugar in this form is a whole food and therefore retains all of the vitamins and minerals found in nature. Sucanat is stirred into the dry ingredients when making baked goods, because it does not emulsify with creamed ingredients. It imparts many of the same characteristics as brown sugar (which can be substituted for Sucanat on a one to one basis), and is found in health food stores nationwide.

Sun-Dried Tomatoes—Ripe tomato halves that have been oven dried, giving them a uniquely intense flavor. I use only the dry variety, which is reconstituted in boiling water, never those that have been packed in oil. Organic sun-dried tomatoes are available in the Sonoma brand.

Sunspire Chocolate Chips—Real chocolate chips that are wholesome and dairy free. They have several varieties, but my favorites are the new Organic Dark Chocolate Chips. These chips are knock-your-socks-off delicious! They are sold in health food stores nationwide.

Tapioca Flour—This flour made from tapioca is an effective thickening agent. It may be substituted for arrowroot.

Veganrella—This vegetarian cream cheese is made from Brazil nuts and imparts texture to chilled dishes. It's available in plain and flavored varieties. I have used only the plain Veganrella in the recipes included here.

Vegetable Broth—Beef- or chicken-flavored vegetarian broth powder is used to reconstitute unflavored TVP. These products are available in some health food stores and through the Harvest Direct and The Mail Order catalogs.

Wheat Gluten—The natural protein derived from wheat and used in bread baking to enhance the rise and flavor, improve the shape, and extend freshness. It is widely used by the baking industry to produce consistent, uniform breads.

White Wheat Flour—A new variety of whole grain flour, produced from hard white wheat. It combines all the fiber of traditional whole wheat and the sweeter, milder taste and baking performance of unbleached flour. White wheat flour is available from King Arthur's Flour Baker's Catalog; organic white wheat flour is available from Arrowhead Mills in healthfood stores nationwide.

Whole Wheat Pastry Flour—The best whole grain flour to use in cakes and quickbreads, this finely milled flour is made from soft wheat. It has a low gluten content and is not used in yeast breads. Organic whole wheat pastry flour is available from Arrowhead Mills in health food stores and some supermarkets.

Wonderslim Cocoa—This is real cocoa, and lower in fat than low-fat regular cocoa. Even better, it is caffeine-free, with the caffeine extracted using a natural process. This cocoa is available in supermarkets and health food stores nationwide. You may use this cocoa in any recipe that calls for cocoa.

Substitutions

Throughout this book, I have indicated some substitute ingredients for those that might be unfamiliar. For instance, brown sugar may be substituted for Sucanat, sugar may replace Florida Crystals, and honey may replace liquid Fruitsource.

Other acceptable substitutions on a one to one basis include dry sherry for mirin; beaten egg whites for EnerG egg replacer powder and water; low-fat cream cheese for Veganrella; and chopped dates instead of date pieces.

To substitute egg whites for egg replacer, use 1/4 cup of beaten egg whites in place of 1 tablespoon of egg replacer powder and 1/4 cup of water. You may also replace any nutmeats listed in a recipe with another you may have on hand. For instance, pecans might replace cashews or walnuts in a quick bread or muffins with tasty results. When substituting honey for liquid Fruitsource, a one to one ratio is a good rule of thumb. However, honey may vary in taste and texture, and honey does not contain the pectins that are present in Fruitsource. Be aware of these variances when substituting honey for the preferred listed ingredient.

These substitutions are offered to make *Soy of Cooking* as user-friendly as possible. However, the nutrition analyses are calculated according to the original ingredient listed, not the substitute ingredient. The original ingredient is the ingredient of choice and the one I recommend for the delectable dishes in this collection. I encourage you to use the suggested ingredients when making these recipes. I do not endorse the use of eggs, refined sugar, or honey. These substitutions are offered solely for your convenience.

Spices: The Variety of Kitchen Life

Spices have long been added to food for flavor and variety. In the past decade, herb and spice consumption has been on the rise. The popularity of ethnic foods and the interest in lowering the fat in our diets has encouraged some of us to try new and unusual herbs and spices. Herbs and spices can be used artfully to boost the flavor of a dish and substantially reduce the amount of fat at the same time. The flavor and aroma of fragrant herbs and spices reduces the need for fat and salt in cooking. Anyone who appreciates fine food, well presented, knows that the clever use of herbs and spices adds depth and dimension to even the most basic assemblage of ingredients.

There are no strict rules governing the use of herbs and spices in cooking—the best route is to experiment. Learning to recognize the particular flavors, aromas, and attributes that distinguish each herb and spice is necessary in order to appreciate the qualities they contribute to a dish. Gourmet cooks know that spice is the variety of kitchen life and the clever use of herbs and spices will make your efforts more appetizing, appealing, and digestible.

Using spices and herbs with confidence is the key to developing interesting menus and enlivening simple fare. Confidence comes from familiarity, and the best way to get to know any spice or herb is by cooking with it. The challenge is that many of us become accustomed to using several herbs and spices with which we are familiar, and we avoid others. We rely on tried and true favorites or blends rather than risk trying something new.

Fresh herbs are a wonderful addition to any dish, and most supermarkets stock the more common herbs like parsley, cilantro, basil, oregano, mint, dillweed, and chives. Specialty markets and ethnic grocers can supply the adventurous cook with more exotic varieties. When using fresh herbs, you will find that they are milder than the dried variety and you can safely substitute three to five times times the amount of dried herb (depending on the strength of the herb) called for in the recipe.

GUIDE TO SPICES AND HERBS

The term "spice" refers to all aromatic plants used to season foods. However, herbs are the leaves of low-growing, non-woody plants or shrubs; spices are generally derived from the bark, root, fruit, or berries of perennial plants and trees. Both spices and herbs may produce aromatic seeds.

Allspice—Pungent spice of a reddish-brown berry found in Central America and the West Indies. Used in pumpkin dishes, spice cakes, applesauce, chutney, and fruits, it has the flavor of cinnamon, nutmeg, and cloves.

Anise—Small, oval shaped, grayish-brown aromatic seed grown in Spain and Mexico. Used in stews, cakes, fruit pies, sweet rolls, Italian coffee, and liquors.

Basil (Sweet Basil)—A powerful herb with a rich and pungent flavor, heady aroma, and an adaptable taste. Indispensable in Italian and Mediterranean cookery, it is native to the Near East and is used in cuisines around the world.

Bay Leaf—Native to the Mediterranean, there are several varieties sold as bay or bay laurel. Ninety percent of all bay leaves sold in this country are of Mediterranean origin because of its smoother, full flavor. Used in sauces, soups, stews, and pickling spices.

Bouquet Garni—Several herbs tied together in a small cheesecloth bag so the herbs can be easily removed. Parsley, thyme, and bay leaf are the basics, but basil, rosemary, chervil, tarragon, or celery leaves can also be included.

Capers—The bud of a bush that grows wild in the Mediterranean, pickled and preserved in brine, vinegar, or salt. It has a sharp, pungent flavor and is used with tomatoes, sauces, gravies, and eggplant dishes.

Caraway—Small, brown, crescent-shaped seed with a mild licorice taste, found in central Europe. Used in rye breads, cabbage and turnip dishes, soups, stews, and pickling spices.

Cardamom—Native to India, and also found in Guatemala and Sri Lanka, cardamom is a perennial of the ginger family. It produces green seedpods that are harvested by hand. Pungent and aromatic, it is a bit like mild ginger with an interesting flowery sweetness. Used extensively in India, it is found in sweets and curry dishes. It is also popular in Scandinavia, where it is used in breads, baked goods, and sweet potatoes.

Cayenne—Dried and ground from the tropical capsicum plant native to Latin American countries. Once processed, a dash of this bright scarlet, very hot chile will bring out the natural flavor in many Mexican, Indian, Latin American, and Cajun dishes.

Celery Seed—Small, light brown aromatic seed with the flavor of celery, found in India and southern France. Actually a member of the parsley family, celery seed is used in stuffing, salad dressings, coleslaw, pickles, soups, and potato dishes.

Chervil—Bright green feathery leaves, resembling parsley, but with a subtle slightly licorice flavor. Used more extensively in France, it is considered a blending herb.

Chili Powder—A ground blend based on a combination of spices and herbs typically including: chili peppers, cumin, coriander, garlic, cloves, paprika, oregano, turmeric, and black pepper.

Chive—A delicate onion-flavored herb with long green tubular leaves, that is available fresh, minced, dried, or frozen. Can be used with baked potatoes, and in dips, soups, salads, and dressings.

Cilantro—Pungent and peppery aroma and flavor, with round, delicately fringed leaves. Sometimes called fresh coriander or Chinese parsley, it adds a sharp, distinctive flavor and is essential to many Mexican, Oriental, and Mediterranean dishes.

Cinnamon—Produced in southern China, Sumatra, Sri Lanka, and Indochina, cinnamon is at the same time sweet and mildly hot. Found in eastern Mediterranean, Indian, and Mexican dishes, and used extensively in baked goods and beverages, it is widely available in powdered and rolled bark (cinnamon sticks).

Clove—The dried, unopened buds of a tropical evergreen native to Indonesia, clove has a strong, sweet, and pungent flavor. Available in whole and ground form, it is widely used in cakes, cookies, custards, pickled fruits, and hot cider.

Coriander—Aromatic seed with a warm, slightly musty taste, somewhat like sage, and a lemon-like undertone. Native to Yugoslavia and French Morocco, coriander is available whole or ground. It's used extensively in Indian cuisine to flavor vegetable dishes or in preparing curry powder.

Crushed Red Pepper—Sometimes referred to as red pepper flakes, it has a hot, strong flavor. It is quite useful in seasoning the oil at the outset of sautéeing, and its heat diminishes somewhat during cooking. These spicy flakes are used sparingly.

Cumin—Strongly aromatic and reminiscent of caraway with a very agreeable flavor, this yellowish-brown seed is ridged and slightly curved. Found in French Morocco and Iran, cumin is available whole or ground. Cumin is an essential ingredient in chili powder and most curries, adding a warm, heady, and robust flavor to many dishes.

Curry Powder—A prepared blend of six or more of the following spices: turmeric, cumin, coriander, ginger, cloves, pepper, fenugreek, mustard, and cardamom.

Dill—Found in California, the seeds are small and tan, and the leaves are feathery light green with a tangy flavor resembling caraway. Used in breads, salads, sauces, and pickling spices.

Fennel—Native to India and Rumania and available as chartreuse seeds or fresh as short, rounded, celery-like bulbs. Having a pronounced licorice flavor that diminishes somewhat as it cooks, fennel is used in casseroles, sweet pickles, and Italian breads and rolls.

Fenugreek—Native to Asia, fenugreek is available as a smooth, red, aromatic seed or in the ground form. It's used in chutneys and curry powders.

Ginger—Contributing a clean, hot, spicy-sweet flavor and a pungent aroma, fresh gingerroot is cultivated extensively in most semitropical regions. Native to Southeast Asia, Jamaican ginger is considered to be of the highest quality. Peel back the skin before grating. It is also available in the more familiar ground form.

Mace—Found in the Moluccas Islands of Indonesia, mace is processed from the fibrous covering of the nutmeg shell. Mace has a flavor similar to nutmeg but it's somewhat milder. It's used in cherry pies, pumpkin breads, pound cakes, and puddings.

Marjoram—Found in France and Portugal, marjoram is actually a member of the mint family. It has a musky flavor, similar to oregano. Available fresh or dried, and it is used in tomato dishes, with green vegetables, in salads, stuffings, and casseroles.

Mint—Found in Belgium, France, and Germany, this herb has emerald green leaves and a warm, menthol flavor. It's available fresh, dried, and as an extract. Mint is used in desserts, cold beverages, hot teas, and jellies, and with chilled fruits.

Mustard—Available as whole seeds or ground, mustard has a tangy, biting quality. The seeds can be white, brown, or black. Black mustard seeds are commonly used in Indian cooking. Sautéed in hot oil until they pop, they add a pungent quality to vegetable, rice, and legume dishes.

Nutmeg—Grown in hot, moist regions of the tropics, like Malaysia and Java. Nutmeg is the oval shaped, dried seed of an apricot-like fruit of an evergreen tree that bears for more than 50 years. Available in whole or ground form, the spicy-sweet flavor is best when using freshly grated nutmeg. Used in desserts, quick breads, cakes, vegetable dishes, and some cream sauces.

Oregano—Stronger and heavier in aroma and flavor than marjoram, this herb adds zip to pizza, pastas, tomato dishes, and vegetables. Another strain of this popular herb is Mexican oregano, an essential ingredient in chili powder.

Paprika—Native to Central America but grown commercially in California, paprika is the dried, stemless pod of a sweet red pepper. Most of the paprika used in the United States is mild and slightly sweet and used as a garnish. Hungarian paprika is more pungent and lighter in color.

Parsley—The curly leaf variety is grown chiefly in California and is the main source of dehydrated parsley flakes. Either fresh or dried, it is used generously to flavor and garnish most foods, sweets being the exception. It has a pleasant mild odor and an agreeable taste. Flat leaf parsley, sometimes called Italian parsley, has a stronger flavor.

Rosemary—A delightfully sweet, fragrant herb, its spiky leaves resemble miniature pine needles. Used in breads (Rosemary Foccacia is one example), or sprinkled on boiled potatoes or green beans, this herb imparts a distinctive flavor and aroma.

Saffron—Widely used in French, Spanish, and Indian dishes, saffron is native to the Mediterranean, primarily imported from Spain. This pleasantly bitter spice is the most expensive spice in the world. It is the whole dried stigma of the saffron crocus. It requires 75,000 blossoms or 225,000 stigmas to make one pound of saffron. It is orange-yellow and used for color as much as flavor. It is used sparingly—a pinch or two will go a long way.

Sage—Native to Albania and the Balkans, sage is available as silver tipped, grayish green leaves or in the ground form. Sage has a slightly bitter and strongly astringent flavor and is used in stuffings, baked dishes, dressings, and stews.

Sesame Seed—The dried hulled fruit of a tropical plant, sesame seed is the source of a cooking oil used widely in the East. This smooth, creamy-white oval-shaped seed is one of the most versatile of the seeds. Its rich, nut-like flavor enhances breads, cookies, noodles, vegetables, salads, and more. When ground into a paste, it is called tahini, which is widely used in Middle Eastern cuisine.

Tamarind—Used in Southeast Asia, India, the Middle East, and Latin America, this flavoring adds a tasty prunelike sourness to curries, chutneys, pickles, and hot and sour soups. It's available in ethnic groceries. You may substitute lemon juice.

Tarragon—A distinctive herb with uniquely sharp, spicy, and aromatic flavor, with undertones of licorice and mint. The word tarragon comes from the French word for little dragon, and the herb grown for culinary use is of the French variety. It's available dried and ground.

Thyme—A strong flavored herb with a heavy, spicy aroma and a pungent clove-like taste. This versatile herb blends well with other herbs, and is found in bouquet garni.

Turmeric—Turmeric is the root of a tropical plant of the ginger family. Used extensively in Indian cooking, turmeric is best known as an ingredient in curry powder, and is available in ground form in supermarkets and Indian groceries. It has a musky, slightly bitter taste. Like saffron, a little turmeric adds a rich golden color to cooked dishes or baked goods.

Vanilla Bean—Long, dark, slender seed pods with a pleasant sweet flavor. Available as whole beans or as an extract, it is used extensively in sweet dishes, baked goods, puddings, and chilled and frozen confections.

Techniques

Here are some useful directions for preparing various ingredients and foods used in *Soy of Cooking.*

BAKING WITHOUT ADDED FAT

I use no added fat in my baked goods. For the most part, I make use of the pectins and sorbitols that are naturally present in fruits. Unsweetened applesauce and prune purée are most effective in replacing the fat in my baked desserts, breads, and muffins. Miso can also be used in essentially the same way to replace fat in yeast breads and savory dishes. A mildly-flavored miso is best in this application; I generally use mellow white miso, as it has a rich natural flavor and a subtle, sweet fragrance. I also use liquid Fruitsource to replace both fat and honey. These ingredients and innovative techniques help to slash fat and calories dramatically.

BLANCHING TOFU

To blanch tofu, drop cakes or cubes into boiling water, and simmer 5 minutes. This will help keep tofu firm and more absorbent. It also keeps it from diluting what it is added to. Placing tofu in the microwave for 2 to 3 minutes after it is cut or mashed into the desired shape will achieve the same, if not better, results.

CHESTNUTS

To blanch: Place chestnuts in boiling water for 2 minutes. Remove a few chestnuts at a time, allow them to cool slightly, and use a paring knife to peel the shell from the nutmeat. If some shells are particularly difficult to remove, boil an additional 2 minutes.

To roast: Preheat oven to 400°. With a sharp knife, cut an "X" through the shell on the flat side of the chestnuts. Spread the chestnuts, cut side up, on a baking sheet. Roast chestnuts until tender, about 20 minutes. Test tenderness with a fork.

DRIED BEANS

Dried beans are of all varieties need to be rehydrated before use. They should be rinsed thoroughly and sorted. Lentils and split peas don't need to be presoaked, but other types of dried beans should be soaked with one of two equally effective methods. The preferred method is to soak the beans overnight. In the case of soybeans, place the bowl in the refrigerator so the beans will not ferment. The second method is to bring the rinsed and sorted beans to a boil, remove from heat, and let stand for an hour, then proceed with cooking. Most dried beans will cook in 1 1/2 to 2 1/2 hours; soybeans and chickpeas require more time. Never salt the beans or add acidics like tomatoes or vinegar during the precooking process, as this will prolong the cooking time.

It is a good idea to discard the soaking water and cook the beans in fresh water for the first 30 minutes, then discard this water and continue the cooking process with fresh water. This will address the digestive problems some associate with consumption of beans. It is also true that as you start to eat beans more often, these digestive problems tend to disappear. A University of California-Berkeley study reported participants had greater tolerance after three weeks of eating beans regularly. It seems that the more often you eat beans, the better the chances of developing the enzymes needed to handle it.

FROZEN TOFU

Freezing tofu can produce excellent results, yielding a "meatier," chewy, coarse textured ingredient, like that of cooked chicken or veal.Freezing will radically change the structure and basic character, as frozen tofu is highly concentrated and readily absorbs flavors, sauces, and marinades much like a sponge.

For frozen tofu, I use firm or extra firm tofu; *regular* silken tofu is not recommended because it tends to disintegrate into a mushy substance. Each recipe specifies the type of tofu best suited for that recipe; however, vacuum-packed nigari tofu and extra firm *lite* silken tofu are generally indicated.

When freezing tofu, remove it from its original packaging and drain slightly, then pat with a paper towel. It's generally best to slice the tofu into cutlets or cubes at this stage to hasten thawing. Wrap the cutlets, cubes, or blocks individually in plastic wrap and place packages in a plastic bag, pressing out the air. I like to use the zipper type, because of their heavier weight. During freezing the color will change from creamy white to yellow and resemble a block of cheese. The longer tofu is frozen the better the texture, so you will want to freeze it for at least a week or two; you can safely freeze tofu for more than six months.

In tofu, water makes up about 85 percent of the weight, and freezing tofu turns the water into ice crystals. When the ice thaws, it leaves a firm network of concentrated protein and solids. I prefer to defrost tofu in the microwave, especially when it has been precut in the cutlets or cubes. Just place the frozen tofu in a bowl, cover, and microwave it, checking it every 2 or 3 minutes, so that it does not cook. Tofu can also be thawed by pouring several quarts of boiling water over the blocks set in a pan. Thawing takes about 15 minutes this way and can be hastened by slicing the block into smaller pieces when partially thawed. I generally replenish the hot water halfway through, which also quickens the process. Frozen tofu can also be thawed in the refrigerator for several hours or overnight.

Some recipes call for shredded tofu after it has been defrosted. Before freezing, the block of tofu should be cut thirds or pieces 1-inch wide. Then, after thawing, squeeze out as much water as possible by gently pressing it between your palms. Gently run the times of a fork through the tofu to produce the desired shape.

Once as much water as possible has been squeezed out, you will have a super absorbent form of tofu. It is in this sponge-like state that tofu fully absorbs flavorful sauces and marinades. At this stage, slice the tofu to the desired size and place it in a bowl that will allow the pieces to be submerged in the marinade. Set it aside for as little as 15 minutes, several hours, or overnight (as indicated in each recipe) and turn occasionally.

LEEKS

Leeks can be very gritty. They often retain sand between their many tight layers, especially where the white bulb joins the tender green shaft. Thorough cleaning is essential in order to avoid unpleasant residue. First, cut off and discard the roots and tough green top. Then, without cutting all the way through, slice the leek in half lengthwise. Fan the layers open, but do not pull the leek apart. Rinse the leek thoroughly under running cold water. Finally, soak the rinsed leeks in a large bowl of cold water, changing the water several times until no grit appears at the bottom of the bowl.

LITE SILKEN TOFU

Lite silken tofu is aseptically packaged. This means that it can be eaten right from the box or incorporated into a chilled recipe without precooking. Always drain tofu by cutting the side flaps where marked and pouring off the liquid. Remove from box, wrap in paper towels of double thickness, and set aside until ready to use.

Always blend lite silken tofu until smooth, before adding other ingredients to the food processor or blender.

(Note: To accurately measure tofu, stir with a fork to break down, and measure as you would flour, leveling with a knife.)

MINCING GARLIC

The best way to mince garlic is to place an unpeeled clove on a cutting board. Lay the flat side of a large, wide-bladed knife over the clove and strike a few times with the heel of your hand; remove the peel. Mince with short chopping motions, grasping both ends of the knife carefully.

MISO SOUP

Miso soup has four basic elements: dashi, vegetables, miso, and garnishes. The preparation of miso soup begins with a traditional stock called dashi. Made with kombu (dried seaweed), a fragrant and flavorful dashi is a fundamental ingredient in good miso soup. I make my dashi with kombu and a combination of western-style vegetables. After simmering the dashi, I generally remove the solids and press them against a wire strainer in order to extract optimal flavor.

Next, I like to add flavored vegetable broth and seasonings. There are many varieties of miso that can be used in miso soup. Using a combination of different miso flavors produces a delightful balance of flavor and aroma. Miso is always mixed with a liquid, most times a ladle or two of hot broth, before being added to the soup. To "cream" the miso, place a cup or so of liquid gradually and blend with a small wire whisk or fork. The soup is then allowed to simmer for several minutes but is never allowed to come to a boil. To do so would destroy the microorganisms and enzymes for which miso soup is so highly prized.

NUTMEATS

I generally purchase nutmeats either whole or in large pieces. I always measure the nuts first and then place them in a plastic bag. I place the closed bag on the kitchen counter and rap it a number of times with the edge of my rolling pin. This enables me to crush nuts smaller than available commercially. I think it makes them go further and seems to increase the volume.

PASTA

Pasta should be cooked in a large pot of boiling water, with at least 4 quarts of water per pound of pasta. Place a tablespoon of oil in the water along with a teaspoon of salt, to help keep the strands from sticking together. Cooking times will vary according to the thickness of the pasta, with filled pastas generally cooking longer. Keep a close watch on boiling pasta, being careful not to overcook. Frequent testing by biting or pinching a test piece is the best method. Pasta has reached what is considered the perfect texture, "al dente," when it is firm but flexible; pasta is gummy when it's overdone.

PEARL ONIONS, PEELING

First blanch the onions by plunging them into boiling water for 2 minutes. Drain immediately, and plunge them into ice water. With a sharp knife, cut off the root and stem ends. The remaining skin should slide off easily with the knife.

PHYLLO DOUGH

Sometimes spelled filo, this versatile pastry is available in the freezer section of most supermarkets. Remove the package from the freezer and place it in the refrigerator overnight. Remove the package from the refrigerator and place it on the kitchen counter, unopened, for 2 to 4 hours before opening. This will bring the dough to room temperature. Remove the number of sheets needed, and freeze the remainder.

Work quickly with each individual layer, keeping the remaining dough covered with a damp cloth. I like to use a water spritzer, like the typical indoor plant sprayer, to keep the cloth from drying while I'm working. Spray lightly; do not drench the cloth or the dough will become gummy, especially around the edges.

Always make the filling for phyllo dough before removing it from its wrapper. If the filling has been cooked, it should be cooled a bit before mounding it onto the prepared layers in order to avoid sogginess. Flavored bread crumbs are sometimes sprinkled between the layers to promote crispness.

If you've never worked with these leaves of dough, you might think they are sheets of translucent paper. They are very delicate and dry out easily, so handle them gingerly. Generally the leaves of dough are brushed with melted butter before placement to promote flakiness. In my approach to low-fat cuisine, I use an oil cooking spray instead. There are flavored mists on the market that will impart the flavor of butter or garlic, however this is not absolutely necessary, especially if butter is not something you normally include in your diet. The use of oil sprays has proven to be a very adequate fat-busting ally.

PIZZA DOUGH

Pizza dough is always made with bread flour, which has a high gluten content and allows the yeast maximum rise. The yeast used in this book is baker's yeast, which is sold in jars in supermarkets across the country. Red Star and Fleishman are two popular brands. This type of yeast is measured in teaspoons rather than packets. A package of yeast contains two and a half teaspoons, and the yeast called for in these recipes is not rapid rise. I keep yeast in the refrigerator to maintain maximum freshness.

I use the food processor to make pizza dough. However, if you prefer to make the dough by hand you may proceed with the standard method:

In a small glass measuring cup, warm the water with the sweetener called for to no more than 110° in the microwave. Sprinkle the yeast into the water and set aside to proof. If the yeast is good, it should foam. In a large bowl, stir together the flours and salt. If a cooked potato is needed, it should be riced before adding to the flour. Make a well in the center of the flour and pour in the yeast mixture. Mix well and knead for 10 to 12 minutes, adding more flour as needed to make a smooth dough. To knead by hand, place the dough on a lightly floured surface and sprinkle the top lightly with flour. Using the heel of your hands, press down and away, and then fold the dough back onto itself. Repeat this action, turning the dough around a little each time. Add only enough flour to prevent the dough from sticking. When the dough is smooth, elastic, and springy, it is ready to rest. At this point, proceed with the recipe.

PRUNE PURÉE

Homemade prune purée is a snap: Simply place 2 cups of pitted prunes in a food processor or blender with 3/4 cup of water and 4 teaspoons of vanilla extract. Blend until smooth, then cover and refrigerate. Prune purée will keep in the refrigerator for more than two weeks.

"SNIPPING" INGREDIENTS

Sometimes a recipe will call for an ingredient to be "snipped." I use my kitchen shears to cut herbs or dried fruits. For basil, I roll the leaves into a tight bunch and cut them into strips. For dried fruits or sun-dried tomatoes, I snip them into halves or thirds, as indicated in the recipe.

SOY BUTTERMILK

Adding lemon or cider vinegar to soymilk lite creates a low-fat ingredient that imparts the same characteristics as traditional buttermilk to baked goods, dressings, and sauces. This marvelous ingredient is easy to make and rich in phytochemicals. It has the same thick texture and tangy flavor as traditional buttermilk.

Simply place soymilk in a glass measuring cup. Add the souring ingredient called for in the recipe, and set aside while assembling remaining ingredients.

Sensational Starters

How do soyfoods find their way into the first course? By using exciting new products that are widely available and easy to use, you can create first-rate appetizers. Here, heart heavy ingredients like sour cream, eggs, and meat products that are high in fat and cholesterol are replaced with heart healthy alternatives. Available in natural food stores and supermarkets across the country, these wholesome alternatives will introduce you to a low-fat, high fiber, and dairy-free cooking style.

Using some of the newest soyfoods on the market and creative techniques, the health conscious cook can replace unhealthy ingredients with those that mimic familiar tastes and textures. Delight your guests with the scrumptious Spanakopitta, a gorgeous Greek spinach pie fashioned from phyllo pastry. You can wrap it up with style making the enticing Sausage Roll-Ups. Adding versatility with a minimum of fuss is easy: just blend, chill, and serve Chick-Pea Dip, Savory Spinach Dip, or Spicy Roasted Pepper Dip with Pita Crisps or crudités.

Whether planning a festive buffet or an intimate dinner, the enticing hot and cold appetizers in this exciting collection will greet your guests with an irresistible invitation to dine. The first course is primarily designed to stimulate the appetite and serve as a prelude to the rest of the meal. When planning your menu, focus on the taste, texture, and color of your choices and how they will be complemented by succeeding courses. Whatever you select, you can be sure these tasty openers are both healthful and delicious. ◆

Chick-Pea Dip With Pita Crisps

Dramatically lower in fat than traditional hummus, this exceptional appetizer tastes rich and delicious.

◆ ABOUT 4 CUPS ◆

DIP

1 1/4 cups lite silken tofu, drained
2 cloves garlic, peeled
15-oz. can garbanzo beans, drained
4 scallions, tops only
2 Tbsp. tahini
1 Tbsp. tamari
1 Tbsp. Dijon mustard

Place tofu in food processor, and blend. Add garlic, and blend. Add remaining ingredients; blend until smooth. Chill until ready to serve.

PITA CRISPS

Vegetable oil cooking spray
12 whole wheat or oat bran pita pockets
granulated garlic

Preheat oven to 400°. Line a baking pan with foil, then coat the foil with cooking spray. Cut each pita pocket into eighths, and place on prepared pan. Coat the top side of each pita lightly with cooking spray, then sprinkle with granulated garlic. Bake 10 minutes. Place under the broiler 3 to 4 minutes; broil until lightly browned. Place dip in a small bowl in center of platter or tray, and surround with pita crisps. Serve immediately.

NUTRITION ANALYSIS
(PER SERVING: 1/3 CUP DIP + 4 PITA CRISPS)

Protein 10 gm., Carbohydrate 31 gm., Fiber 5 gm., Fat 3 gm., Cholesterol 0, Calcium 23 mg., Sodium 258 mg.

Calories 186
From protein: 20%; From carbohydrate: 65%; From fat: 15%

Colorful Guacamole

Serve this easy-to-make starter with blue corn chips.

◆ 12 SERVINGS ◆

2 large ripe avocados
juice of 1 plump lime
2 cloves garlic, minced
1/3 cup sliced scallions
1/3 cup chopped red bell pepper
14 1/2-oz. can diced tomatoes with jalapeños (drained)
1/4 cup snipped fresh cilantro
2 tsp. Bragg liquid aminos

Slice avocados in half and remove pit. Use a melon baller to remove flesh. Place in a medium bowl and mash. Drizzle generously with lime juice. Add garlic, scallions, and bell pepper. Add drained tomatoes and cilantro; mix thoroughly. Cover and chill until ready to serve.

NUTRITION ANALYSIS
(PER 3 1/2-OZ. SERVING)

Protein 2 gm., Carbohydrate 24 gm., Fiber 1 gm., Fat 5 gm., Cholesterol 0, Calcium 9 mg., Sodium 116 mg.

Calories 68
From protein: 4%; From carbohydrate: 67%; From fat: 29%

Cocktail Nibbles

Chunks of broiled tofu hot dogs or squares of lite silken tofu are speared with toothpicks for dipping in a tasty sauce.

◆ 8 SERVINGS ◆

2 12-oz. pkg. tofu hot dogs, cut to 1-inch pieces (see Soyfoods Pantry)

OR

2 pkgs. lite silken tofu* (extra firm), drained and cubed

DIPPING SAUCE:

1 cup fruit-sweetened ketchup
2 Tbsp. dry sherry
1 clove garlic
2 scallions, sliced
3 Tbsp. tomato paste
3 Tbsp. Dijon mustard
1 Tbsp. grated gingerroot

Blend sauce ingredients until smooth (a hand-held blender works best). Place the cut hot dogs under the broiler and cook, turning frequently, about 3 to 4 minutes. Pierce hot dogs with toothpicks. Serve immediately.

SILKEN NIBBLES

Place the cubed tofu on a plate around a bowl of sauce. Diners can spear tofu with toothpicks, dip in sauce, and enjoy.

*Only Mori Nu, aseptically packaged tofu, can be used right from the package. If you're using water packed or vacuum packed tofu, it should be steamed for 10 minutes, then cooled and cubed.

COCKTAIL WIENERS NUTRITION ANALYSIS (PER 4-OZ. SERVING)

Protein 21 gm., Carbohydrate 18 gm., Fiber 3 gm., Fat 1 gm., Cholesterol 0, Calcium 5 mg., Sodium 429 mg.

Calories 174
From protein: 51%; From carbohydrate: 42%; From fat: 6%

SILKEN NIBBLES NUTRITION ANALYSIS (PER 4.5-OZ. SERVING)

Protein 7 gm., Carbohydrate 10 gm., Fiber 0, Fat 1 gm., Cholesterol 0, Calcium 6 mg., Sodium 500 mg.

Calories 77
From protein: 36%; From carbohydrate: 52%; From fat: 12%

Cold Noodles Szechuan

A popular first course at Chinese restaurants, this delightful dish is easy to make at home.

◆ 6 SERVINGS ◆

1/4 cup rice vinegar
3 Tbsp. peanut butter
1 1/2 Tbsp. tamari
1 1/2 tsp. hot pepper sesame oil
1/2 tsp. toasted sesame oil
2 cloves garlic, minced
3 Tbsp. chopped shallots
2 Tbsp. hot water
8 oz. soba noodles
1 cup sliced scallions
1 to 3 Tbsp. Szechuan chili sauce—to taste

In a 2-cup glass measuring cup or small bowl, blend together the first 8 ingredients to prepare dressing. Set aside in refrigerator. Cook noodles according to package directions. Drain noodles and rinse with cold water. Place noodles in a 2-quart. bowl and toss with dressing and scallions. Mix well. Add chili sauce according to taste. Serve immediately.

NUTRITION ANALYSIS
(PER SERVING)

Protein 8 gm., Carbohydrate 33 gm., Fiber 1 gm., Fat 5 gm., Cholesterol 0, Calcium 19 mg., Sodium 509 mg.

Calories 201
From protein: 15%; From carbohydrate: 62%; From fat: 23%

Dilled Artichoke Dip

This creamy dip is delicious served hot from the oven or chilled.

◆ ABOUT 5 1/4 CUPS ◆

1 cup soymilk lite
1 tsp. cider vinegar
1 1/4 cups lite silken tofu (firm), drained
1/2 cup sliced scallions
3 cloves garlic, peeled
2 13.75-oz. cans quartered artichoke hearts, drained
1 Tbsp. dried dillweed, separated
2 Tbsp. very dry sherry
1/4 cup nutritional yeast
1 Tbsp. Dijon mustard

Preheat oven to 350°. Place soymilk in a small measuring cup; add vinegar, and set aside. Place tofu in food processor, and blend. Add scallions and garlic, and process. Add artichokes and soymilk; process. Add 1 tsp. of the dried dillweed along with remaining ingredients. Process to mix. Pour into a 2-quart casserole dish. Sprinkle generously with reserved dillweed. (At this point you may cover and refrigerate for up to 24 hours.) Bake in preheated oven for 35 minutes or until lightly browned and firm to the touch at the center. Serve garnished with fresh dill, with pita crisps (see page 56).

NUTRITION ANALYSIS
(PER 1/3-CUP SERVING)

Protein 4 gm., Carbohydrate 5 gm., Fiber 1 gm., Fat 0, Cholesterol 0, Calcium 7 mg., Sodium 101 mg.

Calories 38
From protein: 40%; From carbohydrate: 50%; From fat: 11%

Especially Onion Dip

This dairy-free variation on a classic is creamy and delicious.

◆ ABOUT 3 CUPS ◆

- 1 1/4 cups lite silken tofu (extra firm), drained
- 3 Tbsp. Veganrella cream cheese or low-fat cream cheese
- 1.75-oz. pkg. dry onion soup mix
- 3 cloves garlic, peeled
- 8-oz. can sliced water chestnuts, drained
- 3 scallions, sliced
- 1/4 cup soymilk lite

Place drained tofu in a food processor, and blend until smooth. Add cream cheese and blend. Add dry soup mix and garlic; blend. Add water chestnuts, scallions, and soymilk. Pulse, just to mix, leaving a chunky consistency. Serve with crudités.

NUTRITION ANALYSIS
(PER 2-OZ. SERVING)

Protein 3 gm., Carbohydrate 6 gm., Fiber 1 gm., Fat 1 gm., Cholesterol 0, Calcium 10 mg., Sodium 408 mg.

Calories 46
From protein: 21%; From carbohydrate: 54%; From fat: 25%

Marvelous Mushroom Pâté

"Meaty" portobello mushrooms and tempeh lend an authentic quality to this fabulous pâté.

◆ 12 SERVINGS ◆

1 1/2 tsp. olive oil
1/4 tsp. crushed red pepper
1 cup sliced scallions
6 cloves garlic, minced
6 oz. portobello mushrooms, cubed
6 oz. cremini mushrooms
4 oz. seasoned tempeh, cubed
3 Tbsp. very dry sherry
1 Tbsp. egg replacer powder*
1/4 cup water
1/3 cup tomato paste
2 Tbsp. Dijon mustard
1 tsp. granulated garlic
2 tsp. rubbed sage
1 Tbsp. tamari
1/4 tsp. ground allspice
1/8 tsp. ground cloves
dash cayenne pepper

Heat oil and crushed red pepper 1 minute, over medium high heat. Add scallions and garlic; sauté 2 minutes. Add the next 3 ingredients and cook, stirring, 5 minutes. Add sherry, and simmer 10 minutes. Cool slightly, then pour mixture into food processor. Whisk egg replacer powder with water in a small bowl until foamy. Add to mushroom mixture along with remaining ingredients. Blend until thick and smooth. Spoon into loaf pan and garnish with fresh basil. Chill 3 hours or overnight. Serve with pita crisps (see page 56).

*Do not substitute with beaten egg whites.

NUTRITION ANALYSIS
(PER 3-OZ. SERVING)

Protein 4 gm., Carbohydrate 6 gm., Fiber 1 gm., Fat 1 gm., Cholesterol 0, Calcium 14 mg., Sodium 80 mg.

Calories 52
From protein: 29%; From carbohydrate: 48%; From fat: 23%

Grilled Marinated Portobellos

These tender, flavorful mushrooms are sometimes described as "vegetarian steak."

◆ 4 SERVINGS ◆

4 portobello mushrooms (about 12 oz.)
Vegetable oil cooking spray

MARINADE:

1/3 cup balsamic vinegar
4 Tbsp. tamari
3 Tbsp. very dry sherry
6 cloves garlic, minced
1 tsp. dried thyme
3 Tbsp. minced shallots
1 Tbsp. olive oil

Remove and discard stems from mushrooms. Wipe caps with damp paper towels and divide in half. Set aside. Whisk together marinade ingredients in a large glass measuring cup. Place mushroom caps in a single layer in a zipper lock plastic bag (1-gallon size). Pour marinade in bag, close, and turn bag several times to soak mushrooms. Set aside, allowing mushrooms to marinate at room temperature for at least 2 or 3 hours. Turn bag every 30 minutes, if possible.

Spray a broiler pan with cooking spray, and place mushrooms in preheated broiler. Broil mushrooms 3 to 5 minutes on each side. Lightly spray second side when turning them over. Check mushrooms often. Remove mushrooms, slice thinly, keeping slices together, and serve.

NUTRITION ANALYSIS
(PER SERVING)

Protein 4 gm., Carbohydrate 9 gm., Fiber 1 gm., Fat 4 gm., Cholesterol 0, Calcium 27 mg., Sodium 816 mg.

Calories 83
From protein: 18%; From carbohydrate: 42%; From fat: 40%

Pita Crisps

These low-fat alternatives to chips are terrific with any dip.

◆ 12 SERVINGS ◆

Vegetable oil cooking spray
12 whole wheat or oat bran pita pockets
granulated garlic

Preheat oven to 400°. Line a baking pan with foil, and spray with cooking spray. Cut pita pockets into eighths, and place on prepared pan. Lightly spray the top side of the pita bread, and sprinkle with granulated garlic. Bake 10 minutes. Place under the broiler 3 to 4 minutes or until lightly browned. Serve immediately.

NUTRITION ANALYSIS
(PER SERVING: 8 PITA CRISPS)

Protein 5 gm., Carbohydrate 25 gm., Fiber 3 gm., Fat 1 gm., Cholesterol 0, Calcium 15 mg., Sodium 172 mg.

Calories 122
From protein: 15%; From carbohydrate: 77%; From fat: 8%

Spicy Roasted Pepper Dip

This is a delicious, savory dip that is low in calories and fat.

◆ 3 CUPS ◆

1 1/4 cups lite silken tofu (firm), drained
1/3 cup tofu mayonnaise (see Soyfoods Pantry)
4 cloves garlic, peeled
3/4 cup roasted sweet red and yellow peppers (drained)
2 Tbsp. red wine vinegar
1/2 tsp. Tabasco sauce
2 tsp. tamari
1/2 tsp. dried basil
1/2 tsp. dried marjoram

Place tofu in food processor, and blend. Add tofu mayonnaise, garlic, and peppers; pulse to mix. Add remaining ingredients, and pulse until blended but chunky. Refrigerate several hours or overnight. Serve **well chilled** with crudités and pita crisps (see page 56).

NUTRITION ANALYSIS
(PER 3-OZ. SERVING)

Protein 2 gm., Carbohydrate 4 gm., Fiber 1 gm., Fat 1 gm., Cholesterol 0, Calcium 20 mg., Sodium 69 mg.

Calories 28
From protein: 24%; From carbohydrate: 51%; From fat: 25%

Sausage Roll-Ups

These roll-ups are so authentic in taste, appearance, and texture, you could fool even the most avid meat eater. You can make them in advance, if you wish, then reheat and slice just before serving.

◆ 24 HORS D'OEUVRES ◆

FILLING:

1 1/2 tsp. olive oil

1/8 tsp. crushed red pepper

1 medium, sweet onion (Vidalia, Texas, Maui), chopped

5 large cloves garlic, minced

14-oz. pkg. Gimme Lean, sausage flavor

10-oz. pkg. frozen spinach, thawed, drained, and pressed in colander

1/4 cup very dry sherry

1 tsp. thyme

DOUGH:

1/2 cup soymilk lite

2 Tbsp. lemon juice

2 cups whole wheat flour

1/2 tsp. salt

2 1/2 tsp. baking powder

1/3 cup lite silken tofu, drained

1 Tbsp. liquid Fruitsource or honey

1 1/2 tsp. olive oil

Preheat oven to 350°. Heat oil and crushed pepper in a 10" frying pan over medium-high heat for 1 minute. Add onions and garlic, and sauté 3 minutes. Add Gimme Lean and well drained spinach; mix thoroughly. Sauté 10 minutes, stirring frequently. Add sherry and thyme, and lower to simmer. Combine soymilk and lemon juice in a cup; set aside. Place next 3 dough ingredients in food processor; process to mix. Add tofu, and process to crumb. Add Fruitsource; blend, then add soymilk through feed tube while processing.

Place dough on floured board. Oil hands lightly, and knead dough 5 minutes, until elastic. Divide dough in two, and roll 1/2- to 1/4-inch thick. Spread 1 1/2 cups filling on dough, and roll up, tucking in ends as you go. Repeat with second half of dough and remaining filling. Place roll-ups in a baking pan coated with cooking spray. Bake 20 minutes, then serve immediately, or wrap in foil, and refrigerate. Reheat in foil 15 minutes at 325° before serving.

NUTRITION ANALYSIS
(PER SERVING)

Protein 5 gm., Carbohydrate 12 gm., Fiber 2 gm., Fat 1 gm., Cholesterol 0, Calcium 25 mg., Sodium 142 mg.

Calories 73
From protein: 25%; From carbohydrate: 65%; From fat: 10%

Soybeans in the Pod

One of my favorite ways to enjoy soybeans is to eat them right out of the pod. Hold one end of the pod between two fingers, place the pod between your teeth and pull gently. The delicious soybeans will slide out. Discard the pod. They're so tasty, you won't be able to stop eating them.

◆ 4 SERVINGS ◆

5 quarts water
1 tsp. salt
16-oz. pkg. green vegetable soybeans (Edamamé)

Bring water to boil in a large saucepan. Add salt and frozen pods. Do not defrost pods before cooking. Simmer pods for 5 minutes. Drain, and serve hot or cold.

NUTRITION ANALYSIS
(PER SERVING)

Protein 14 gm., Carbohydrate 15 gm., Fiber 3 gm., Fat 4 gm., Cholesterol 0, Calcium 82 gm., Sodium 272 mg.

Calories 142
From protein: 36%; Calories from carbohydrate: 39%; From fat: 24%

Soynuts

Roasted soynuts are easy to make in your own kitchen. They make a great snack and a deliciously crunchy addition to an hors d'oeuvres buffet.

◆ 2 1/2 CUPS ◆

1 cup dried soybeans
1 quart cold water
Vegetable oil cooking spray
1/2 tsp. salt

Rinse beans thoroughly. Sort and discard any stones or debris that remain. Place beans in a bowl, and cover with cold water. Soak beans 3 to 4 hours on the counter or overnight in the refrigerator. Drain the beans, and pat dry with paper towels.

Preheat oven to 350°. Spray a baking sheet with cooking spray. Place beans in a single layer on the baking sheet. Bake 35 to 45 minutes, stirring often, until well browned. Place in a bowl, and salt to taste. Serve warm, or store in a covered container in the refrigerator. You may reheat at 325° until hot, if desired.

NUTRITION ANALYSIS
(PER 1-OZ. SERVING)

Protein 9 gm., Carbohydrate 7 gm., Fiber 3 gm., Fat 5 gm., Cholesterol 0, Calcium 68 mg., Sodium 57 mg.

Calories 102
From protein: 33%; From carbohydrate: 27%; From fat: 40%

(The percentage of calories from fat seems high because the calories are so low.)

Spanakopitta

This savory Greek pie made with flaky phyllo pastry is as delectable as it is beautiful.

◆ 16 SERVINGS ◆

- 16-oz. pkg. phyllo pastry
- Vegetable oil cooking spray
- 2 1/2 cups lite silken tofu (extra firm), drained and patted dry
- 1/2 cup nutritional yeast
- 2 Tbsp. mellow white miso
- 2 Tbsp. mirin
- 4 10-oz. pkg. frozen spinach, thawed, drained, and pressed in a colander
- 6 cloves garlic, minced
- 2/3 cup chopped scallions
- 2 tsp. dried dillweed
- 1/4 tsp. ground nutmeg
- 1/4 tsp. lemon pepper
- 1/2 cup whole wheat bread crumbs

Prepare phyllo pastry using techniques on pg. 43. Preheat oven to 350°. Spray a 9" x 13" pan with cooking spray. Place tofu in a large bowl. Use a potato masher to mash it into curds. Stir in nutritional yeast. Blend miso with mirin in a small bowl until smooth. Add to tofu mixture. Add drained spinach, and mix thoroughly. Mix in garlic, scallions, dill weed, nutmeg, and lemon pepper. Set aside.

Gently place one pastry leaf across the bottom of the pan, leaving an overlap. Spray lightly with cooking spray and sprinkle with bread crumbs. Repeat until half of the phyllo leaves are used. Spread spinach mixture over dough, then fold the pastry in over the filling. Top with the remaining pastry, using the cooking spray and bread crumbs between the leaves in the same way. Trim the pastry around the edges to a one inch overhang. Then tuck the top pastry in down the sides, using a rubber spatula to make room. Use a sharp knife to make a diamond pattern cutting just through the top pastry. Bake for one hour; serve warm.

NUTRITION ANALYSIS (PER SERVING)

Protein 12 gm., Carbohydrate 32 gm., Fiber 2 gm., Fat 2 gm., Cholesterol 0, Calcium 112 mg., Sodium 274 mg.

Calories 170
From protein: 24%; From carbohydrate: 66%; From fat: 10%

Spinach Balls

These delicious hors d'oeuvres are easy to make. They can be assembled in advance and popped into the oven just before serving.

◆ ABOUT 50 SPINACH BALLS ◆

Vegetable oil cooking spray
1 1/4 cups lite silken tofu (extra firm), drained
2 Tbsp. mellow white miso
1 1/2 Tbsp. very dry sherry
2 Tbsp. egg replacer powder
1/4 cup water
1 Tbsp. Dijon mustard
1/4 cup nutritional yeast
1 tsp. granulated garlic
1 tsp. dried parsley
1 tsp. tamari
10-oz. pkg. frozen spinach, thawed and well drained

Preheat oven to 350°. Spray 2 baking sheets with cooking spray. Place tofu in food processor, and blend. Add miso and sherry, and blend. Whisk egg replacer powder and water in a small bowl until frothy; add to the mixture. Add the next 5 ingredients, and blend. Add the spinach, and pulse to mix. Place rounded tablespoonfuls of the spinach mixture on the prepared baking sheets. Bake for 15 minutes, then broil until brown. Serve hot.

NUTRITION ANALYSIS
(PER SERVING: 4 SPINACH BALLS)

Protein 4 gm., Carbohydrate 4 gm., Fiber 1 gm., Fat 1 gm., Cholesterol 0, Calcium 8 mg., Sodium 80 mg.

Calories 34
From protein: 48%; From carbohydrate: 40%; From fat: 12%

Savory Spinach Dip

A most popular dip at get-togethers, this creamy, flavorful, and rich-tasting dip is low in calories and fat. Serve with crudités and pita crisps to rave reviews.

◆ 4 1/2 CUPS ◆

1 1/4 cups lite silken tofu (extra firm), drained
1.75-oz. pkg. onion soup mix
1/2 cup tofu mayonnaise
3 large cloves garlic, peeled
10-oz. pkg. frozen, chopped spinach, thawed, drained, and pressed in a colander
8-oz. can sliced water chestnuts, drained
1/4 cup thinly sliced scallions

Drain tofu, and pat with paper towels. Place tofu in food processor, and blend until smooth. Add dry soup mix, mayonnaise, and garlic; blend. Add spinach, and blend. Add water chestnuts and scallions; pulse just until chunky. Refrigerate for at least an hour before serving.

NUTRITION ANALYSIS
(PER 2.25-OZ. SERVING)

Protein 2 gm., Carbohydrate 4 gm., Fiber 1 gm., Fat 2 gm., Cholesterol 0, Calcium 30 mg., Sodium 103 mg.

Calories 42
From protein: 21%; From carbohydrate: 41%; From fat: 38%

Savory Stuffed Mushrooms

The hearty filling for these popular appetizers can be made in advance, refrigerated, and then stuffed just before baking.

◆ 8 SERVINGS ◆

Vegetable oil cooking spray
30 large mushrooms
1 1/2 tsp. olive oil
1/8 tsp. crushed red pepper
1 1/2 cups chopped red onion
1 cup finely grated carrot (1 large carrot)
1 cup dry TVP granules, ground-beef style
1/3 cup water
1 Tbsp. vegetable boullion powder, beef flavor
1/2 cup white wine
1 tsp. granulated garlic
1/4 cup nutritional yeast
1 Tbsp. Bragg Liquid Aminos

Preheat oven to 375°. Spray a baking pan lightly with cooking spray. Rinse, brush or damp-wipe mushrooms, then dry thoroughly. Gently remove stems; chop, and set aside.

Heat oil and crushed pepper in a 10" frying pan over medium-high heat for 1 minute. Add onion, carrot, and chopped mushroom stems. Sauté 5 minutes. Stir in dry TVP granules. Cook 2 minutes. Add water, boullion, and wine. Lower heat to simmer, then add garlic, nutritional yeast, and liquid aminos. Simmer 5 to 8 minutes, stirring occasionally. Mound filling into mushroom caps, and place on prepared pan. Bake for 12 minutes, then broil for 3 minutes or just until browned. Serve hot.

NUTRITION ANALYSIS
(PER SERVING)

Protein 10 gm., Carbohydrate 51 gm., Fiber 4 gm., Fat 1 gm., Cholesterol 0, Calcium 11 mg., Sodium 134 mg.

Calories 106
From protein: 15%; From carbohydrate: 79%; From fat: 5%

Chili 'n Chips

Serve this spicy filling with pita crisps or blue corn chips, and Colorful Guacamole (page 49).

◆ 16 SERVINGS ◆

1 1/2 tsp. olive oil
1/8 tsp. crushed red pepper
1 cup chopped red onion
6 cloves garlic, minced
1/3 cup chopped red bell pepper
1 cup zucchini, cut into julienne strips
1 1/2 cups chopped carrots
1 cup chopped mushrooms
2 10-oz. pkgs. Ready Ground Tofu, Hot & Spicy
15 1/2-oz. can chili beans with chipotle peppers
14 1/2-oz. can diced tomatoes and jalapeños
1 tsp. dried thyme
1 tsp. Mexican oregano
1 tsp. ground cumin
1/3 cup snipped fresh cilantro

In a 4-quart saucepan, heat oil and crushed pepper for 1 minute over medium-high heat. Add the next 3 ingredients and sauté 2 minutes. Add zucchini, carrots, and mushrooms. Cook 5 minutes, stirring frequently. Stir in tofu. Lower heat to medium and cook 3 minutes, then add remaining filling ingredients. Lower heat and simmer 10 minutes, stirring frequently. Keep warm until ready to serve.

NUTRITION ANALYSIS
(PER 4 1/2-OZ. SERVING)

Protein 5 gm., Carbohydrate 10 gm., Fiber 2 gm., Fat 2 gm., Cholesterol 0, Calcium 15 mg., Sodium 179 mg.

Calories 69
From protein: 27%; From carbohydrate: 49%; From fat: 25%

Sweet and Sour "Meatballs"

This delicious dish is always a crowd pleaser. Serve it as an appetizer or as a main course over rice or noodles.

◆ 16 APPETIZER SERVINGS OR 8 MAIN-COURSE SERVINGS ◆

SAUCE:

1 Tbsp. olive oil
1/8 tsp. crushed red pepper
1 Tbsp. grated fresh gingerroot
3/4 cup chopped red onion
1/3 cup chopped red bell pepper
5 large cloves garlic, minced
2 28-oz. cans crushed tomatoes
1 large bay leaf
2 Tbsp. cider vinegar
1 tsp. tamari
1/2 tsp. ground ginger
2 Tbsp. liquid Fruitsource or honey
1/4 cup frozen apple juice concentrate, thawed
2 Tbsp. lemon juice

"MEATBALLS":

2 14-oz. pkg. Gimme Lean, ground beef style
1/2 cup ketchup
2 Tbsp. egg replacer powder
1/2 cup water
1/4 cup whole wheat bread crumbs
1 1/2 tsp. ground allspice
2 tsp. granulated garlic
Vegetable oil cooking spray

Heat olive oil and crushed pepper in a 4-quart saucepan over medium-high heat. Add the next 4 ingredients, and sauté 3 minutes. Add the tomatoes and bay leaf, and simmer 5 minutes. Whisk together the next 6 ingredients in a small bowl; add to the sauce. Cover, and simmer, stirring occasionally.

Preheat oven to 400°. Place the Gimme Lean in a large bowl with ketchup, and mix with a fork. Place egg replacer powder and water in a small bowl. Whisk until foamy. Add remaining meatball ingredients; mix thoroughly. Coat a baking pan with cooking spray. Form meatball mixture into about 30 balls (2 to 3 inches in diameter) and place on prepared pan. Spray meatballs lightly with cooking spray. Bake 15 minutes. Place under broiler to brown during the last few minutes of baking. Place browned meatballs in the sauce, and simmer 30 to 45 minutes or until ready to serve.

NUTRITION ANALYSIS (PER APPETIZER-SIZE SERVING)

Protein 10 gm., Carbohydrate 22 gm., Fiber 3 gm., Fat 1 gm., Cholesterol 0, Calcium 35 mg., Sodium 410 mg.

Calories 129
From protein: 29%; From carbohydrate: 63%; From fat: 8%

Veggie Nachos

Your guests will be incredulous to learn that there are no meat or dairy products in this intensely flavorful and appealing Southwestern treat!

◆ 12 SERVINGS ◆

TVP LAYER

- 3 cups TVP, ground beef style
- 1 1/2 cups beef-flavored vegetable broth, boiling
- 1 1/2 tsp. olive oil
- 1/2 cup chopped red onion
- 1/4 cup chopped green pepper
- 3 cloves garlic, minced
- 2 15-oz. cans Mexican-style stewed tomatoes
- 1/4 cup tomato paste
- 1/4 cup burgundy
- 1 tsp. ground cumin
- 1/4 cup chopped fresh cilantro

BEAN LAYER

- 1 1/2 tsp. olive oil
- 1/2 cup chopped red onion
- 1/4 cup chopped green pepper
- 1 clove garlic, minced
- 2 15-oz. cans black beans
- 6 Tbsp. tomato paste
- 1 bay leaf
- 1 1/2 tsp. ground cumin
- 1/2 tsp. ground coriander
- dash cayenne pepper

CHEESE SAUCE

- 1 1/4 cups lite silken tofu (extra firm), drained
- 2 Tbsp. lemon juice
- 2 cloves garlic, peeled
- 3/4 soymilk lite
- 1/3 cup nutritional yeast
- 1 tsp. Bragg Liquid Aminos

1 10-oz. bag blue corn tortilla chips
1 avocado, sliced into wedges, drizzled with 2 Tbsp. lime juice

TVP LAYER

Place TVP in a medium bowl, cover with boiling broth, stir, and set aside for 10 minutes. Heat oil in a 10" skillet over medium-high heat. Sauté the next 3 ingredients for 3 minutes. Add reconstituted TVP and sauté mixture 10 minutes, stirring frequently. Add remaining TVP layer ingredients, and continue to cook over low heat 10 minutes or until ready to assemble. Stir occasionally.

BEAN LAYER

Heat oil in a medium saucepan over medium-high heat. Add the next 3 ingredients and sauté 3 minutes. Stir in the beans and cook 2 minutes. Add remaining bean layer ingredients. Lower heat and simmer mixture 10 minutes, stirring occasionally.

CHEESE LAYER

Place tofu in food processor and blend until smooth. Add remaining sauce ingredients and blend until smooth.

ASSEMBLY

Preheat oven to 350°. On a large pizza pan, place a generous layer of corn chips. Top with TVP layer. Add bean layer over TVP. Arrange avocado slices attractively over top layer. Pour cheese sauce over all.

Bake 20 minutes or until heated through and sauce is bubbly. Scoop onto individual plates.

NUTRITION ANALYSIS (PER SERVING)

Protein 22 gm., Carbohydrate 40 gm., Fiber 10 gm., Fat 5 gm., Cholesterol 0, Calcium 34 mg., Sodium 583 mg.

Calories 224
From protein: 30%; From carbohydrate: 55%; From fat: 15%

Soups, Stews, and Salads

In this chapter we will prepare flavorful, well-seasoned soups and stews which offer exceptional nutritional value utilizing versatile soyfoods. There's a special warmth about the inviting aroma of a steaming bowl of soup or a robust stew, especially at the end of a tiring day. These savory soups and stews served with a hearty bread and crisp salad combine to make a meal that is satisfying and complete.

Classically elegant Vichyssoise, hearty Basque Stew, and creamy Mushroom Miso Soup are just a few of the irresistible recipes in this collection, which get a nutritional boost from the mighty soybean. Miso is a savory, high-protein seasoning that is used to add unparalleled nutrition and flavor to recipes throughout this book. Long touted for its health giving properties, some Japanese doctors and scientists believe that the amino acids in miso can provide protection against air pollution and other toxins like tobacco smoke.

Salads have always appealed to the health conscious and those concerned with physical fitness. Contemporary salads have become more than just a plate of crisp greens, tomatoes, and snipped herbs. Often they are artful compositions with colorful ingredients like radicchio, arugula, endive, and enoki mushrooms. However, the natural goodness of fresh, raw vegetables is often eclipsed by high-fat dressings which accompany them. Here is a perfect opportunity to replace the heavy ingredients found in traditional dressings with—you guessed it—*soyfoods.* Dressings like Garlic Basil, "Honey" Mustard Dill, and Raspberry Walnut are some of the tasty dressings featured here that are incredibly low in fat and calories. ◆

Salad Greens

Salads no longer have to be monochromatic bowls of chopped iceberg lettuce with sliced tomatoes. Salad making now presents an opportunity to create a colorful array of salad greens from a much broader spectrum than was once available.

When shopping for any kind of lettuce, choose those which are crisp and free of blemishes. Salad greens should always be washed thoroughly and drained, and then either blotted with paper towels or dried in a salad spinner. Never allow the greens to soak, as this will cause the leaves to soften and lose their treasured crunch. One exception is spinach, which, after rinsing, may be soaked briefly in a series of bowls of cold water to remove grit. The following is a list of salad greens that are readily available in supermarkets across the country.

ARUGULA

Sometimes called rocket lettuce, arugula is a tender salad green with a spicy mustard flavor and small, elongated leaves that sometimes have serrated edges.

BELGIAN ENDIVE
(or Witloof Chicory)

This endive is pleasantly bitter, with firm, slender, creamy white leaves edged in pale yellow.

BUTTER LETTUCE

The delicately ruffled leaves of this green have a buttery flavor.

CHINESE CABBAGE

This cabbage has mildly flavored pale green leaves on a long, tight head.

CURLY ENDIVE OR CHICORY

Another green with a pleasantly bitter flavor, curly endive has crisp, dark green leaves with curly edges.

ESCAROLE

This broad-leaf variety of endive has a mildly bitter flavor.

GREEN LEAF LETTUCE

This is a popular variety of loose-leaf lettuce with a delicate flavor.

ICEBERG LETTUCE

The crisp texture and very mild flavor of iceberg lettuce make it the best selling of all types of salad greens.

RADICCHIO

Sometimes called Italian Chicory, this colorful salad component has purplish-red to burgundy leaves with white ribs, shaped around a small round head. Hardy and flavorful, with a taste similar to escarole, this is a fine choice for a gourmet salad mix.

RED CABBAGE

This tastes much like green cabbage, but its bright reddish-purple leaves add a colorful contrast when shredded into a salad.

RED LEAF LETTUCE

This popular variety's tender, dark, red-tinged leaves are a mild and colorful addition to any salad.

ROMAINE

This favorite has dark green outer leaves which lighten toward the center. It has a particularly succulent midrib and a crisp and crunchy texture.

SPINACH

The earthy, lemony, slightly bitter taste of raw spinach is prized in salads. Fresh spinach is available year-round and should be thoroughly rinsed because it is usually very gritty.

WATERCRESS

A member of the mustard family, watercress has small, crisp, deep green leaves and a slightly bitter, peppery flavor. It can be used as an interesting addition to salads or as a garnish.

Basque Stew

This aromatic stew is bursting with the flavors of potatoes, tomatoes, robust herbs, and sausage. This hearty entrée is extraordinary with Saffron Couscous (page 179).*

◆ 12 SERVINGS ◆

1 Tbsp. olive oil
1/4 tsp. crushed red pepper
14-oz. pkg. Gimme Lean, sausage flavor (see Soyfoods Pantry)
4 cups unpeeled potatoes, cut into 2-inch wedges
2 cups baby carrots, cut into thirds
4 medium to large leeks, well rinsed (see Techniques)
8 cloves garlic, minced
1/3 cup chopped orange bell pepper
1 cup white wine
3 cups beef-flavored vegetable broth, boiling
4 1/2 cups chunky tomato sauce
1 large bay leaf
5 to 6 large basil leaves, snipped
2 Tbsp. drained capers
2 tsp. dried thyme
2 Tbsp. cornstarch
2 Tbsp. cold water
1 tsp. dried parsley

Preheat oven to 350°. Heat the crushed pepper in oil in a large stovetop- and oven-proof casserole over medium-high heat. Add Gimme Lean, breaking apart while stirring frequently, about 3 to 5 minutes. Add the next 5 ingredients. Sauté 8 minutes or until vegetables are crisp tender, stirring frequently. Add wine, and cook 3 minutes. Add broth, tomato sauce, and the next four ingredients. Cover stew, and place in oven. Bake 45 minutes. Remove casserole from oven. Make a paste of the cornstarch and water in a small bowl. Add to the stew along with parsley. Cover, and return to the oven for 15 minutes or until ready to serve.

*I use Gimme Lean for a healthy alternative to the sausage that is a traditional ingredient in Basque cuisine.

NUTRITION ANALYSIS
(PER SERVING)

Protein 10 gm., Carbohydrate 43 gm., Fiber 5 gm., Fat 1 gm., Cholesterol 0, Calcium 49 mg., Sodium 394 mg.

Calories 225
From protein: 17%; From carbohydrate: 77%; From fat: 6%

TVP Beef Stew

This homey favorite has tender chunks of TVP and colorful vegetables in a flavorful gravy.

◆ 8 SERVINGS ◆

- 2 cups beef-flavored vegetable broth, boiling
- 1 1/2 cups TVP steak strips
- 1 1/2 tsp. olive oil
- 1/4 tsp. crushed red pepper
- 1 cup chopped red onion
- 4 cloves garlic, minced
- 2 cups sliced baby carrots, 1-inch chunks
- 4 cups cubed, unpeeled potato
- 3 cups zucchini, cut into slices, then quartered
- 2 cups sliced mushrooms
- 1 cup white wine
- 4 cups beef-flavored vegetable broth
- 2 Tbsp. tamari
- 1 tsp. granulated garlic
- 1/4 cup beef-flavored vegetable broth, cold
- 3 Tbsp. cornstarch
- 1 tsp. dried thyme
- 1 tsp. dried marjoram

Combine broth and TVP in a medium glass bowl; steep for 5 minutes. Microwave for 3 minutes; set aside. Sauté oil and crushed pepper in a medium saucepan over medium-high heat for 2 minutes. Add onion and garlic; sauté 3 minutes. Add the next 4 ingredients, and sauté 5 minutes, stirring occasionally. Add wine, and cook 5 minutes. Add reconstituted TVP, 4 cups broth, tamari, and granulated garlic. Lower heat, and simmer 20 minutes, stirring occasionally. Blend cold broth with cornstarch in a small bowl; add to stew. Add thyme and marjoram. Simmer 10 minutes or until ready to serve.

NUTRITION ANALYSIS (PER SERVING)

Protein 12 gm., Carbohydrate 38 gm., Fiber 6 gm., Fat 1 gm., Cholesterol 0, Calcium 39 mg., Sodium 323 mg.

Calories 211
From protein: 23%; From carbohydrate: 72%; From fat: 6%

Italian Sausage Stew

You will savor this delightful stew with its succulent chunks of Italian sausage (vegetarian, of course) in a richly flavored sauce laced with vermouth.

◆ 8 SERVINGS ◆

1 Tbsp. olive oil
1/4 tsp. crushed red pepper
1 small onion, chopped, about 1 cup
5 cloves garlic, minced
1/2 cup chopped red bell pepper
11.2-oz. pkg. Lean Links Italian, cut in 1/2-inch pieces
2 cups baby carrots, halved crosswise
4 cups diced, peeled potatoes
1 small zucchini, sliced and cut in half (about 1 1/2 cups)
1/3 cup vermouth
2 cups boiling beef-flavored vegetable broth
1 bay leaf
3 cups chunky tomato sauce

Heat oil and crushed red pepper in a 4- to 5-quart saucepan over medium-high heat for 2 minutes. Add the next 3 ingredients, and sauté for 2 minutes. Add sausage, and sauté about 8 minutes. Add the next 3 ingredients, and cook mixture 10 minutes, stirring frequently. Stir in vermouth, and cook for 2 minutes. Lower heat to simmer and add remaining ingredients. Simmer for 25 minutes or until ready to serve, stirring occasionally. Serve accompanied by a rice or couscous dish.

NUTRITION ANALYSIS
(PER SERVING)

Protein 10 gm., Carbohydrate 48 gm., Fiber 4 gm., Fat 4 gm., Cholesterol 0, Calcium 28 mg., Sodium 375 mg.

Calories 270
From protein: 15%; From carbohydrate: 72%; From fat: 13%

Creamy Tomato Orzo Soup

This soup is so delicious, you'll want to make it often. Try adding a few drops of hot pepper sauce at the table for an extra zing!

◆ ABOUT 4 1/2 QUARTS ◆

- 1 piece kombu
- 2 quarts water
- 1 medium onion, chopped
- 4 cloves garlic, minced
- 1/3 cup chopped green bell pepper
- 1 Tbsp. grated fresh gingerroot
- 1 cup sliced carrots
- 2 cups beef-flavored vegetable broth, boiling
- 14.5-oz. can Italian-style stewed tomatoes
- 1 tsp. granulated garlic
- 1 tsp. dried basil
- 1 Tbsp. tamari
- 3/4 cup orzo (uncooked)
- 1/3 cup mellow white miso
- 1/2 cup white wine

Place kombu and water in a 5-quart pot. Soak kombu overnight or for at least 15 minutes. Add the next 5 ingredients, and bring to a boil. Reduce heat, and simmer 15 minutes, stirring occasionally. Remove kombu,* then add hot broth, tomatoes, and seasonings. Bring to a boil again, and add orzo. Simmer 15 minutes, stirring occasionally. Place miso in a small bowl and cream with wine. When smooth, add to soup; simmer 5 minutes or until ready to serve. Do not boil.

*Cooked kombu can be a delicious addition to a vegetable dish. You may store in refrigerator for future use or discard.

NUTRITION ANALYSIS
(PER 2-CUP SERVING)

Protein 2 gm., Carbohydrate 24 gm., Fiber 3 gm., Fat 1 gm., Cholesterol 0, Calcium 57 mg., Sodium 405 mg.

Calories 128
From protein: 7%; From carbohydrate: 76%; From fat: 5%

Golden Split Pea Curry

This aromatic stew has a lovely golden hue and rich flavor. Serve this hearty stew with brown rice for a satisfying meal.

◆ 8 SERVINGS ◆

2 cups yellow split peas, sorted and rinsed
6 cups chicken-flavored vegetable broth
1 1/2 tsp. olive oil
1 tsp. black mustard seeds
1 cup chopped red onion
4 cloves garlic, minced
2 ribs celery, sliced
2 cups sliced carrots
2 cups peeled and cubed potatoes
1 Tbsp. grated gingerroot
1/2 tsp. turmeric
1 tsp. ground coriander
1 cup white wine
1/2 cup plus 2 Tbsp. lite silken tofu (extra firm), drained
1/2 cup soymilk lite
1/4 tsp. asafetida

Combine split peas with broth in a 5-quart saucepan; bring to a boil. Reduce heat and simmer 20 minutes, skimming foam from surface, and stirring occasionally. Heat oil over medium high heat in a 10" frying pan. Stir in mustard seeds, and cook until they begin to pop, about 2 minutes. Add the next 5 ingredients, stirring after each addition. Sauté for 5 minutes. Stir in the next 3 ingredients and continue to cook 5 minutes longer. Add the wine; reduce heat to medium low. Cover and cook until vegetables are soft, stirring occasionally.

Place the tofu in food processor, and blend. Add soymilk and asafetida, and blend until smooth, about 1 minute. Stir tofu mixture into frying pan, and simmer a few minutes. Add the vegetable tofu mixture to the peas, mixing thoroughly. Simmer until ready to serve.

NUTRITION ANALYSIS
(PER 1 1/2-CUP SERVING)

Protein 16 gm., Carbohydrate 52 gm., Fiber 7 gm., Fat 2 gm., Cholesterol 0, Calcium 66 mg., Sodium 220 mg.

Calories 303
From protein: 22%; From carbohydrate: 72%; From fat: 7%

Golden Vegetable Dill Soup

This soup is simply "dill-ightful."

◆ ABOUT 4 QUARTS ◆

1 1/2 tsp. olive oil
1 large onion, chopped (about 2 cups)
4 large cloves garlic, minced
1 large rib celery, sliced
2 cups sliced baby carrots
2 cups sliced summer squash
8 cups beef-flavored vegetable broth (hot)
1 1/2 cups frozen corn, thawed
1 1/4 cups lite silken tofu, drained
1 cup nutritional yeast
3 Tbsp. tapioca flour or arrowroot
1/4 cup soymilk lite
1 Tbsp. Bragg liquid aminos
1 Tbsp. tamari
1/2 cup chopped fresh dill
1 tsp. granulated garlic
1 tsp. dried tarragon
1 tsp. ground coriander

Heat oil in a 5-quart saucepan over medium-high heat for 1 minute. Add the next 4 ingredients; sauté 3 minutes. Add squash; sauté 2 minutes. Add broth and corn, then lower heat to simmer. Cover and cook until vegetables soften, about 20 minutes.

Blend tofu in food processor until smooth. Add nutritional yeast, and blend again. Scoop out 1 1/2 cups of soup vegetables with a slotted spoon, and purée with tofu. Add purée to soup pot gradually, stirring with a wire whisk. Blend flour with soymilk in a small bowl; stir into soup. Season with remaining ingredients. Simmer for 15 minutes or until ready to serve.

NUTRITION ANALYSIS
(PER 2-CUP SERVING)

Protein 16 gm., Carbohydrate 68 gm., Fiber 3 gm., Fat 2 gm., Cholesterol 0, Calcium 44 mg., Sodium 291 mg.

Calories 200
From protein: 18%; From carbohydrate: 76%; From fat: 6%

Italian Vegetable Soup

This is a delicious way to use the overflow of zucchini from your garden.

◆ ABOUT 4 1/2 QUARTS ◆

- 1 1/2 tsp. olive oil
- 1 large red onion, chopped
- 6 cloves garlic, minced
- 4 cups sliced zucchini, cut in half
- 2 cups sliced baby carrots, 1/2-inch slices
- 1 rib celery, including top, sliced
- 1 cup dry vermouth
- 6 cups chicken-flavored vegetable broth
- 2 14.5-oz. cans Italian-flavored tomatoes, peeled and diced
- 10 large fresh basil leaves, snipped
- 1/2 cup dry TVP, ground poultry style
- 2 tsp. chicken-flavored vegetable bouillon powder
- 1 Tbsp. Bragg Liquid Aminos

Heat oil over medium-high heat in a 5-quart saucepan. Add the onion and garlic, and sauté 3 minutes. Add the next 3 ingredients and sauté until crisp tender, about 5 minutes. Add vermouth, and cook 3 minutes. Add broth, tomatoes, and basil; lower heat. Simmer 30 minutes.

Add TVP granules and remaining ingredients. Simmer an additional 20 minutes or until ready to serve.

NUTRITION ANALYSIS
(PER 2 1/4-CUP SERVING)

Protein 6 gm., Carbohydrate 57 gm., Fiber 4 gm., Fat 1 gm., Cholesterol 0, Calcium 70 mg., Sodium 490 mg.

Calories 134
From protein: 9%; From carbohydrate: 87%; From fat: 5%

Mushroom Miso Soup

A delectable soup with a velvety smooth texture, this nutritious, flavorful, dairy-free cream of mushroom soup is wonderful.

◆ 8 SERVINGS ◆

1 1/2 tsp. olive oil
1 1/2 cups chopped sweet onion (Vidalia, Maui, or red)
6 cloves garlic, minced
1/2 cup chopped green pepper
6 oz. cremini mushrooms, sliced
1 cup white wine
4 cups beef-flavored vegetable broth, hot
2 medium red potatoes, parboiled, quartered, and peeled
1 1/2 Tbsp. olive oil
3 Tbsp. whole wheat flour
1 cup soymilk lite
1/3 cup country barley miso
1/3 cup nutritional yeast
1 rounded Tbsp. dehydrated mushroom powder

Sauté onion, garlic, and pepper in olive oil in a 5-quart saucepan over medium-high heat for 3 minutes. Add sliced mushrooms, and sauté about 5 minutes. Add wine, and cook 3 minutes. Add hot vegetable broth. Lower heat, then add potatoes and simmer 45 minutes.

Heat 1 1/2 tablespoons oil in a small saucepan over medium-high heat. Stir in flour to form a roux. Whisk in soymilk. Lower heat to simmer; stir until white sauce thickens. Set aside.

Remove potatoes and two-thirds of the vegetables to food processor, and blend until smooth. Add miso to processor, and blend again. Scrape mixture into soup, and stir until blended. Whisk white sauce into soup, and mix thoroughly. Whisk yeast and mushroom powder into soup. Heat *just* until it comes to a boil. Remove from heat. Serve.

NUTRITION ANALYSIS
(PER 1 1/2-CUP SERVING)

Protein 7 gm., Carbohydrate 23 gm., Fiber 2 gm., Fat 4 gm., Cholesterol 0, Calcium 20 mg., Sodium 290 mg.

Calories 175
From protein: 16%; From carbohydrate: 54%; From fat: 18%

Good Morning Miso Soup

Considered a nutritional keystone, miso soup is an integral part of the traditional Japanese breakfast. It's delicious any time of the day or evening.

◆ ABOUT 3 QUARTS ◆

1 piece of kombu
2 quarts water
3/4 cup chopped onion
3 cloves garlic, minced
1 large tomato, chopped
1/3 cup chopped green bell pepper
2 Tbsp. grated fresh gingerroot
2 cups chicken-flavored vegetable broth
1 tsp. granulated garlic
1/2 tsp. ground ginger
1/2 cup lite silken tofu (optional)
1/3 cup mellow white miso
1/4 cup country barley miso

Place kombu in water in a 4-quart saucepan. Let it soak while chopping vegetables (you may also soak the kombu overnight). Add the next 5 ingredients, and bring mixture to a boil. Simmer 15 minutes; remove kombu. Use a wire strainer with a handle to remove solids. Continue to simmer broth as you press the solids firmly against the strainer with the back of a large spoon, squeezing the juices back into the soup; discard solids. Add the vegetable broth, garlic, and ginger to the simmering broth.

Cut tofu into a 1/2-inch slice for each serving. Cut each slice into small cubes, and place the cubes in the bottom of soup bowls. Combine both varieties of miso in a small bowl. Gradually add a cup of the broth, blending with a small whisk or fork, until the mixture is creamed. Add the mixture back to the soup, and simmer gently 2 minutes. Serve immediately.

When reheating the soup, heat gently, just until the first bubbles appear.

NUTRITION ANALYSIS
(PER 1 1/2-CUP SERVING)

Protein 2 gm., Carbohydrate 7 gm., Fiber 1 gm., Fat 0, Cholesterol 0, Calcium 12 mg., Sodium 306 mg.

Calories 41
From protein: 21%; From carbohydrate: 69%; From fat: 10%

Morning Miso II

The predominant flavor in this richly-flavored, savory soup is hatcho miso. Most of the vegetables are left in this version of miso soup, giving it a chunkier texture.

◆ ABOUT 3 QUARTS ◆

1 piece kombu
2 quarts water
1 medium tomato, diced
1 cup chopped onion
4 cloves garlic, minced
1/2 cup chopped green bell pepper
1 Tbsp. grated gingerroot
1 cup diced zucchini
2 cups chicken-flavored vegetable broth, hot
1 tsp. granulated garlic
1/2 tsp. ground ginger
1/4 cup hatcho miso
1/4 cup mellow white miso
2 Tbsp. mellow barley miso
1/2 cup plus 2 Tbsp. lite silken tofu (optional), drained

Soak kombu at least 15 minutes or overnight in water. Add the next 6 ingredients, bring to a boil, then simmer 15 minutes. Remove the kombu. Remove a third of the vegetables from the broth, and press against a strainer with the back of a spoon, squeezing the juices back into the soup; discard solids. Add the hot broth, garlic, and ginger, and continue to simmer. Place the miso varieties in a small bowl, and gradually blend in about a cup of the hot broth. Cream the miso with the broth until smooth. Add the creamed miso to the soup, and simmer gently. *Do not allow to boil!*

Slice the tofu into 1/4-inch slices. Cut each slice into small cubes, and place the cubes in each soup bowl. Ladle soup over the tofu. Serve hot.

NUTRITION ANALYSIS
(PER 1/2-CUP SERVING)

Protein 3 gm., Carbohydrate 9 gm., Fiber 1 gm., Fat 1 gm., Cholesterol 0, Calcium 17 mg., Sodium 360 mg.

Calories 53
From protein: 20%; From carbohydrate: 70%; From fat: 10%

Soybeans Polynesian

Soybeans are at the heart of this luscious stew. It takes its Hawaiian character from the sweet Maui onions and pineapple chunks that blend so well with the cinnamon-spiced sauce.

◆ 10 SERVINGS ◆

1 cup dried soybeans
6 cups water
1 1/2 tsp. olive oil
1/4 tsp. crushed red pepper
1 medium Maui onion, chopped (or other sweet onion)
6 cloves garlic, minced
2 Tbsp. grated gingerroot
1 medium gold bell pepper, chopped
2 medium Yukon Gold potatoes, unpeeled, diced
2 cups sliced baby carrots
1/2 pound. mushrooms, sliced
3 large fresh tomatoes, diced
20-oz. can pineapple chunks in juice, drained, reserve juice
1 bay leaf
1/4 cup mirin or dry sherry
1 cinnamon stick
1 Tbsp. Bragg Liquid Aminos
1/2 tsp. ground ginger
8 large fresh basil leaves

Precook soybeans (see Techniques). Heat oil with crushed pepper in a 6-quart saucepan over medium-high heat. Add the next 4 ingredients, and sauté 2 minutes. Add potatoes and carrots; sauté 5 minutes, stirring frequently. Add mushrooms, tomatoes, pineapple chunks, and bay leaf. Cook 5 minutes over medium heat, stirring occasionally. Add mirin, 1/4 cup of reserved pineapple juice, and cinnamon stick. Add cooked soybeans and remaining ingredients. Lower heat, and simmer for an hour, stirring occasionally, or until ready to serve. Serve with Pungent Basmati Rice (see page 142).

NUTRITION ANALYSIS
(PER 2-CUP SERVING)

Protein 11 gm., Carbohydrate 67 gm., Fiber 6 gm., Fat 5 gm., Cholesterol 0, Calcium 84 mg., Sodium 101 mg.

Calories 219
From protein: 12%; From carbohydrate: 76%; From fat: 13%

Split Pea Soup With Ham

This split pea soup is hearty and flavorful. Chunky vegetables and vegetarian bacon make this authentic-tasting remake quite remarkable.

◆ ABOUT 4 QUARTS ◆

- 1-pound. pkg. dry split peas, rinsed and sorted
- 7 cups chicken-flavored vegetable broth
- 1 1/2 tsp. olive oil
- 1/4 tsp. crushed red pepper
- 6 cloves garlic, minced
- 1 large red onion, chopped (about 3 cups)
- 2 cups sliced baby carrots
- 2 cups zucchini cut into julienne strips
- 6-oz. pkg. veggie Canadian bacon, diced
- 1 cup white wine
- 2 bay leaves
- 1/2 tsp. dried thyme
- 2 Tbsp. dried parsley
- 1 Tbsp. Bragg Liquid Aminos

Combine the peas with the broth in a 5-quart saucepan. Bring to a boil, then lower to simmer, covered. Heat olive oil and crushed red pepper in a 10" frying pan for 1 minute. Add the next 4 ingredients, and sauté over medium-high heat 10 minutes or until vegetables soften and the juices are rendered. Using a slotted spoon, remove the veggies and place in soup pot, leaving juices in frying pan. Add the diced bacon to the frying pan, and cook 5 minutes. Add bacon to soup pot, and deglaze the frying pan with wine, stirring up any browned bits that remain at the bottom. Add to pot. Add the remaining ingredients, and simmer, stirring occasionally, until the peas are tender (from 30 to 45 minutes) or until ready to serve.

NUTRITION ANALYSIS
(PER 1/2-CUP SERVING)

Protein 17 gm., Carbohydrate 68 gm., Fiber 6 gm., Fat 1 gm., Cholesterol 0, Calcium 61 mg., Sodium 323 mg.

Calories 242
From protein: 20%; From carbohydrate: 77%; From fat: 4%

Tempting Tomato Vegetable Soup

The wonderful flavors of leeks, mushrooms, zucchini, and carrots, along with a broth enriched with miso, combine to make this soup especially delicious.

◆ ABOUT 5 QUARTS ◆

1 Tbsp. olive oil
1/4 tsp. crushed red pepper
2 leeks, cleaned and cut into 1/4-inch slices (see Techniques)
6 cloves garlic, minced
1 1/4 cups green beans, cut into 1 1/2-inch pieces
1 1/2 cups baby carrots, halved crosswise
2 medium Yukon gold potatoes, unpeeled, cut into 1-inch chunks
2 cups zucchini, cut into julienne strips
2 cups sliced mushrooms, stems intact
1 1/4 cups white wine
14.5-oz. can Italian-flavored tomatoes, peeled and diced
10 cups beef-flavored vegetable broth
1/4 cup mellow white miso
1 tsp. Bragg Liquid Aminos
1 tsp. dried basil
1 tsp. dried marjoram

Heat oil and crushed pepper in a 6-quart saucepan. Add the leeks and garlic; sauté 3 minutes. Add the next 3 ingredients. Sauté 7 minutes, stirring frequently. Add zucchini and mushrooms; cook over medium-high heat 5 minutes. Stir in wine, and cook mixture 3 minutes. Add tomatoes and broth. Lower heat, and simmer 30 to 45 minutes. Place miso in a small bowl. Gradually stir in 1/2 cup of hot soup broth. Add creamed miso to soup along with remaining ingredients. Simmer 3 minutes—do not allow to boil. Serve immediately.

NUTRITION ANALYSIS
(PER 2 1/2-CUP SERVING)

Protein 5 gm., Carbohydrate 81 gm., Fiber 4 gm., Fat 2 gm., Cholesterol 0, Calcium 60 mg., Sodium 315 mg.

Calories 180
From protein: 5%; From carbohydrate: 90%; From fat: 5%

Vichyssoise

The irresistible yet subtle flavor of leeks is at the heart of this classic soup. Generally served chilled, this soup is also good hot.

◆ ABOUT 3 1/2 QUARTS ◆

- 1 Tbsp. olive oil
- 4 medium leeks, cleaned and cut into 1/4-inch slices (see Techniques)
- 3 cloves garlic, minced
- 1 cup chopped red onion
- 5 Yukon Gold potatoes, peeled and cubed (about 6 cups)
- 1/3 cup chopped gold bell pepper
- 4 cups chicken-flavored vegetable broth
- 1 1/4 cups lite silken tofu (firm), drained
- 3/4 cup soymilk lite
- 2 Tbsp. lemon juice
- 1 Tbsp. nutritional yeast
- 2 tsp. Bragg Liquid Aminos
- 1/4 tsp. white pepper
- fresh parsley for garnish

Heat oil in a 5-quart saucepan over medium-high heat. Sauté the leeks, garlic, onion, potatoes, and bell pepper until vegetables are crisp tender, about 10 minutes. Add broth. Lower heat, and simmer 25 minutes or until vegetables are tender. Using a slotted spoon, place vegetables in food processor; purée. Set puréed vegetables aside in a large bowl. Blend tofu in food processor. Add the soymilk and the liquid from the soup, and blend. Add the remaining ingredients (except parsley) to the tofu, and blend. Combine the tofu mixture with the puréed vegetables.

If you're serving hot vichyssoise, return the mixture to the soup pot to heat until hot. Garnish with chopped fresh parsley. For the traditional cold vichyssoise, chill until ready to serve. You may want to adjust the seasonings or add more soymilk to thin before serving. The texture should be velvety smooth.

NUTRITION ANALYSIS
(PER 1 2/3-CUP SERVING)

Protein 8 gm., Carbohydrate 71 gm., Fiber 3 gm., Fat 3 gm., Cholesterol 0, Calcium 47 mg., Sodium 190 mg.

Calories 236
From protein: 9%; From carbohydrate: 83%; From fat: 7%

Chunky Chick-Pea Salad

This high-protein, low-fat salad is a wonderful lunchbox stuffer. Try it on hearty whole wheat bread with lettuce, sprouts, and tomato. Now that's a sandwich that will see you through the day.

◆ 8 SERVINGS ◆

4 15-oz. cans garbanzo beans, drained
1 stalk celery, chopped
2 scallions, sliced
1/2 cup chopped red onion
1/3 cup chopped green bell pepper
1/2 tsp. salt
1 1/4 cups lite silken tofu (firm), drained
1/4 cup lemon juice
3 Tbsp. cider vinegar
1 Tbsp. liquid Fruitsource or honey
2 Tbsp. Dijon mustard
2 Tbsp. capers, drained

Place garbanzo beans in a large bowl. Mash with a potato masher or fork. Add the next 5 ingredients. Place the tofu in food processor, and blend. Add the next 4 ingredients, and process until smooth. Add the tofu mixture to the garbanzo mixture; add capers. Mix well, and chill 4 hours or until ready to serve.

NUTRITION ANALYSIS
(PER 1 1/4-CUP SERVING)

Protein 15 gm., Carbohydrate 36 gm., Fiber 8 gm., Fat 3 gm., Cholesterol 0, Calcium 8 mg., Sodium 220 mg.

Calories 236
From protein: 25%; From carbohydrate: 62%; From fat: 13%

Couscous Salad

I like to serve this delicious salad at room temperature, but it can also be served chilled, scooped onto a bed of fresh greens.

◆ 8 SERVINGS ◆

- 1 1/2 cups chicken-flavored vegetable broth
- 1 cup couscous
- 2 cups broccoli florets, sliced into 1/4-inch cuts
- 1/2 cup lite silken tofu (firm), drained
- 1/4 cup tofu mayonnaise (see Soyfoods Pantry)
- 1 clove garlic, peeled
- 2 Tbsp. lemon juice
- 1/2 tsp. dried cilantro
- 1/2 tsp. ground cumin
- 1/2 tsp. ground coriander
- 14.5-oz. can peeled and diced tomatoes, well drained
- 1/3 cup sliced scallions
- 1/4 cup chopped red bell pepper
- dried mint for garnish

Place broth and couscous in a medium saucepan. Cover and bring to a boil; stir, and remove from heat. Set aside. Blanch broccoli florets very briefly, no more than a minute. Remove to a bowl of ice water to stop cooking, then drain in a colander. Blend tofu in food processor. Add mayonnaise and garlic; blend until smooth. Add lemon juice, cilantro, cumin, and coriander, and blend thoroughly. Place cooked couscous in a large bowl, and fluff with a fork. Add drained tomatoes, scallions, and bell pepper. Mix well. Fold in tofu mixture, and mix thoroughly. Sprinkle with mint, and serve, or chill before serving.

NUTRITION ANALYSIS
(PER 1-CUP SERVING)

Protein 6 gm., Carbohydrate 24 gm., Fiber 3 gm., Fat 2 gm., Cholesterol 0, Calcium 44 mg., Sodium 88 mg.

Calories 137
From protein: 18%; From carbohydrate: 68%; From fat: 14%

Creamy Herbed Potato "Chill"

Chilled red potato slices nestle in a delectably creamy herb sauce for an intriguing alternative to the all-too-familiar potato salad.

◆ 10 SERVINGS ◆

5 medium new red potatoes, unpeeled (about 2 1/2 pound.)
2 Tbsp. olive oil
1 1/4 cups chopped red onion
2 large cloves garlic, minced
1/2 cup chopped orange or yellow bell pepper
1 rib celery, sliced
1/4 cup whole wheat flour
1/4 cup dry vermouth
1 cup soymilk lite
1 1/4 cups lite silken tofu (extra firm), drained
2 Tbsp. mellow white miso
2 Tbsp. dry vermouth
1 Tbsp. lemon juice
2 Tbsp. nutritional yeast
6 large basil leaves, snipped
1 tsp. dried marjoram
1/2 tsp. dried tarragon
1/2 tsp. dried thyme
1 cup frozen peas, cooked

Place whole, unpeeled potatoes in a large saucepan. Add water to cover. Bring to a boil; cook 45 minutes or until fork tender to the center. Set aside to cool in a colander. Cut into 1/4-inch slices (unpeeled). Chill.

Heat oil over medium-high heat in a medium saucepan. Add the next 4 ingredients, and sauté until tender, about 5 minutes. Add flour, and stir to coat vegetables, about 3 minutes. Add vermouth, and stir to a paste, about 2 minutes. Lower heat to simmer. Add soymilk 1/4 cup at a time. Stir frequently until thickened. Place tofu in a food processor; blend. Blend miso with vermouth in a small bowl. Add to tofu along with lemon juice and nutritional yeast; blend. Stir tofu mixture gently into white sauce, then add herbs and peas. Fold vegetables and herbed cream into chilled potato slices. Chill 1 hour or until ready to serve.

NUTRITION ANALYSIS
(PER SERVING)

Protein 8 gm., Carbohydrate 37 gm., Fiber 3 gm., Fat 4 gm., Cholesterol 0, Calcium 18 mg., Sodium 94 mg.

Calories 213
From protein: 15%; From carbohydrate: 70%; From fat: 16%

Curried Tofu & Basmati Rice Salad

Savory baked tofu and delicate basmati rice in a creamy curry dressing are especially appealing when served on a bed of colorful red leaf lettuce. Garnished with starfruit, this dish makes an impressive presentation.

◆ 6 SERVINGS ◆

DRESSING:

1 1/4 cups lite silken tofu (extra firm), drained
2 large shallots, peeled and quartered
1/4 cup soymilk lite
1 Tbsp. grated fresh gingerroot
1/2 tsp. ground cumin
1/2 tsp. ground coriander
1/4 tsp. turmeric
2 1/2 Tbsp. lemon juice
1 Tbsp. Dijon mustard
1 tsp. tamari
3 Tbsp. chopped fresh cilantro
2 Tbsp. nutritional yeast

1 1/2 cups chicken-flavored vegetable broth
1/2 cup basmati rice, rinsed
1/4 tsp. turmeric
1/4 tsp. granulated garlic
3 6-oz. pkgs. savory baked tofu
2 ripe carambola (starfruit)
salad greens
fresh cilantro

Place tofu in food processor; blend until smooth. Add the next 6 ingredients, and process to blend. Add remaining dressing ingredients, and blend until smooth. Refrigerate, covered.

Bring broth to a boil. Add basmati rice, then bring to a second boil; add seasonings. Reduce heat and simmer 15 minutes or until tender and liquid is absorbed. Set rice aside to cool. Slice the tofu lengthwise, dividing the width. Slice crosswise into julienne strips. Toss with dressing, then add cooled rice, and toss again. Chill the salad several hours or overnight (if allowed to sit overnight, the tofu will develop an even meatier consistency). Place torn salad greens on individual serving plates. Scoop salad onto greens, and garnish with thin slices of starfruit and sprigs of fresh cilantro.

NUTRITION ANALYSIS
(PER SERVING)

Protein 26 gm., Carbohydrate 31 gm., Fiber 3 gm., Fat 3 gm., Cholesterol 0, Calcium 29 mg., Sodium 620 mg.

Calories 253
From protein: 41%; From carbohydrate: 49%; From fat: 10%

Ravishing Rice Salad

Plump and creamy Great Northern beans join vegetarian Canadian bacon and brown rice in this delicious salad.

◆ 8 SERVINGS ◆

3 cups cooked brown rice, cooled
2/3 cup sliced scallions
2 cloves garlic, minced
1/2 cup chopped green bell pepper
4.25-oz. can chopped black olives, drained
6-oz. pkg. veggie Canadian bacon, diced
15-oz. can Great Northern beans, drained

DRESSING:
1/2 cup plus 2 Tbsp. lite silken tofu (extra firm), drained
2 Tbsp. Dijon mustard
1 Tbsp. liquid Fruitsource or honey
1 1/2 Tbsp. mellow white miso
1/2 tsp. dried thyme
1/4 tsp. ground coriander
1/4 tsp. Tabasco sauce

Place cooked rice in a medium bowl. Add the next 6 ingredients, and mix thoroughly. Set aside.

Place tofu in food processor, and blend until smooth. Add the remaining dressing ingredients; pulse to mix, then blend until smooth. Fold dressing into rice mixture. Cover and refrigerate for at least an hour. Serve chilled.

NUTRITION ANALYSIS
(PER SERVING)

Protein 13 gm., Carbohydrate 30 gm., Fiber 5 gm., Fat 3 gm., Cholesterol 0, Calcium 28 mg., Sodium 596 mg.

Calories 183
From protein: 26%; From carbohydrate: 62%; From fat: 12%

Colorful Garden Mix

This is a beautiful salad—a study in contrasts—especially when accented with delectable Raspberry Walnut Dressing (page 96).

◆ 8 SERVINGS ◆

1 head red leaf lettuce, torn
1 pound. fresh spinach, well rinsed and torn
1 medium red onion, thinly sliced
1/2 ripe avocado, peeled, pitted, thinly sliced, and drizzled with lime juice
1/2 cup chopped red bell pepper
1/2 cup chopped orange bell pepper
6 large Calimyrna figs, sliced
2 Tbsp. chopped fresh parsley

Mix the lettuce and spinach in a large salad bowl, then layer the remaining ingredients in the order listed. Pass the dressing to guests at the table.

NUTRITION ANALYSIS
(PER SERVING)

Protein 4 gm., Carbohydrate 15 gm., Fiber 5 gm., Fat 2 gm., Cholesterol 0, Calcium 107 mg., Sodium 54 mg.

Calories 87
From protein: 15%; From carbohydrate: 63%; From fat: 22%

Shredded Tofu and Artichoke Salad

Hearty and colorful, this salad is delicious!

◆ 6 SERVINGS ◆

2 1/2 cups lite silken tofu (extra firm), frozen, defrosted, and shredded
1/2 cup sliced scallions
1/3 cup chopped green pepper
2 cups chopped fresh spinach
15-oz. can garbanzo beans, drained
13 3/4-oz. can quartered artichoke hearts, drained and sliced

DRESSING:

1 1/4 cups lite silken tofu, firm
2 cloves garlic, peeled
1 cup soymilk lite
1 Tbsp. cider vinegar
1 Tbsp. Bragg Liquid Aminos
1/4 cup nutritional yeast
1/2 tsp. dried thyme
1/2 tsp. dried marjoram
1/2 tsp. ground coriander
1/4 tsp. turmeric
1/2 tsp. granulated garlic
dash cayenne, to taste

Place shredded tofu (see Techniques) in a medium bowl and mix with the next 5 ingredients. Set aside.

Place 1 1/4 cups drained tofu in food processor and blend until smooth. Add the next 9 ingredients and blend until smooth. Fold dressing into the shredded tofu mixture; mix thoroughly. Add granulated garlic and cayenne, and mix well. Cover and chill 4 hours or overnight.

NUTRITION ANALYSIS
(PER SERVING)

Protein 20 gm., Carbohydrate 73 gm., Fiber 5 gm., Fat 3 gm., Cholesterol 0, Calcium 72 mg., Sodium 440 mg.

Calories 202
From protein: 20%; From carbohydrate: 73%; From fat: 7%

Tofu 'n Rice Salad

An appealing salad garnished with fresh tomato wedges and sprinkled with fragrant basil and thyme.

◆ 8 SERVINGS ◆

3 cups chicken-flavored vegetable broth, boiling
1 cup short grain brown rice
2 1/2 cups frozen lite silken tofu, (extra firm) defrosted
1/3 cup sliced scallions
1/3 cup chopped green pepper
6 large mushrooms, slice caps and chop stems (about 1 1/4 cups)

DRESSING:

1 1/4 cups lite silken tofu (firm), drained
2 cloves garlic, peeled
2 Tbsp. mellow white miso
1 cup soymilk lite
1 Tbsp. Dijon mustard
1 Tbsp. tamari
2 1/2 Tbsp. lemon juice
8-oz. can sliced water chestnuts, drained
1 medium tomato, sliced into thin wedges
dried basil and dried thyme

Place brown rice in boiling broth and bring to a second boil. Cover saucepan, and simmer for 40 minutes, or until all liquid is absorbed. Shred defrosted tofu (see Techniques). Mix shredded tofu in a medium bowl with the next 3 ingredients; set aside. Place 1 1/4 cups drained tofu in food processor and blend until smooth. Add the next 6 ingredients and blend until smooth. Add the water chestnuts and pulse to mix, leaving the mixture chunky. Fold the dressing into the shredded tofu mixture. Arrange the tomato wedges around the edge of the bowl and sprinkle with basil and thyme. Cover and chill 4 hours or overnight.

NUTRITION ANALYSIS
(PER SERVING)

Protein 11 gm., Carbohydrate 29 gm., Fiber 2 gm., Fat 2 gm., Cholesterol 0, Calcium 53 mg., Sodium 315 mg.

Calories 177
From protein: 25%; From carbohydrate: 63%; From fat: 12%

Raspberry Walnut Dressing

Delightfully flavorful, the secret ingredient in this creamy dressing is dried cherries, which add a special zing. Try this tangy dressing on the Colorful Garden Mix (page 93).

◆ 3 CUPS ◆

1/2 cup plus 2 Tbsp. lite silken tofu (extra firm), drained
1/2 cup soymilk lite
1 Tbsp. olive oil
3 Tbsp. raspberry vinegar
1 clove garlic, peeled
2 scallions, minced
2 Tbsp. dried cherries
2 Tbsp. walnut pieces
1 Tbsp. liquid Fruitsource or honey
2 Tbsp. mellow white miso
1 tsp. dried parsley

In food processor, blend tofu until smooth. Add the next 5 ingredients, and process. Add the next 5 ingredients, and first pulse, then blend. Chill at least one hour. Dressing should be smooth with bits of fruit and parsley.

NUTRITION ANALYSIS
(PER 2-TABLESPOON SERVING)

Protein 1 gm., Carbohydrate 3 gm., Fiber 0, Fat 2 gm., Cholesterol 0, Calcium 3 mg., Sodium 36 mg.

Calories 32
From protein: 18%; From carbohydrate: 35%; From fat: 47%
(The percentage of calories from fat seems high because the calories are so low.)

Garlic Basil Dressing

This creamy, rich-tasting dressing will complement a salad of your favorite greens with tomatoes and colorful bell peppers.

◆ ABOUT 2 CUPS ◆

1/2 cup plus 2 Tbsp. lite silken tofu (extra firm), drained
1/2 cup soymilk lite
1 clove garlic, peeled
2 Tbsp. mellow white miso
2 Tbsp. cider vinegar
1 Tbsp. olive oil
1 Tbsp. liquid Fruitsource or honey
1 tsp. dried basil
1 tsp. Bragg Liquid Aminos

Place drained tofu in food processor, and blend. Add the soymilk and garlic, and pulse to mix. Add the remaining ingredients, and process to mix thoroughly. Dressing should be creamy-smooth with bits of basil. Refrigerate for at least an hour to allow the flavors to blend.

NUTRITION ANALYSIS
(PER 2-TABLESPOON SERVING)

Protein 1 gm., Carbohydrate 11 gm., Fiber 0, Fat 1 gm., Cholesterol 0, Calcium 4 mg., Sodium 63 mg.

Calories 27
From protein: 8%; From carbohydrate: 71%; From fat: 21%

"Honey" Mustard Dill Dressing

This delightful dressing is excellent, whether livening up a tossed salad or a grilled vegetable sandwich on a whole wheat bun.

◆ ABOUT 2 CUPS ◆

1/2 cup plus 2 Tbsp. lite silken tofu (firm), drained
1/2 cup soymilk lite
1 clove garlic, peeled
1/4 cup Dijon mustard
3 Tbsp. liquid Fruitsource or honey
1 1/2 tsp. olive oil
1 Tbsp. cider vinegar
1 Tbsp. lemon juice
2 Tbsp. mellow white miso
1/4 cup sliced scallions
1 Tbsp. dried dillweed

Place drained tofu in food processor, and blend. Add the next 6 ingredients, and pulse to mix. Add the remaining ingredients, and process to mix thoroughly. Dressing should be creamy-smooth with bits of dill. Refrigerate for at least an hour to allow the flavors to blend.

NUTRITION ANALYSIS
(PER 2-TABLESPOON SERVING)

Protein 1 gm., Carbohydrate 4 gm., Fiber 0, Fat 1 gm., Cholesterol 0, Calcium 10 mg., Sodium 89 mg.

Calories 28
From protein: 17%; From carbohydrate: 55%; From fat: 28%

Lemon Poppy Seed Dressing

Try this delicious dressing on a salad of baby greens topped with thinly sliced red onion.

◆ ABOUT 2 CUPS ◆

1 1/2 Tbsp. poppy seeds
1/2 cup plus 2 Tbsp. lite silken tofu (extra firm), drained
1/2 cup soymilk lite
1/4 cup lemon juice
1 Tbsp. liquid Fruitsource or honey
1 Tbsp. olive oil
2 scallions, sliced
1 large shallot, quartered
1 clove garlic, peeled
2 Tbsp. mellow white miso

Place poppy seeds in a small frying pan, and toast lightly about 3 minutes over medium heat, shaking pan gently. Set aside. Place tofu in food processor, and blend until smooth. Add soymilk, and blend. Add remaining ingredients and process to mix. Add poppy seeds. Blend. Chill until ready to serve.

NUTRITION ANALYSIS
(PER 2-TABLESPOON SERVING)

Protein 1 gm., Carbohydrate 3 gm., Fiber 0, Fat 1 gm., Cholesterol 0, Calcium 14 mg., Sodium 34 mg.

Calories 23
From protein: 19%; From carbohydrate: 45%; From fat: 37%
(The percentage of calories from fat seems high because the calories are so low.)

Bountiful Breads

Nothing compares with the tantalizing aroma or the taste of home-baked bread. Alas, how many of us have the luxury of time to guide yeast bread through the hours of preparation required to produce a fine loaf of homemade bread? In this chapter you will find recipes for baking delightful yeast breads that are a cinch, using your bread machine. Bread machines present a terrific contemporary approach to bread baking. All you need do is combine the ingredients according to the machine manufacturer's directions, set the controls, and press "start." As so many of us are discovering bread machine magic these days, I wanted to share my favorite recipes.

In my approach to soy-centered cuisine, making bread offers the splendid opportunity to enhance the nutritive value of this ever present staple. Not only can you avoid unhealthful ingredients, you can impart the wholesome goodness of soy into every slice. Together with soy these wonderful breads are made with whole grains. My favorite, White Wheat Bread, is very light in color and has a bouncy, airy texture not usually found in whole wheat bread.

There are also quick breads which use leavening agents like baking soda and baking powder. Tea breads, snack bars, and muffins are also included in this chapter. Whole Wheat Dinner Muffins, delightful Blueberry Tea Bread, and Peanut Butter Banana Squares are just a few of the easy to assemble quick breads included here. All are made using soy products, and contain no added fat, eggs, or dairy products. These easy-to-make, wholesome baked goods contribute healthful soy protein with each delicious bite! ◆

Apple Raisin Muffins

These muffins are great right out of the oven or split and toasted for breakfast.

◆ 18 MUFFINS ◆

Vegetable oil cooking spray
1 cup soymilk lite
2 Tbsp. lemon juice
1 2/3 cups whole wheat pastry flour
1/3 cup soy flour
1/4 cup soy grits
1 tsp. baking soda
1 tsp. baking powder
1/2 tsp. salt
1 tsp. cinnamon
1/4 cup unsweetened applesauce
1/3 cup Florida Crystals or sugar
1 Tbsp. egg replacer powder
1/4 cup water
1 tsp. vanilla extract
1 medium Pippin or Granny Smith apple, peeled, diced, and drizzled with lemon juice
1/2 cup golden raisins
cinnamon
ground nutmeg

Preheat oven to 375°. Spray muffin pans with cooking spray. Place soymilk in a small glass measuring cup; add lemon juice. Set aside. Mix together the next 7 ingredients (dry ingredients) in a medium bowl. Set aside.

Place applesauce in a large bowl, and cream with Florida Crystals. In a small bowl, whisk egg replacer powder with water until foamy. Add to creamed applesauce. Add soymilk and vanilla to liquid ingredients, and mix thoroughly. Fold wet ingredients into dry, and combine just until mixed. Fold in apples and raisins. Do not overmix. Spoon into muffin cups, filling the empty cups 1/3 with water. Sprinkle with cinnamon and nutmeg. Bake 15 minutes or until lightly browned and a toothpick inserted in the center comes out clean.

NUTRITION ANALYSIS
(PER MUFFIN)

Protein 4 gm., Carbohydrate 18 gm., Fiber 2 gm., Fat 1 gm., Cholesterol 0, Calcium 31 mg., Sodium 158 mg.

Calories 90
From protein: 16%; From carbohydrate: 78%; From fat: 7%

Blueberry Muffins

Dried blueberries and a touch of cornmeal give these muffins a special sweetness and crunch. They're delicious fresh from the oven or toasted under the broiler!

◆ 18 MUFFINS ◆

Vegetable oil cooking spray
1 1/2 cups whole wheat pastry flour
1/2 cup yellow cornmeal
1/3 cup soy grits
1 tsp. baking soda
1 tsp. baking powder
1/4 tsp. salt
1 tsp. ground cinnamon
1/2 cup unsweetened applesauce
1/3 cup Florida Crystals or sugar
1 Tbsp. egg replacer powder
1/4 cup water
1 cup soymilk lite
1 tsp. vanilla extract
1/4 cup walnut pieces
2 Tbsp. soy grits
1 cup dried blueberries

Preheat oven to 350.° Coat 18 muffin cups with cooking spray. Mix whole wheat flour with the next 6 ingredients (dry ingredients) in a medium bowl. Set aside. Cream applesauce and Florida Crystals in a large bowl. Whisk egg replacer with water in a small bowl until foamy; whisk into creamed applesauce. Add soymilk and vanilla, and mix thoroughly. Fold the wet ingredients into the dry ingredients just until mixed. Mix walnut pieces with soy grits, and add to batter along with blueberries. Do not overbeat. Spoon batter into muffin cups, filling empty cups 1/3 full with water. Bake 15 minutes or until toothpick inserted in the center comes out clean.

NUTRITION ANALYSIS
(PER MUFFIN)

Protein 5 gm., Carbohydrate 24 gm., Fiber 2 gm., Fat 1 gm., Cholesterol 0, Calcium 27 mg., Sodium 129 mg.

Calories 126
From protein: 14%; From carbohydrate: 76%; From fat: 10%

Blueberry Tea Bread

Sweet blueberries and buttery cashews make a superb combination!

◆ 12 SERVINGS ◆

Vegetable oil cooking spray
3/4 cup soymilk lite
2 Tbsp. lemon juice
1 1/2 cups whole wheat pastry flour
3/4 cup rolled oats
1/4 cup soy flour
1 tsp. baking soda
1 tsp. baking powder
1/4 tsp. salt
1/2 cup unsweetened applesauce
1 1/4 cups Florida Crystals or sugar
1 Tbsp. egg replacer powder
1/4 cup water
1 tsp. vanilla extract
1 tsp. grated lemon rind
1/3 cup cashew pieces
1/3 cup soy grits
1 1/2 cups fresh or thawed frozen blueberries

Preheat oven to 350°. Spray a 9" x 5" loaf pan with cooking spray. Place soymilk in a small glass measuring cup; add lemon juice. Set aside. Mix together the next 6 ingredients (dry ingredients) in a medium bowl. Set aside. Cream the applesauce and Florida Crystals together in a large bowl. In a small bowl, whisk egg replacer powder with water until foamy. Whisk into creamed applesauce along with vanilla and lemon rind. Add soymilk mixture to liquid ingredients; mix thoroughly. Fold wet ingredients into dry ingredients, just until mixed. Mix cashew pieces with soy grits, and add to batter along with blueberries. Do not overmix. Pour into prepared loaf pan, and bake for 50 to 60 minutes or until toothpick inserted in center comes out clean.

NUTRITION ANALYSIS
(PER SLICE)

Protein 7 gm., Carbohydrate 35 gm., Fiber 3 gm., Fat 3 gm., Cholesterol 0, Calcium 44 mg., Sodium 192 mg.

Calories 186
From protein: 14%; From carbohydrate: 72%; From fat: 14%;

Buttermilk Wheat Bread

This bread machine recipe makes a terrific bread for sandwiches or toast.

SMALL LOAF (1 LB.)

3/4 cup soymilk lite
1 1/2 tsp. cider vinegar
1 Tbsp. unsweetened applesauce
2 Tbsp. Sucanat or brown sugar
1/4 tsp. salt
1/4 tsp. baking soda
1 Tbsp. vital wheat gluten
2 cups whole wheat flour
1 tsp. yeast

LARGE LOAF (1 1/2 LB.)

1 1/2 cups soymilk lite
1 Tbsp. cider vinegar
2 Tbsp. unsweetened applesauce
1/4 cup Sucanat or brown sugar
1/2 tsp. salt
1/2 tsp. baking soda
2 Tbsp. vital wheat gluten
4 cups whole wheat flour
2 tsp. yeast

Place soymilk in small measuring cup, and add vinegar. Set aside for 5 minutes. Place the ingredients in the bread machine pan in the order recommended by the machine's manufacturer. Set the controls, close the lid, and press "start."

NUTRITION ANALYSIS
(PER 1-OZ. SLICE)

Protein 3 gm., Carbohydrate 14 gm., Fiber 2 gm., Fat 0,
Cholesterol 0, Calcium 7 mg., Sodium 65 mg.

Calories 67
From protein: 16%; From carbohydrate: 79%; From fat: 5%

Cranberry Tea Bread

Dusted with powdered sugar and served with tea or coffee, Cranberry Tea Bread hits the spot!

◆ 12 SERVINGS ◆

Vegetable oil cooking spray
2/3 cup soymilk lite
1 Tbsp. lemon juice
2 cups whole wheat pastry flour
1/4 cup yellow cornmeal
1/4 cup soy flour
1 tsp. baking soda
1 tsp. baking powder
1/4 tsp. salt
1 tsp. cinnamon
1/2 cup unsweetened applesauce
1 1/4 cups Florida Crystals or sugar
1 Tbsp. egg replacer powder
1/4 cup water
1 tsp. vanilla extract
1 cup fresh or thawed frozen cranberries
1/4 cup walnut pieces
1/4 cup soy grits

Preheat oven to 350.° Coat a loaf pan lightly with cooking spray. Place the soymilk in a small measuring cup, and add lemon juice. Set aside. Mix together the next 7 ingredients (dry ingredients) in a medium bowl; set aside. Cream the applesauce and the Florida Crystals in a large bowl. Whisk the egg replacer powder and water in a small bowl until foamy. Add to applesauce mixture along with the vanilla; mix thoroughly. Fold the dry ingredients into the applesauce mixture alternately with soymilk. Mix walnut pieces with soy grits. Fold into the batter with cranberries; do not overmix. Bake 55 minutes or until toothpick inserted in center comes out clean.

NUTRITION ANALYSIS (PER SLICE)

Protein 6 gm., Carbohydrate 34 gm., Fiber 3 gm., Fat 2 gm., Cholesterol 0, Calcium 46 mg., Sodium 191 mg.

Calories 177
From protein: 13%; From carbohydrate: 74%; From fat: 12%

"Honey" Wheat Bread

This high-rising bread machine bread uses no fat-replacer other than the Fruitsource, which is a source of pectins.

SMALL LOAF (1 LB.)

3/4 cup soymilk lite
1/4 cup liquid Fruitsource or honey
1/4 tsp. salt
1 Tbsp. vital wheat gluten
2 cups whole wheat flour
1 1/4 tsp. yeast

LARGE LOAF (1 1/2 LB.)

1 1/2 cups soymilk lite
1/2 cup liquid Fruitsource or honey
1/2 tsp. salt
2 Tbsp. vital wheat gluten
4 cups whole wheat flour
2 1/2 tsp. yeast

Place the ingredients in the bread machine pan in the order recommended by the machine's manufacturer. Set the controls, close the lid, and press "start."

NUTRITION ANALYSIS
(PER 1-OZ. SLICE)

Protein 3 gm., Carbohydrate 16 gm., Fiber 2 gm., Fat 0, Cholesterol 0, Calcium 6 mg., Sodium 41 mg.

Calories 74
From protein: 14%; From carbohydrate: 81%; From fat: 5%

Jam-in-the-Middle Muffins

These muffins have a great taste and texture with a dollop of apricot jam baked into the center.

◆ 12 MUFFINS ◆

Vegetable oil cooking spray
3/4 cup soymilk lite
1 Tbsp. lemon juice
1 1/2 cups whole wheat pastry flour
1/2 cup yellow cornmeal
1/3 cup soy grits
1 tsp. baking powder
1 tsp. baking soda
1/4 cup Sucanat or brown sugar
1 tsp. cinnamon
1/2 cup prune purée
1/3 cup liquid Fruitsource or honey
1 Tbsp. egg replacer powder
1/4 cup water
1 tsp. vanilla extract
1/3 cup fruit-sweetened apricot jam

Preheat oven to 350°. Spray a muffin pan with cooking spray. Place soymilk in a small glass measuring cup, and add lemon juice. Set aside. Mix together the next 7 ingredients (dry ingredients) in a medium bowl. Set aside. Place prune purée in a large bowl. Add Fruitsource, and mix well. Whisk egg replacer powder with water in a small bowl until foamy; whisk into creamed prune mixture. Add soymilk and vanilla; mix thoroughly. Fold dry ingredients into liquid ingredients just until mixed. Spoon half of the batter into muffin cups. Drop 1 1/2 teaspoons jam in center of each cup. Top with remaining batter. Bake 12 minutes or until toothpick inserted in the center comes out clean.

NUTRITION ANALYSIS
(PER MUFFIN)

Protein 4 gm., Carbohydrate 36 gm., Fiber 3 gm., Fat 1 gm., Cholesterol 0, Calcium 41 mg., Sodium 162 mg.

Calories 165
From protein: 9%; From carbohydrate: 84%; From fat: 7%

Light 'n Lovely Whole Wheat Bread

Equal parts whole wheat flour and unbleached flour give this bread machine recipe a lighter texture.

SMALL LOAF (1 LB.)

3/4 cup soymilk lite
1 Tbsp. unsweetened applesauce
1 Tbsp. mellow white miso
1 1/2 tsp. egg replacer powder
2 Tbsp. water
1 1/2 Tbsp. liquid Fruitsource or honey
1 Tbsp. vital wheat gluten
3 Tbsp. soy grits
1 cup unbleached flour
1 cup whole wheat flour
1 1/4 tsp. yeast

LARGE LOAF (1 1/2 LB.)

1 1/2 cups soymilk lite
2 Tbsp. unsweetened applesauce
2 Tbsp. mellow white miso
1 Tbsp. egg replacer powder
1/4 cup water
3 Tbsp. liquid Fruitsource or honey
2 Tbsp. vital wheat gluten
1/3 cup soy grits
2 cups unbleached flour
2 cups whole wheat flour
2 1/2 tsp. yeast

Place ingredients in bread machine pan in the order recommended by the machine's manufacturer. Set the controls, close the lid, and press "start."

NUTRITION ANALYSIS
(PER 1-OZ. SLICE)

Protein 3 gm., Carbohydrate 12 gm., Fiber 1 gm., Fat 0, Cholesterol 0, Calcium 4 mg., Sodium 14 mg.

Calories 62
From protein: 16%; From carbohydrate: 77%; From fat: 7%

Maple Wheat Bread

This delicious bread machine loaf rises nicely and slices well for sandwiches.

SMALL LOAF (1 LB.)
- 3/4 cup soymilk lite
- 1 Tbsp. unsweetened applesauce
- 2 Tbsp. maple syrup
- 2 Tbsp. liquid Fruitsource or honey
- 1/4 tsp. salt
- 1 Tbsp. vital wheat gluten
- 2 cups whole wheat flour
- 1 tsp. yeast

LARGE LOAF (1 1/2 LBS.)
- 1 1/2 cups soymilk lite
- 2 Tbsp. unsweetened applesauce
- 1/4 cup maple syrup
- 1/4 cup liquid Fruitsource or honey
- 1/2 tsp. salt
- 2 Tbsp. vital wheat gluten
- 4 cups whole wheat flour
- 2 tsp. yeast

Place ingredients in bread machine pan in the order recommended by the machine's manufacturer. Set the controls, close the lid, and press "start."

NUTRITION ANALYSIS
(PER 1-OZ. SLICE)

Protein 3 gm., Carbohydrate 16 gm., Fiber 2 gm., Fat 0,
Cholesterol 0, Calcium 7 mg., Sodium 42 mg.

Calories 75
From protein: 14%; From carbohydrate: 81%; From fat: 5%

Nutty Oat Bread

Thanks to my neighbor Rosemary Campagna and her garden, I have a constant supply of zucchini in the summer. The zucchini contributes to the moist texture of this delightful bread.

SMALL LOAF (1 LB.)	LARGE LOAF (1 1/2 LB.)
1/2 cup soymilk lite	1 cup soymilk lite
6 Tbsp. shredded zucchini	3/4 cup shredded zucchini
2 Tbsp. prune purée	1/4 cup prune purée
2 Tbsp. liquid Fruitsource or honey	1/4 cup liquid Fruitsource or honey
1/4 tsp. salt	1/2 tsp. salt
1/2 tsp. cinnamon	1 tsp. cinnamon
1/8 tsp. ground nutmeg	1/4 tsp. ground nutmeg
6 Tbsp. rolled oats	3/4 cup rolled oats
2 Tbsp. oat bran	1/4 cup oat bran
1 Tbsp. vital wheat gluten	2 Tbsp. vital wheat gluten
1 1/2 cups whole wheat flour	3 cups whole wheat flour
1 1/4 tsp. yeast	2 1/2 tsp. yeast

Place ingredients in bread machine pan in the order recommended by the machine's manufacturer. Set the controls, close the lid, and press "start."

NUTRITION ANALYSIS
(PER 1-OZ. SLICE)

Protein 3 gm., Carbohydrate 14 gm., Fiber 2 gm., Fat 0, Cholesterol 0, Calcium 7 mg., Sodium 40 mg.

Calories 66
From protein: 15%; From carbohydrate: 79%; From fat: 6%

Oat Bran Raisin Muffins

This sweet bran muffin contributes to a tasty breakfast.

◆ 18 MUFFINS ◆

Vegetable oil cooking spray
3/4 cup soymilk lite
1 Tbsp. lemon juice
1 1/3 cups whole wheat pastry flour
1/2 cup oat bran
1/4 cup yellow cornmeal
1/4 cup soy grits
1/4 cup Sucanat or brown sugar
1 tsp. baking powder
1 tsp. baking soda
1/4 tsp. salt
1 tsp. cinnamon
1/2 cup prune purée
1/4 cup liquid Fruitsource or honey
1 Tbsp. egg replacer powder
1/4 cup water
1 Tbsp. grated lemon zest
1 tsp. vanilla extract
1 cup golden raisins, tossed with 1 tsp. flour

Preheat oven to 350°. Spray 18 muffin cups with cooking spray. Place soymilk and lemon juice in a small measuring cup. Set aside. Mix the next 9 ingredients (dry ingredients) in a medium bowl. Set aside. Combine prune purée and Fruitsource in a large bowl; mix well. Whisk egg replacer powder with water in a small bowl until foamy. Add to prune mixture, and whisk together. Add lemon zest, vanilla, and soymilk. Mix well. Fold the dry ingredients into the wet ingredients just until mixed. Add raisins. Spoon into muffin cups, filling empty cups 1/3 full with water. Bake 10 minutes or until toothpick inserted in center comes out clean.

NUTRITION ANALYSIS
(PER MUFFIN)

Protein 3 gm., Carbohydrate 27 gm., Fiber 3 gm., Fat 1 gm., Cholesterol 0, Calcium 33 mg., Sodium 137 mg.

Calories 118
From protein: 9%; From carbohydrate: 85%; From fat: 6%

Oat Wheat Bread

This light and flavorful bread has just a hint of oats. It rises nicely and is perfect for sandwiches.

SMALL LOAF (1 LB.)	LARGE LOAF (1 1/2 LBS.)
3/4 cup soymilk lite	1 1/2 cups soymilk lite
3 Tbsp. liquid Fruitsource or honey	1/3 cup liquid Fruitsource or honey
1 Tbsp. mellow white miso	2 Tbsp. mellow white miso
1 Tbsp. vital wheat gluten	2 Tbsp. vital wheat gluten
1/2 cup rolled oats	1 cup rolled oats
3 Tbsp. soy flour	1/3 cup soy flour
1 1/3 cups white wheat flour	2 2/3 cups white wheat flour
1 1/4 tsp. yeast	2 1/2 tsp. yeast

Place ingredients in bread machine pan in the order recommended by the machine's manufacturer. Set the controls, close the lid, and press "start."

NUTRITION ANALYSIS
(PER 1-OZ. SLICE)

Protein 2 gm., Carbohydrate 13 gm., Fiber 2 gm., Fat 1 gm., Cholesterol 0, Calcium 3 mg., Sodium 17 mg.

Calories 66
From protein: 14%; From carbohydrate: 77%; From fat: 9%

Perfect Pumpernickel

In my quest for a great pumpernickel bread, I hit upon this bread machine recipe after many tries. Look for a medium rise, firm crust, and soft interior in this fragrant bread.

SMALL LOAF (1 LB.)	LARGE LOAF (1 1/2 LB.)
3/4 cup soymilk lite	1 1/2 cups soymilk lite
1 Tbsp. prune purée	2 Tbsp. prune purée
1 Tbsp. mellow white miso	2 Tbsp. mellow white miso
2 Tbsp. mild molasses	1/4 cup mild molasses
1 Tbsp. unsweetened cocoa powder	2 Tbsp. unsweetened cocoa powder
1 Tbsp. vital wheat gluten	2 Tbsp. vital wheat gluten
1/2 cup oat flour	1 cup oat flour
1/2 cup rye flour	1 cup rye flour
1 1/4 cups whole wheat flour	2 1/2 cups whole wheat flour
1 1/4 tsp. yeast	2 1/2 tsp. yeast

Place ingredients in bread machine pan in the order recommended by the machine's manufacturer. Set the controls, close the lid, and press "start."

NUTRITION ANALYSIS (PER SLICE)

Protein 2 gm., Carbohydrate 13 gm., Fiber 2 gm., Fat 0, Cholesterol 0, Calcium 25 mg., Sodium 20 mg.

Calories 64
From protein: 14%; From carbohydrate: 79%; From fat: 7%

Peanut Butter Banana Squares

Low in fat and high in carbohydrates, these squares could be called "energy bars."

◆ 25 SQUARES ◆

Vegetable oil cooking spray
3/4 cup soymilk lite
1 Tbsp. lemon juice
2 1/2 cups whole wheat pastry flour
1/2 cup soy grits
1 1/2 tsp. baking soda
1 1/2 tsp. baking powder
1/4 tsp. salt
1 tsp. cinnamon
1/3 cup crunchy peanut butter
1/3 cup prune purée
1 cup mashed banana (2 medium)
1/2 cup liquid Fruitsource or honey
1 Tbsp. egg replacer powder
1/4 cup water
1/2 cup date nuggets (see page 24)
cinnamon
nutmeg

Preheat oven to 350°. Spray a 9" x 13" pan with cooking spray. Place soymilk and lemon juice in a small measuring cup; set aside. Mix together the next 6 ingredients in a large bowl; set aside. Blend peanut butter, prune purée, and banana in a medium bowl. Add Fruitsource, and blend well. Place egg replacer and water in a small bowl. Whisk until frothy, and add to peanut butter mixture. Fold liquid ingredients into the dry ingredients alternately with soymilk. Pour batter into prepared pan. Sprinkle generously with cinnamon and nutmeg. Bake 35 to 40 minutes or until toothpick inserted in center comes out clean.

NUTRITION ANALYSIS
(PER SQUARE)

Protein 5 gm., Carbohydrate 22 gm., Fiber 2 gm., Fat 2 gm., Cholesterol 0, Calcium 30 mg., Sodium 127 mg.

Calories 116
From protein: 15%; From carbohydrate: 70%; From fat: 15%

Spiced Carrot Muffins

Fragrant with fresh ginger, cinnamon, and other spices, these muffins are a treat!

◆ 12 MUFFINS ◆

Vegetable oil cooking spray
1/2 cup cup soymilk lite
1 Tbsp. lemon juice
1 1/2 cups whole wheat pastry flour
1 tsp. baking powder
1 tsp. baking soda
1 tsp. cinnamon
1/2 tsp. ground nutmeg
1/2 tsp. ground ginger
1/8 tsp. ground cloves
1/4 tsp. salt
1 1/2 cups Sucanat or brown sugar
1/2 cup prune purée
2 Tbsp. egg replacer powder
1/2 cup cold water
1 Tbsp. grated fresh gingerroot
1 1/2 cups grated carrots
1/2 cup golden raisins or currants

Preheat oven to 375°. Spray muffin pan with cooking spray. Place soymilk in a measuring cup. Add lemon juice; set aside. In a medium bowl, stir together flour with next 8 ingredients. Set aside. Measure prune purée into a large bowl. Whisk egg replacer powder with water in a small bowl. Whisk into prune purée. Add grated gingerroot and soymilk. Mix thoroughly. Add liquid ingredients to dry, mixing just until blended. Fold in grated carrots and raisins. Spoon into muffin cups. Bake for 12 minutes or until a toothpick inserted in the center comes out clean.

NUTRITION ANALYSIS
(PER MUFFIN)

Protein 3 gm., Carbohydrate 44 gm., Fiber 3 gm., Fat 0, Cholesterol 0, Calcium 63 mg., Sodium 245 mg.

Calories 184
From protein: 6%; From carbohydrate: 92%; From fat: 2%

Josh's Banana Bread

I made this streusel-filled banana bread for Susie Boch on the day her son was born.

◆ 12 SERVINGS ◆

Vegetable oil cooking spray
3/4 cup soymilk lite
1 Tbsp. lemon juice
2 cups whole wheat pastry flour
1/4 cup soy flour
1 tsp. baking soda
1 tsp. baking powder
1/4 tsp. salt
1 tsp. cinnamon
1/3 cup prune purée
1 cup mashed bananas (2 to 3 bananas)
3/4 cup Florida Crystals or sugar
1 Tbsp. egg replacer powder
1/4 cup water
1 tsp. vanilla extract

STREUSEL:

1/3 cup walnut pieces
2 Tbsp. soy grits
2 Tbsp. brown sugar
1/2 tsp. cinnamon
1/4 tsp. ground nutmeg

Preheat oven to 350.° Coat a 9" x 5" loaf pan with cooking spray. Place soymilk in a small glass measuring cup, and add lemon juice. Set aside. Mix together the next 6 ingredients. Set aside. Place prune purée in a large bowl. Add mashed bananas and Florida Crystals. Whisk together egg replacer powder and water in a small bowl until foamy. Add egg replacer and vanilla to the prune/banana combination. Mix thoroughly. Fold liquid ingredients into dry ingredients alternately with soymilk. Mix together streusel ingredients. Pour half the batter into the prepared pan. Top with streusel, then add remainder of the batter. Sprinkle generously with cinnamon and nutmeg. Bake 50 to 55 minutes or until toothpick inserted in center comes out clean.

NUTRITION ANALYSIS
(PER SLICE)

Protein 5 gm., Carbohydrate 35 gm., Fiber 4 gm., Fat 3 gm., Cholesterol 0, Calcium 49 mg., Sodium 196 mg.

Calories 180
From protein: 10%; From carbohydrate: 74%; From fat: 16%

White Wheat Bread

Whole grain white wheat flour is naturally light in color. This high-rising bread machine bread has a fine crumbed, creamy interior, unlike the hearty, whole grain density one expects from whole wheat bread.

SMALL LOAF (1 LB.)

3/4 cup soymilk lite
2 Tbsp. liquid Fruitsource or honey
1 Tbsp. mellow white miso
1 1/2 tsp. egg replacer powder
2 Tbsp. water
1 Tbsp. vital wheat gluten
2 Tbsp. soy flour or soy grits
2 cups white wheat flour
1 1/4 tsp. yeast

LARGE LOAF (1 1/2 LBS.)

1 1/2 cups soymilk lite
1/4 cup liquid Fruitsource or honey
2 Tbsp. mellow white miso
1 Tbsp. egg replacer powder
1/4 cup water
2 Tbsp. vital wheat gluten
1/4 cup soy flour or soy grits
3 3/4 cups white wheat flour
2 1/2 tsp. yeast

Place the first 3 ingredients in the bread machine pan. Place egg replacer powder in a small bowl, and whisk in water until foamy. Add to pan, then add the remaining ingredients in the order listed unless the manufacturer of your bread machine recommends a different order. Close the lid, set the controls, and press "start."

NUTRITION ANALYSIS
(PER 1-OZ. SLICE)

Protein 2 gm., Carbohydrate 13 gm., Fiber 2 gm., Fat 0,
Cholesterol 0, Calcium 1 mg., Sodium 15 mg.

Calories 60
From protein: 14%; From carbohydrate: 79%; From fat: 7%

Whole Wheat Dinner Muffins

Simple to prepare and bursting with flavor, these tasty muffins are perfect with dinner. If you have any left over, just split and pop under the broiler, top with your favorite jam, and enjoy at breakfast.

◆ 12 MUFFINS ◆

Vegetable oil cooking spray
1 cup soymilk lite
1 tsp. cider vinegar
2 cups whole wheat pastry flour
1/4 cup soy grits
1 tsp. baking soda
1 tsp. baking powder
1/2 tsp. salt
1/4 cup unsweetened applesauce
1/4 cup Florida Crystals or sugar
1 Tbsp. egg replacer powder
1/4 cup water
3/4 cup wheat germ

Preheat oven to 375°. Spray muffin pan with cooking spray. Place soymilk in a small measuring cup; add vinegar. Set aside. Stir together the next 5 ingredients in a large bowl. Set aside. Place applesauce in a medium bowl. Stir in Florida Crystals. Whisk egg replacer with water in a small bowl until foamy. Add to applesauce mixture. Make a well in the dry ingredients, and pour liquid in all at once. Fold quickly together, just until blended but still lumpy. Do not overbeat. Spoon into prepared muffin cups. Sprinkle with wheat germ. Bake for 15 to 20 minutes or until lightly browned.

NUTRITION ANALYSIS
(PER MUFFIN)

Protein 5 gm., Carbohydrate 20 gm., Fiber 3 gm., Fat 1 gm., Cholesterol 0, Calcium 37 mg., Sodium 236 mg.

Calories 105
From protein: 19%; From carbohydrate: 76%; From fat: 5%

Exceptional Entrées

Soyfoods are at the heart of the entrées in this irresistible collection. Hearty, richly flavored meals, needn't be heavy with fat and cholesterol. Rich-tasting cream sauces and delicate quiche are a snap when you know how to make the most of products like lite silken tofu and soymilk lite. The recipes offered in this section use the nutritional powerhouse of soyfoods to mimic a variety of dairy products and to create familiar fare using some new and ingenious products made from soybeans.

Healthful entrées that are flavorful and satisfying are highlighted in this chapter, using a wide variety of the new lower fat soyfoods. Textured vegetable protein, veggie Canadian bacon, tempeh, Ready Ground Tofu, and Gimme Lean are just some of the intriguing products that are used to make delectable dishes your family will love. You will also be introduced to some innovative techniques that change the texture of tofu to a chewier substance that will readily absorb well-seasoned marinades.

Traditional meals that were once made with high-fat, low-fiber, cholesterol-laden ingredients are just as delicious when made with these wholesome alternatives. Fiesta Scramblers, Savory Stuffed Peppers, and Oven-Baked Tempeh are just a few of the delightful dishes in this collection that demonstrate the undeniable versatility of the remarkable soybean. Highly authentic flavor and texture coupled with impressive nutritional content are the signature here. These exceptional entrées were created for the discriminating palate, and here you will learn to make delectable meals that are wholesome, satisfying, and delicious. ◆

Broiled Tofu Cutlets With Brown Rice

Firm Nigari tofu is used in this delightful entrée or first course.

◆ 4 SERVINGS ◆

3 cups cooked brown rice
1 cup frozen peas, cooked
1 tsp. dried thyme
1 tsp. dried basil
1 tsp. Bragg liquid aminos
2 8-oz. pkg. Nigari tofu (firm), drained

MARINADE:
1/4 cup hatcho miso
1/3 cup burgundy wine
1 cup beef-flavored vegetable broth
2 Tbsp. balsamic vinegar
2 Tbsp. tomato paste
1 tsp. granulated garlic
1/2 tsp. dried thyme
1/2 tsp. dried Mexican oregano

Slice each block of tofu along the width into three 1/4-inch cutlets. Blend marinade ingredients in a blender (a hand-held blender works fine). Pour marinade over tofu cutlets. Cover, and refrigerate overnight.

The next day, toss brown rice with peas, herbs, and aminos; keep warm. Spoon extra marinade over the tofu cutlets. Place in preheated broiler. Cook 3 to 4 minutes, then turn cutlets over and spoon additional marinade over cutlets. Cook an additional 3 to 4 minutes. Serve with rice dish.

NUTRITION ANALYSIS
(PER SERVING)

Protein 21 gm., Carbohydrate 77 gm., Fiber 9 gm., Fat 5 gm., Cholesterol 0, Calcium 52 mg., Sodium 310 mg.

Calories 349
From protein: 19%; From carbohydrate: 71%; From fat: 10%

Bubbling Potato Casserole

This aromatic, hearty dish is wonderful with whole grain bread and a crisp salad.

◆ 8 SERVINGS ◆

- 1 Tbsp. olive oil
- 1 cup chopped onion
- 4 cloves garlic, minced
- 14-oz. pkg. Gimme Lean, sausage flavor
- 6-oz. pkg. Yves veggie Canadian bacon, chopped
- 5 medium unpeeled russet potatoes, quartered and cut into 1/4-inch slices
- 2 cups zucchini cut into 1/2-inch-wide julienne strips
- 1/2 cup white wine
- 1 cup beef-flavored vegetable broth, boiling
- 25-oz. jar fat-free tomato sauce
- 1 cup frozen peas, thawed
- 1 large bay leaf

Preheat oven to 350°. Heat oil in a large oven- and stovetop-safe casserole dish. Add the onions and garlic; sauté 2 minutes. Stir in the Gimme Lean, breaking it apart with a wooden spoon as it cooks. Add the veggie bacon, and sauté the mixture 5 minutes. Add the potatoes and zucchini. Continue to cook over medium-high heat, stirring frequently, until the vegetables soften, about 8 minutes. Add wine, and stir 2 minutes. Add boiling broth; reduce heat to low. Cook 5 minutes, stirring occasionally. Add remaining ingredients. Cook 5 minutes longer. Cover the dish. Bake 1 hour or until ready to serve.

NUTRITION ANALYSIS
(PER SERVING)

Protein 20 gm., Carbohydrate 55 gm., Fiber 5 gm., Fat 2 gm., Cholesterol 0, Calcium 21 mg., Sodium 651 mg.

Calories 318
From protein: 25%; From carbohydrate: 69%; From fat: 6%

Creamed Chicken (TVP) and Corn

Tender chunks of chicken TVP in a delectable sake-laced sauce make a lovely presentation when served with basmati rice.

◆ 6 SERVINGS ◆

2 cups TVP chicken chunks
1 3/4 cups chicken-flavored vegetable broth, boiling
1 1/2 tsp. olive oil
1/4 cup scallions, sliced thin
3 cloves garlic, minced
1/4 cup chopped green pepper
1/4 cup sake
1 Tbsp. tamari
2 cups corn
1/2 tsp. granulated garlic
1 tsp. dried marjoram
1 cup nutritional yeast
2/3 cup soymilk lite
dash cayenne
dash lemon pepper

Place TVP in a medium bowl. Cover with boiling broth; set aside. Heat oil in a 4-quart saucepan over medium-high heat for 1 minute. Add scallions, garlic, and green pepper. Sauté 3 minutes. Add reconstituted TVP and any remaining liquid. Cook over medium heat 5 minutes, stirring frequently. Add sake and tamari, and continue cooking 5 minutes. Stir in corn and granulated garlic. Cook for 5 minutes. Gradually add remaining ingredients, stirring to blend. Lower heat and simmer 10 minutes, stirring occasionally.

NUTRITION ANALYSIS (PER SERVING)

Protein 30 gm., Carbohydrate 34 gm., Fiber 6 gm., Fat 3 gm., Cholesterol 0, Calcium 9 mg., Sodium 226 mg.

Calories 268
From protein: 42%; From carbohydrate: 48%; From fat: 10%

Fiesta Scrambler

Serve this tequila-laced entrée with black beans and rice for a quick and easy Mexican fiesta!

◆ 4 SERVINGS ◆

- 2 1/2 cups lite silken tofu (firm or extra firm), drained
- 1 1/2 tsp. olive oil
- 1/8 tsp. crushed red pepper
- 3 scallions, sliced
- 3 large cloves garlic, minced
- 1/3 cup chopped green bell pepper
- 1/4 tsp. turmeric
- 1 Tbsp. tamari
- 3/4 cup chunky medium-hot salsa, drained
- 3 to 4 Tbsp. tequila
- 1 Tbsp. lime juice
- 1/4 cup chopped fresh cilantro

Drain tofu, and pat dry. Place tofu in a microwave-safe medium bowl, and use potato masher to mash tofu. Microwave on high for 2 1/2 minutes. Place tofu in a fine mesh colander. Heat olive oil and crushed pepper in a 10" frying pan over medium-high heat. Add scallions, garlic, and bell pepper. Sauté for 3 minutes or until crisp tender. Add drained tofu, and continue to cook for 5 minutes, stirring frequently. Stir in remaining ingredients. Reduce heat, and simmer 5 minutes or until ready to serve. Serve with warm whole wheat tortillas and extra salsa.

NUTRITION ANALYSIS
(PER SERVING)

Protein 12 gm., Carbohydrate 7 gm., Fiber 2 gm., Fat 4 gm., Cholesterol 0, Calcium 20 mg., Sodium 396 mg.

Calories 126
From protein: 39%; From carbohydrate: 21%; From fat: 26%

Gourmet Soyburgers

A cast of exceptional ingredients joins soybeans in this tasty burger.

◆ 10 BURGERS ◆

1 cup dried soybeans
6 cups water
Vegetable oil cooking spray3/4 cup roasted chestnuts, peeled
6-oz. pkg. portobello mushrooms, cubed
1/2 cup chopped red bell pepper
2 cups fresh spinach leaves, firmly packed
8 cloves garlic, peeled
2/3 cup sliced scallions
3 Tbsp. egg replacer powder
2/3 cup water
1 cup cooked basmati rice
2 Tbsp. Dijon mustard
1/4 cup whole wheat bread crumbs
1/4 cup nutritional yeast

Rinse and sort soybeans. Soak in 4 cups of water overnight in the refrigerator. Discard soaking water. Bring beans to boil in 6 cups of water. Reduce heat, and simmer for 3 hours, stirring occasionally; drain.

Preheat oven to 375.° Spray baking pans with cooking spray. Place chestnuts and next 5 ingredients in food processor; pulse just to mix. Whisk egg replacer powder with 2/3 cup water in a small bowl until foamy. Add to processor along with soybeans, and pulse just to mix; do not purée. Scrape mixture into a large bowl, and add basmati rice. Mix well. Add mustard, bread crumbs, and yeast; mix thoroughly. Form mixture into burgers. Place burgers on baking pans; bake 25 minutes. Spray top of burgers lightly with cooking spray, then brown under the broiler. You may also panfry these burgers using cooking spray along with olive oil, with very good results.

NUTRITION ANALYSIS
(PER BURGER)

Protein 12 gm., Carbohydrate 28 gm., Fiber 4 gm., Fat 4 gm., Cholesterol 0, Calcium 83 mg., Sodium 25 mg.

Calories 175
From protein: 25%; From carbohydrate: 56%; From fat: 19%

Dilled Artichoke Dip ◆ *page 52*
Savory Spinach Dip ◆ *page 63*
Spanakopitta ◆ *page 61*
Savory Stuffed Mushrooms ◆ *page 64*

Basque Stew ◆ *page 74*

Saffron Couscous ◆ *page 179*

Sauced Five-Spice Tofu With Sun-Dried Tomatoes & Cauliflower ◆ *page 141*
Pungent Basmati Rice ◆ *page 142*

Pumpkin Ravioli ◆ *page 197*

Tempeh Shish Kebobs ◆ *page 152*
Minted Orzo—"Mimi" ◆ *page 177*

Spicy Pizza Abbondanza ◆ *page 194*

Savory Stuffed Peppers ◆ *page 145*

Lime 'n Ginger Chicken ◆ *page 132*

Brussels Sprouts and Chestnuts in a Savory Sauce ◆ *page 164*

Split Pea Soup With Ham ◆ *page 85*

Curried Tofu & Basmati Rice Salad ◆ *page 91*

Broccoli Lasagna Rolls ◆ *page 185*

White Wheat Bread ◆ *page 118*
Whole Wheat Dinner Muffins ◆ *page 119*

Lemon Blueberry Delite ◆ *page 234*

Glazed Apple Custard Pie ◆ *page 230*

Pumpkin Fudge Brownies ◆ *page 241*

Fudgy Chocolate Walnut Ring ◆ *page 227*

Hearty Shepherd's Pie

The Ready Ground Tofu adds a nice texture to this peasant dish, and the portobello mushrooms and sliced baby carrots elevate it to new heights.

◆ 8 SERVINGS ◆

1 1/2 tsp. olive oil
1/4 tsp. crushed red pepper
1 cup chopped red onion
2 cups sliced baby carrots
4 cloves garlic, minced
6 oz. portobello mushrooms, cut to 1-inch cubes (about 2 1/4 cups)
3 Tbsp. whole wheat flour
2 1/2 cups beef-flavored vegetable broth, hot (separated)
2 10-oz. pkg. savory garlic Ready Ground Tofu, drained
1 cup frozen peas, thawed
1/4 cup nutritional yeast
1 Tbsp. dehydrated ground mushrooms
1 Tbsp. tamari

MASHED POTATO TOPPING:

2 1/4 cups water
1 cup soymilk lite
1/2 tsp. salt
2 1/4 cups mashed potato flakes
1/4 tsp. lemon pepper
paprika

Preheat oven to 350°. Heat oil and crushed pepper over medium-high heat 2 minutes in a 3- or 4-quart ovenproof and stovetop-safe casserole. Add onion, carrots, and garlic. Sauté 5 minutes, stirring frequently. Add mushrooms; cover and sauté another 3 minutes. Stir in flour. Add 1 1/2 cups hot broth, and stir until thickened, about 3 minutes. Lower heat; add ground tofu and peas. Add remaining broth, nutritional yeast, dehydrated mushrooms, and tamari.

Bring water to a boil in a medium pan. Turn off heat, and add soymilk. Stir in potato flakes and salt, stirring until smooth. Add lemon pepper. Arrange mashed potatoes over top of stew. Sprinkle with paprika. Bake for 15 minutes, then place under broiler for 3 minutes to brown.

NUTRITION ANALYSIS
(PER SERVING)

Protein 14 gm., Carbohydrate 34 gm., Fiber 4 gm., Fat 5 gm., Cholesterol 0, Calcium 29 mg., Sodium 326 mg.

Calories 214
From protein: 23%; From carbohydrate: 58%; From fat: 19%

Homestyle Veggie Loaf

This delicious baked loaf is easy to prepare and goes well with pasta and a salad.

◆ 8 SERVINGS ◆

Vegetable oil cooking spray
1 1/2 cups beef-flavored vegetable broth
1 cup soy grits
4 cloves garlic, minced
2/3 cup chopped onion
1 cup whole wheat bread crumbs
1 cup grated carrots
1 1/2 cups grated zucchini
1 1/4 cups frozen corn, thawed
1/4 cup nutritional yeast
2 Tbsp. Dijon mustard
2 Tbsp. tamari
2 Tbsp. egg replacer powder
1/2 cup water
1 tsp. dried thyme
1 tsp. dried basil
1 tsp. dried marjoram

Preheat oven to 350°. Lightly coat a 9" x 5" loaf pan with cooking spray. Place broth and soy grits in a medium saucepan, and bring to a boil. Reduce heat, cover, and simmer, stirring occasionally, 10 to 15 minutes or until liquid is absorbed. Cool slightly. Place cooked grits in a large bowl, and add the next 9 ingredients, mixing well after each addition. Whisk egg replacer with water in a small bowl until foamy. Add to vegetable mixture; mix. Add the herbs, and mix thoroughly. Turn into the prepared pan. Sprinkle with additional thyme, basil, and marjoram. Bake for 45 minutes.

NUTRITION ANALYSIS
(PER SERVING)

Protein 17 gm., Carbohydrate 46 gm., Fiber 5 gm., Fat 3 gm., Cholesterol 0, Calcium 27 mg., Sodium 218 mg.

Calories 173
From protein: 24%; From carbohydrate: 65%; From fat: 10%

Jasmine Chicken TVP

TVP chicken chunks in a vermouth-laced tomato sauce form the basis for this delicious mélange of vegetables and fragrant jasmine rice.

◆ 6 SERVINGS ◆

1 1/4 cups chicken-flavored vegetable broth, boiling
2 cups chunk chicken-style TVP
1 1/2 tsp. olive oil
1/8 tsp. crushed red pepper
1 1/2 cups chopped sweet onion (like Vidalia or Maui)
4 cloves garlic, minced
3 large mushroom caps, sliced
3 cups sliced yellow squash
1/3 cup dry vermouth
25-oz. jar fat-free tomato sauce
1 bay leaf
1 tsp. dried marjoram
1 1/2 cups cooked jasmine rice

Combine boiling broth and TVP; set aside. Heat oil and crushed pepper in a 5-quart saucepan over medium-high heat for 1 minute. Add onion and garlic; sauté 2 minutes. Add mushrooms and squash; cook 5 minutes. Add reconstituted TVP, and cook 3 minutes. Add vermouth, tomato sauce, bay leaf, and marjoram. Reduce heat to simmer. Gently stir in cooked rice, and simmer 10 minutes or until ready to serve.

NUTRITION ANALYSIS
(PER SERVING)

Protein 19 gm., Carbohydrate 43 gm., Fiber 9 gm., Fat 2 gm., Cholesterol 0, Calcium 37 mg., Sodium 232 mg.

Calories 248
From protein: 28%; From carbohydrate: 66%; From fat: 6%

Jungle Curry

This Thai classic loses nothing in the translation. Highly saturated coconut milk has been replaced with a clever blend of wholesome ingredients.

◆ 8 SERVINGS ◆

1 1/2 tsp. olive oil
1 medium red onion, quartered and cut into thin slices
6 cloves garlic, minced
1 green bell pepper, cut into thin strips
2 cups sliced mushrooms
1 medium zucchini, thinly sliced
2 cups green beans, cut into 2-inch pieces
1 1/2 cups shredded cabbage
15 large fresh basil leaves
1/2 cup white wine
15-oz. can peeled and diced tomatoes
3 Tbsp. fresh lime juice (juice of 1 lime)
1 Tbsp. grated lemon zest
1/2 cup plus 2 Tbsp. lite silken tofu (firm), drained
1/2 cup soymilk lite
1 tsp. coconut extract
1 jalapeño pepper
1 Tbsp. tamari

Heat oil in a 5-quart saucepan over medium-high heat. Add the next 3 ingredients, and sauté 3 minutes. Add the next 4 ingredients, and cook 5 minutes. Add basil leaves, white wine, tomatoes, lime juice, and lemon zest. Reduce heat to medium, and cover, stirring occasionally. Place tofu in food processor; blend. Add soymilk and coconut extract. Working with rubber-gloved hands, remove stem from jalapeño pepper, and quarter. Add pepper, along with seeds, to food processor (to reduce heat, omit seeds). Pulse to blend. Fold tofu mixture into pot, and reduce to simmer. Add tamari. Serve with jasmine rice.

NUTRITION ANALYSIS (PER SERVING)

Protein 5 gm., Carbohydrate 14 gm., Fiber 3 gm., Fat 2 gm., Cholesterol 0, Calcium 55 mg., Sodium 207 mg.

Calories 89
From protein: 21%; From carbohydrate: 62%; From fat: 17%

Lentils 'n Sausage

This high-protein dish is delicious served with pasta.

◆ 8 SERVINGS ◆

2 cups brown lentils
4 cups water
1 1/2 tsp. olive oil
1/8 tsp. crushed red pepper
3/4 cup chopped onion
6 cloves garlic, minced
2 cups sliced baby carrots
14 oz. pkg. Gimme Lean Sausage
1/4 cup dry sherry
14.5 oz. can Mexican-style stewed tomatoes

Rinse and sort lentils, and place them in a 4-quart saucepan with the water. Bring to a boil, stir, and reduce heat. Simmer 20 minutes or until liquid is absorbed. In a 10" frying pan, heat oil and crushed pepper over medium-high heat 2 minutes. Add onion and garlic, and sauté 2 minutes. Add carrots and cook 5 minutes or until vegetables are crisp tender. Add the vegetarian sausage and cook mixture 10 to 12 minutes, stirring often and breaking up sausage. Add sausage mixture to cooked lentils. Add sherry, then stir in tomatoes. Simmer 10 minutes, stirring often.

NUTRITION ANALYSIS
(PER SERVING)

Protein 23 gm., Carbohydrate 44 gm., Fiber 10 gm.,
Cholesterol 0, Calcium 64 mg., Sodium 296 mg.

Calories 276
From protein: 32%; From carbohydrate: 63%; From fat: 5%

Lime 'n Ginger Chicken

Hearty chunks of TVP chicken, carrots, sweet peas, and zesty seasonings combine in this lively, Caribbean-inspired dish.

◆ 8 SERVINGS ◆

3 cups TVP chicken chunks
2 cups chicken-flavored vegetable broth, boiling, separated
1 1/2 tsp. olive oil
6 cloves garlic, minced
2 Tbsp. grated fresh gingerroot
1 jalapeño pepper, chopped, with seeds*
1 1/2 cups chopped red onion
1 rib celery, sliced
2 cups sliced baby carrots
juice of 1 lime (about 3 to 4 Tbsp.)
3/4 cup white wine
1/3 cup mango chutney, chopped
1 cup frozen peas, thawed
1 tsp. dried thyme
2 Tbsp. Bragg liquid aminos

Immerse TVP in 1 1/2 cups boiling broth, reserving 1/2 cup. Heat oil in a 5-quart saucepan over medium-high heat for 1 minute. Add the next 5 ingredients, and sauté 3 minutes. Add the carrots, and cook 3 minutes. Add reconstituted TVP. Cook 5 minutes, stirring frequently. Add the lime juice and white wine; cook 3 minutes. Add the remaining ingredients plus the reserved 1/2 cup of broth; lower heat. Simmer 12 to 15 minutes, stirring occasionally, or until the vegetables and TVP are tender.

*Always wear rubber gloves when working with jalapeño peppers. The addition of seeds will increase the heat of the dish; you may omit.

NUTRITION ANALYSIS
(PER SERVING)

Protein 18 gm., Carbohydrate 102 gm., Fiber 9 gm., Fat 1 gm., Cholesterol 0, Calcium 41 mg., Sodium 318 mg.

Calories 182
From protein: 15%; From carbohydrate: 83%; From fat: 3%

Moussaka

This popular Greek casserole can be served warm or at room temperature.

◆ 8 SERVINGS ◆

vegetable oil cooking spray
5 medium russet potatoes
1 2/3 cups beef-flavored vegetable broth, boiling
3 cups TVP, ground beef style
1 1/2 tsp. olive oil
1 cup chopped red onion
6 cloves garlic, minced
28-oz. can peeled and diced tomatoes
1 tsp. dried basil
1/4 tsp. lemon pepper
cayenne to taste
1/3 cup whole wheat bread crumbs (reserve 3 Tbsp.)

WHITE SAUCE:

1 Tbsp. olive oil
2 large shallots, chopped (1/4 cup)
3 Tbsp. whole wheat flour
1/2 cup white wine
1 1/2 cups soymilk lite
1 cup nutritional yeast
2 Tbsp. cornstarch
3 Tbsp. water
1/8 tsp. ground nutmeg

Preheat oven to 350°. Spray a 9" x 13" baking pan with cooking spray. Cut unpeeled potatoes in 1/4-inch slices, and parboil for 10 minutes. Set aside. Pour boiling broth over TVP in a medium bowl. Set aside. Heat olive oil in a 5-quart saucepan over medium-high heat. Add onion and garlic; sauté for 3 minutes. Stir in reconstituted TVP, and cook mixture 3 minutes. Add tomatoes and seasonings. Reduce heat to simmer, stirring occasionally. Heat olive oil in a medium saucepan. Add shallots, and sauté 3 minutes. Stir in flour to form a paste. Add wine; stir until smooth. Gradually add soymilk, then whisk in yeast 1/3 cup at a time. Blend cornstarch with water, and add to sauce. Simmer until thickened. Sprinkle half of the bread crumbs along the bottom and sides of the prepared pan. Layer the potato slices along the bottom of the pan, overlapping slightly. Top with the TVP mixture. Pour the sauce over all, then sprinkle with nutmeg and reserved bread crumbs. Bake for 30 minutes, then cool 20 minutes before serving.

NUTRITION ANALYSIS
(PER SERVING)

Protein 33 gm., Carbohydrate 60 gm., Fiber 7 gm., Fat 5 gm., Cholesterol 0, Calcium 22 mg., Sodium 242 mg.

Calories 345
From protein: 32%; From carbohydrate: 58%; From fat: 10%

Outrageous Oatmeal

The soymilk in this oatmeal recipe makes it so very creamy, and the sweet dried fruit, cinnamon, and nutmeg start your day with a smile.

◆ 3 SERVINGS ◆

1 3/4 cups soymilk lite
1 cup rolled oats (5-minute variety)
1/8 tsp. salt
vanilla soy milk or rice milk to taste
1/4 cup snipped dried apricots
2 Tbsp. dried fruit, such as golden raisins, blueberries, or cranberries
1 mashed banana
3 large fresh strawberries, sliced
pure maple syrup to taste
cinnamon and nutmeg to taste

Place soymilk in medium saucepan. Heat over medium heat 2 minutes. Stir in rolled oats, and reduce heat to low. Cook 3 minutes, stirring occasionally. When mixture begins to thicken, add fruit of your choice, cinnamon, and nutmeg. Continue to cook, stirring occasionally, 2 to 3 minutes or until liquid is absorbed and oatmeal is thick and creamy. Spoon into bowls. Serve with syrup and extra milk.

NUTRITION ANALYSIS
(PER 8-OZ. SERVING)

Protein 7 gm., Carbohydrate 59 gm., Fiber 4 gm., Fat 3 gm., Cholesterol 0, Calcium 40 mg., Sodium 156 mg.

Calories 285
From protein: 10%; From carbohydrate: 80%; From fat: 10%

Oven-Baked Tempeh

This dish has a flavor reminiscent of baked chicken and vegetables.

◆ 6 SERVINGS ◆

1 1/2 tsp. olive oil
1/8 tsp. crushed red pepper
1 leek, well rinsed, and cut into 1/8-inch slices (see Techniques)
1/3 cup sliced shallots
1/2 cup chopped red bell pepper
4 cloves garlic
2 cups baby carrots, halved
1 cup diced zucchini
8-oz. pkg. tempeh, seasoned (see Soyfoods Pantry)
1/2 cup dry sherry
1 medium tomato, diced
1 Tbsp. tamari

Preheat oven to 350°. Place oil and crushed pepper in a stovetop-safe and oven-proof casserole dish. Sauté over medium-high heat 1 minute. Add the next 4 ingredients, and sauté 3 minutes. Add carrot chunks and zucchini. Sauté, stirring frequently, 5 minutes. Add tempeh, and sauté 5 minutes. Add sherry, diced tomato, and tamari; cook mixture 5 minutes. Cover casserole, and bake 30 minutes.

NUTRITION ANALYSIS
(PER SERVING)

Protein 11 gm., Carbohydrate 16 gm., Fiber 3 gm., Fat 3 gm., Cholesterol 0, Calcium 39 mg., Sodium 288 mg.

Calories 144
From protein: 31%; From carbohydrate: 47%; From fat: 23%

Pasta de Patate

This is a delightful dish loosely based on an Italian potato pie. This version features light phyllo pastry, marinated mushrooms, and a delectable layered filling. Don't be discouraged by the individual preparation of the separate layers. It all comes together quite easily and results in an exceptional entrée.

◆ 12 SERVINGS ◆

MUSHROOM MARINADE:

2 6-oz. pkgs. sliced portobello mushrooms
1 cup white wine
3 Tbsp. tamari
2 Tbsp. Dijon mustard
1 tsp. granulated garlic
1 Tbsp. cider vinegar
1 Tbsp. mild molasses
2 Tbsp. vegetarian Worcestershire sauce

3 large russet potatoes, unpeeled, cut into 1/4-inch slices
3 oz. sun-dried tomatoes, snipped
1 cup boiling water

"CHEEZY" WINE SAUCE:

2 Tbsp. olive oil
1/4 cup whole wheat flour
1 cup white wine
1 cup soymilk lite
1/2 cup nutritional yeast
1 tsp. dried marjoram
1/2 tsp. granulated garlic

2 1/2 cups lite silken tofu (extra firm), drained
1/3 cup sliced scallions
1 tsp. granulated garlic
2 cups frozen corn, thawed

vegetable oil cooking spray
1/2 pound. phyllo pastry
6-oz. pkg. Yves veggie Canadian bacon, cut to 1/4-inch julienne strips

Clean mushrooms, and place in a large ziplock bag. Whisk together marinade ingredients, and pour over mushrooms. Set aside, turning a few times during marinating. Parboil the potatoes 10 minutes in 1 quart of boiling salted water. Set aside in colander. Steep sun-dried tomatoes in boiling water; set aside.

Heat olive oil in a medium saucepan over medium heat. Whisk in flour. Stir 3 minutes. Whisk in wine, then when mixture starts to thicken, add soymilk. Lower heat, and simmer 3 minutes. Whisk in remaining wine sauce ingredients. Simmer 3 minutes, then set aside.

Place the tofu in a large bowl. Mash with a potato masher. Add scallions, garlic, corn, and sun-dried tomatoes (reserving liquid). Set aside.

Spray a 10" frying pan with cooking spray. Using a slotted spoon, remove mushrooms from the marinade, and sauté 10 minutes, over medium-high heat, until browned on both sides and and remaining marinade is re-absorbed. Set aside.

Preheat oven to 350°. Spray a 9" x 13" baking pan with cooking spray. Prepare phyllo pastry (see Techniques). Spray 8 phyllo leaves with cooking spray, then place them in the 9" x 13" pan. Place a single layer of potato slices on the phyllo leaves. Top with a layer of veggie bacon. Spread with tofu mixture, then top with a layer of the remaining potatoes. Pour the reserved sun-dried tomato soaking water over the potato layer. Pour the wine sauce over all. Top with 8 leaves of phyllo pastry, spraying each with cooking spray, as in the bottom crust. Spray the top of the pastry with cooking spray, and tuck the top leaves under the bottom into the sides of the pan. Score the top layers with a diamond pattern, being careful not to cut through to the filling. Bake 35 to 40 minutes, or until lightly browned. Serve with a rice dish.

NUTRITION ANALYSIS (PER SERVING)

Protein 14 gm., Carbohydrate 44 gm., Fiber 3 gm., Fat 3 gm., Cholesterol 0, Calcium 14 mg., Sodium 383 mg.

Calories 293
From protein: 20%; From carbohydrate: 61%; From fat: 10%

Quiche Lorraine

This outstanding rendition of a classic is both egg- and dairy-free.

◆ 8 SERVINGS ◆

CRUST

1 cup rolled oats
1 cup whole wheat flour
1/4 tsp. salt
1/3 cup lite silken tofu (firm), drained
1 Tbsp. canola oil
1 Tbsp. liquid Fruitsource or honey
1/4 cup ice water

Place oats, wheat flour, and salt in food processor; blend to mix. Add tofu, and process. Add oil and Fruitsource; pulse to blend. Slowly add ice water, with the machine running, until the dough begins to form a ball. Knead the dough a few times, and shape into a ball. Chill in a plastic bag in the refrigerator. Remove from the refrigerator an hour or so before needed.

FILLING

1 1/2 tsp. olive oil
1/3 cup sliced scallions
2 large cloves garlic, minced
1/4 cup chopped green pepper
6-oz. pkg. Yves veggie Canadian bacon, diced
2 1/2 cups lite silken tofu (extra firm), drained
1/4 cup mirin or dry sherry
2 Tbsp. mellow white miso
1/3 cup mashed potato flakes (see Quick Guide to Ingredients)
1/3 cup nutritional yeast
1/4 tsp. ground nutmeg
1/4 tsp. turmeric
1/2 cup soymilk lite
1 Tbsp. lemon juice

Preheat oven to 400°. Heat oil in a 10" frying pan. Add scallions, garlic, and green pepper. Sauté 3 minutes. Add bacon, and sauté 2 minutes, or until the vegetables are crisp tender. Blend tofu in the food processor. Place the mirin and miso in a small bowl, and blend. Add with the next 4 ingredients to the food processor; process. Add soymilk and lemon juice, and blend until smooth. Fold into the vegetables and bacon.

Roll out dough 1/4-inch thick on a cutting board sprinkled with flour. Press the dough into a pie pan. Fill with tofu mixture. Bake in the center of the oven 25 to 30 minutes. Serve at room temperature.

NUTRITION ANALYSIS (PER SERVING)

Protein 20 gm., Carbohydrate 29 gm., Fiber 3 gm., Fat 5 gm., Cholesterol 0, Calcium 17 mg., Sodium 401 mg.

Calories 232
From protein: 33%; From carbohydrate: 48%; From fat: 18%

Roghan Josh

This version of a popular, spicy curried East Indian dish is as aromatic and delicious as can be.

◆ 8 SERVINGS ◆

1 1/2 cups beef-flavored vegetable broth, boiling
3 cups TVP steak strips
1 Tbsp. olive oil
1/4 tsp. crushed red pepper
2 bay leaves
2 cinnamon sticks
1 rounded Tbsp. grated gingerroot
2 cups chopped red onion
2 ribs celery, sliced
1 1/2 cups sliced baby carrots
2 cups cubed zucchini
1 tsp. granulated garlic
1/8 tsp. asafetida
1/2 tsp. ground coriander
1/2 tsp. ground cardamom
1/2 tsp. ground cumin
1/2 tsp. ground ginger
1 1/2 tsp. dried cilantro
6 cherry tomatoes, halved
1 1/4 cups lite silken tofu (firm), drained
2 Tbsp. lemon juice
1 clove garlic, peeled
1/2 cup soymilk lite
1 1/2 Tbsp. country barley miso
1/4 cup white wine (Chablis is nice)
2 Tbsp. Brinjal Pickle (spicy eggplant relish)

Place TVP in boiling broth, and set aside. Heat the oil with crushed red pepper in a 5-quart saucepan for 1 minute. Add the next 7 ingredients; sauté 5 minutes. Then add garlic and the following 7 ingredients; simmer. Place tofu in food processor, and blend until smooth. Add the next 3 ingredients; blend. Blend miso with wine in a small bowl. Add to tofu mixture. Fold tofu mixture into vegetable/TVP mixture in saucepan. Stir in eggplant relish. Serve.

NUTRITION ANALYSIS
(PER SERVING)

Protein 20 gm., Carbohydrate 22 gm., Fiber 8 gm., Fat 3 gm., Cholesterol 0, Calcium 43 mg., Sodium 217 mg.

Calories 176
From protein: 41%; From carbohydrate: 45%; From fat: 14%

Sauced Five-Spice Tofu With Sun-Dried Tomatoes & Cauliflower

This tempting dish is easy to assemble and very delicious. Serve it with Pungent Basmati Rice (recipe follows).

◆ 6 SERVINGS ◆

1 cup halved sun-dried tomatoes
1 1/3 cups boiling water
1 1/2 tsp. olive oil
1/4 tsp. crushed red pepper
1 cup chopped onion
6 cloves garlic, minced
1 Tbsp. grated gingerroot
1/2 cup chopped red bell pepper
6-oz. pkg. Five-Spice Baked Tofu, drained, cut into 1/4-inch slices
1 medium head cauliflower, broken into florets
1/4 cup mirin or dry sherry
6 large basil leaves, snipped
1 Tbsp. Bragg liquid aminos
1 Tbsp. cornstarch
2 Tbsp. water

Steep sun-dried tomatoes in boiling water; set aside. Heat olive oil and crushed pepper in a medium saucepan over medium-high heat for 1 minute. Add the next 4 ingredients, and sauté 3 minutes. Add tofu, and sauté 3 minutes, stirring frequently. Add cauliflower, and sauté 3 minutes. Add mirin, basil, and liquid aminos. Lower heat, and simmer 10 minutes, stirring frequently. Blend cornstarch and water in a small bowl. Add to saucepan, and simmer 5 minutes or until ready to serve, stirring occasionally.

NUTRITION ANALYSIS
(PER SERVING)

Protein 16 gm., Carbohydrate 86 gm., Fiber 11 gm., Fat 1 gm., Cholesterol 0, Calcium 35 mg., Sodium 341 mg.

Calories 203
From protein: 16%; From carbohydrate: 82%; From fat: 2%

Pungent Basmati Rice

This delightful rice variety is enhanced by Indian spices in this quick and easy treatment.

◆ 6 SERVINGS ◆

1 cup basmati rice, rinsed thoroughly
2 1/2 cups chicken-flavored broth, boiling
1/4 tsp. turmeric
1/2 tsp. ground coriander

Place rinsed rice in the boiling broth; stir and bring to a second boil. Stir, add remaining ingredients, and reduce heat. Cover and simmer, undisturbed, for 20 minutes. Liquid should be absorbed. Serve.

NUTRITION ANALYSIS
(PER 1/2-CUP SERVING)

Protein 3 gm., Carbohydrate 24 gm., Fiber 0, Fat 0, Cholesterol 0, Calcium 3 mg., Sodium 3 mg.

Calories 114
From protein: 10%; From carbohydrate: 90%; From fat: 0%

Sausage Scrambler

Fragrant and delicious, this great Sunday brunch dish owes its abundant flavor to savory vegetarian sausage. Serve with pita pockets and a dollop of salsa.

◆ 6 SERVINGS ◆

2 1/2 cups lite silken tofu (extra firm), drained
1 1/2 tsp. olive oil
1/8 tsp. crushed red pepper
5 cloves garlic, minced
1/2 cup sliced scallions
1/2 cup chopped green pepper
14-oz. pkg. Gimme Lean, sausage style
1/4 tsp. turmeric
1/2 tsp. dried thyme
2 Tbsp. dry sherry
1 Tbsp. tamari
14.5-oz. can Mexican-style stewed tomatoes, well drained

Drain and pat dry the tofu. Place in a microwave-safe, medium bowl. Using a potato masher, press tofu into curds. Cover and heat in the microwave 3 minutes. Pour tofu curds in a colander to drain. Set aside. Heat oil and crushed pepper in a 4-quart saucepan 1 minute over medium-high heat. Add garlic, scallions, and pepper; sauté 2 minutes. Add Gimme Lean. Sauté, stirring and breaking sausage apart. Cook 5 minutes or until sausage is brown. Add drained tofu. Stir in spices, sherry, and tamari. Cook mixture 2 minutes. Add drained tomatoes; lower heat, and simmer 5 minutes.

NUTRITION ANALYSIS
(PER SERVING)

Protein 19 gm., Carbohydrate 17 gm., Fiber 3 gm., Fat 2 gm., Cholesterol 0, Calcium 38 mg., Sodium 560 mg.

Calories 167
From protein: 45%; From carbohydrate: 41%; From fat: 13%

Savory Sausage Patties

These delicious vegetarian patties are very low in fat and contain no cholesterol.

◆ 8 PATTIES ◆

vegetable oil cooking spray
14-oz. pkg. Gimme Lean, sausage style
2 cloves garlic, minced
1/4 cup whole wheat bread crumbs
1/4 cup soy grits
1 Tbsp. country Dijon mustard
1 Tbsp. egg replacer powder
1/4 cup water

Preheat oven to 400°. Spray a baking sheet with cooking spray. Place Gimme Lean in a large bowl. Add the next 4 ingredients; mix well. Whisk egg replacer with water in a small bowl. Add to sausage mixture, and mix thoroughly. Form into 8 patties, and place on baking sheet. Bake 15 to 20 minutes, turning over after 8 minutes to brown second side.

NUTRITION ANALYSIS
(PER PATTY)

Protein 11 gm., Carbohydrate 16 gm., Fiber 2 gm., Fat 1 gm., Cholesterol 0, Calcium 3 mg., Sodium 256 mg.

Calories 92
From protein: 39%; From carbohydrate: 56%; From fat: 6%

Savory Stuffed Peppers

This colorful dish is tasty and satisfying.

◆ 8 SERVINGS ◆

2 quarts boiling water
4 bell peppers (2 green and 2 gold or orange), halved lengthwise and seeded
1 1/2 tsp. olive oil
1 medium red onion, chopped
5 cloves garlic, minced
14-oz. pkg. Gimme Lean, sausage flavor
2 cups cooked brown rice
2 tsp. dried thyme
4 fresh basil leaves, snipped
1/2 cup white wine
25-oz. jar fat-free tomato sauce
14.5-oz. can Italian-style stewed tomatoes
1 bay leaf
4 fresh basil leaves, snipped
1 tsp. granulated garlic

Preheat oven to 375°. Place halved peppers in boiling water, and blanch 5 minutes. Remove to colander, and rinse with cold water; set aside. Heat oil in a 10" frying pan over medium-high heat for 1 minute. Add onions and garlic; sauté 3 minutes. Add Gimme Lean. Cook for 5 minutes, using a large spoon to break it apart as it cooks. Add the next 3 ingredients, and cook 3 minutes. Add wine, and simmer 5 minutes or until ready to stuff peppers.

In a medium saucepan, heat the tomato sauce with the remaining ingredients for 10 minutes. Spread about half the sauce on the bottom of a 9" x 13" baking pan. Spoon filling into each pepper half and place in pan. Top with remaining sauce. Cover with foil. Bake 30 minutes. Remove foil, and continue to bake an additional 10 to 15 minutes.

NUTRITION ANALYSIS
(PER SERVING)

Protein 13 gm., Carbohydrate 42 gm., Fiber 7 gm., Fat 2 gm., Cholesterol 0, Calcium 55 mg., Sodium 409 mg.

Calories 232
From protein: 22%; From carbohydrate: 72%; From fat: 6%

Savory Tofu Bake

Savory tofu is baked with fresh vegetables to create this flavorful mélange.

◆ 8 SERVINGS ◆

1 1/2 tsp. olive oil
1/8 tsp. crushed red pepper
6 cloves garlic, minced
1/2 cup sliced scallions
1/3 cup chopped shallots
2 1/2 cups sliced carrots
2 pounds green beans, cut into 2-inch pieces
6 oz. cremini mushrooms, sliced
12 cherry tomatoes, halved lengthwise
2 6-oz. pkgs. savory baked tofu, cut into julienne strips
1/4 cup very dry sherry
1 Tbsp. tamari
6 large basil leaves, snipped

Preheat oven to 350°. Heat oil and crushed pepper in a large stovetop- and oven-safe casserole over medium-high heat for 1 minute. Add the next 3 ingredients, and sauté 2 minutes. Add carrots and green beans, and cook 5 minutes. Add mushrooms, tomatoes, and tofu, and cook 5 minutes. Add sherry and remaining ingredients; stir and cook 2 minutes. Cover, and bake 30 minutes. Serve with a rice or noodle dish.

NUTRITION ANALYSIS
(PER SERVING)

Protein 13 gm., Carbohydrate 23 gm., Fiber 7 gm., Fat 2 gm., Cholesterol 0, Calcium 70 mg., Sodium 380 mg.

Calories 162
From protein: 31%; From carbohydrate: 56%; From fat: 12%

Scrumptious Stewed Tempeh

This tasty combination of seasoned tempeh, fresh green beans, and cremini mushrooms is a real treat!

◆ 6 SERVINGS ◆

1 1/2 tsp. olive oil
1/8 tsp. crushed red pepper
1/2 cup chopped onions
6 cloves garlic, minced
1/3 cup chopped red bell pepper
1/3 cup chopped green bell pepper
8 oz. pkg. seasoned tempeh, cubed (see page 148)
6 oz. cremini mushrooms (caps only)
2 cups fresh green beans, cut into 1-inch pieces
1/3 cup dry sherry
14.5-oz. can Italian-style stewed tomatoes
4 fresh basil leaves, snipped
1 Tbsp. cornstarch
1 Tbsp. water

Heat oil and crushed pepper in a 4-quart saucepan over medium-high heat for 1 minute. Add the next 4 ingredients, and sauté 2 minutes. Add the tempeh, and sauté 3 minutes. Add the mushroom caps and green beans. Cook 10 minutes, stirring frequently. Add sherry, and cook 3 minutes. Add the tomatoes and basil. Reduce heat, and simmer for 15 minutes. Blend cornstarch with water in a small bowl. Add to the sauce. Simmer 5 to 8 minutes, stirring frequently. Serve with Garlic Mashed Potatoes (page 175), a rice dish, or noodles.

NUTRITION ANALYSIS
(PER SERVING)

Protein 11 gm., Carbohydrate 16 gm., Fiber 4 gm., Fat 3 gm., Cholesterol 0, Calcium 49 mg., Sodium 144 mg.

Calories 141
From protein: 31%; From carbohydrate: 46%; From fat: 22%

Seasoned Tempeh

Some cooks like to steam tempeh before use, but I've found that seasoning tempeh before using it in a recipe enhances the flavor and texture. This recipe will provide enough tempeh for use in 2 to 4 recipes. It will keep for up to a week in the refrigerator.

◆ 8 SERVINGS ◆

2 8-oz. pkg. soy tempeh
3 1/2 cups water
2 Tbsp. tamari
1 piece of kombu, cut in two

Divide each 8-ounce block of tempeh into 2 or 4 pieces. Place in a medium saucepan with remaining ingredients. Bring to a boil; reduce heat. Simmer about 30 to 45 minutes or until tempeh is fragrant and liquid is almost absorbed. As it simmers, gently rotate tempeh from time to time so it's equally submerged. Cool slightly. Cover, and refrigerate. Seasoned tempeh can be used with any tempeh recipe.

NUTRITION ANALYSIS
(PER SERVING)

Protein 13 gm., Carbohydrate 5 gm., Fiber 1 gm., Fat 3 gm., Cholesterol 0, Calcium 2 mg., Sodium 196 mg.

Calories 98
From protein: 52%; From carbohydrate: 21%; From fat: 28%

South-of-the-Border Scrambler

This Mexican-spiced scrambler is colorful, flavorful, and filling.

◆ 6 SERVINGS ◆

2 1/2 cups lite silken tofu (extra firm), drained

1 1/2 tsp. olive oil

1/4 tsp. crushed red pepper

1 cup chopped onion

4 cloves garlic, minced

1/2 cup chopped green bell pepper

4 oz. seasoned tempeh, cubed (see page 148)

1/4 tsp. turmeric

1 Tbsp. tamari

14.5-oz. can diced tomatoes and jalapeños, drained

1 medium baked potato, unpeeled, cubed (Yukon Gold is a good choice)

Place drained tofu in microwave-safe bowl, and mash with potato masher. Cover, and cook 3 minutes. Place in colander to drain; set aside. Heat oil and crushed pepper in a 4-quart saucepan over medium-high heat for 1 minute. Add onion, garlic, and green pepper. Cook and stir 2 minutes. Crumble tempeh, add to mixture, and cook 3 minutes. Add drained tofu, turmeric, and tamari. Stir to mix. Add drained tomatoes and potato. Lower heat, and simmer 10 minutes, stirring occasionally, or until ready to serve.

NUTRITION ANALYSIS
(PER SERVING)

Protein 14 gm., Carbohydrate 18 gm., Fiber 1 gm., Fat 3 gm., Cholesterol 0, Calcium 13 mg., Sodium 448 mg.

Calories 151
From protein: 35%; From carbohydrate: 45%; From fat: 20%

Tempeh Burgers

Serve these hearty, flavorful burgers with french fries and a salad – very tasty!

◆ 6 BURGERS ◆

15-oz. can low-sodium garbanzo beans, drained
8 ounces seasoned tempeh (see page 148)
4 cloves garlic, minced
1/4 cup whole wheat bread crumbs
2 Tbsp. Dijon mustard
1 Tbsp. ketchup
2 Tbsp. tamari
1 Tbsp. egg replacer powder
1/4 cup water
vegetable oil cooking spray
1 Tbsp. olive oil

Place garbanzo beans in a large bowl, and mash with a fork. Crumble seasoned tempeh into the bowl; mix with mashed beans. Add the next 5 ingredients and mix well. Whisk egg replacer with water in a small bowl until foamy. Add to the tempeh mixture; mix thoroughly. (At this point, you may cover mixture and set aside in the refrigerator before proceeding.)

Spray a 10-inch frying pan with cooking spray. Add a tablespoon of olive oil. Form mixture into 6 burgers. Cook over medium heat until browned on both sides, about 15 minutes. If necessary, use additional cooking spray on the pan to keep the burgers from sticking.

NUTRITION ANALYSIS
(PER BURGER)

Protein 16 gm., Carbohydrate 26 gm., Fiber 3 gm., Fat 4 gm., Cholesterol 0, Calcium 6 mg., Sodium 402 mg.

Calories 191
From protein: 32%; From carbohydrate: 50%; From fat: 19%

Tempeh in Brown Gravy

Fresh shiitake mushrooms and colorful vegetables accent succulent chunks of tempeh in a rich brown sauce.

◆ 6 SERVINGS ◆

- 1 Tbsp. olive oil
- 1 cup chopped red onion
- 6 cloves garlic, minced
- 1 rib celery, sliced
- 2 1/2 cups sliced carrots
- 8 ounces seasoned tempeh, cubed (see page 148)
- 3 oz. fresh shiitake mushrooms, sliced
- 3 Tbsp. whole wheat flour
- 1 1/3 cups beef-flavored vegetable broth, hot
- 1/4 cup white wine
- 2 Tbsp. tamari
- 1 cup frozen peas, thawed
- 1/2 tsp. dried thyme

Heat olive oil in a 4-quart saucepan over medium-high heat. Add the next 3 ingredients; cook and stir 2 minutes. Add the carrots, and cook 3 minutes. Add the tempeh, and sauté 5 minutes. Add mushrooms, and continue to cook 3 minutes. Sprinkle with flour; stir to coat. Pour hot broth over the mixture, and stir until thickened. Stir in wine and remaining ingredients. Simmer 10 minutes or until ready to serve.

NUTRITION ANALYSIS
(PER SERVING)

Protein 13 gm., Carbohydrate 22 gm., Fiber 4 gm., Fat 5 gm., Cholesterol 0, Calcium 44 mg., Sodium 476 mg.

Calories 181
From protein: 28%; From carbohydrate: 48%; From fat: 24%

Tempeh Shish Kebobs

Chunks of succulent, marinated tempeh and vegetables are skewered and baked, then finished under the broiler. This dish makes an impressive presentation.

◆ 6 KEBOBS ◆

- 1/3 cup hot barbecue sauce
- 1/3 cup mild hickory barbecue sauce
- 1/4 cup ketchup
- 2 Tbsp. Dijon mustard
- 3 Tbsp. lemon juice
- 3 Tbsp. frozen apple juice concentrate
- 1 Tbsp. tamari
- 1 tsp. dried basil
- 1/2 tsp. granulated garlic
- 1/2 tsp. dried thyme
- cayenne pepper to taste
- 8 ounces seasoned tempeh (see page 148)
- 1/4 pound. button mushrooms, stems intact
- 2 small zucchini, cut into 1/2-inch rounds
- 1 medium yellow onion, cut into 3/4-inch wedges
- 12 cherry tomatoes
- 6 bamboo skewers, soaked 20 minutes in hot water

Mix together the first 11 ingredients in a medium bowl. Set aside. Cut the tempeh into 24 cubes. Skewer the tempeh and vegetables in an alternating pattern, beginning and ending with a mushroom at each end. Place in a 9" x 13" baking pan. Spoon marinade over kebobs, turning to coat both sides. Cover pan with foil, and refrigerate for at least an hour. Preheat oven to 400° Bake in covered pan for 20 minutes. Remove kebobs from pan and place on broiler rack. Spoon marinade over kebobs; place under broiler. Broil kebobs for 5 minutes, then turn them over and recoat with marinade. Broil for about 5 more minutes or until tempeh and vegetables are browned.

NUTRITION ANALYSIS
(PER SERVING)

Protein 13 gm., Carbohydrate 25 gm., Fiber 7 gm., Fat 2 gm., Cholesterol 0, Calcium 37 mg., Sodium 426 mg.

Calories 167
From protein: 30%; From carbohydrate: 57%; From fat: 13%

Tempeh Teriyaki

This easy-to-assemble dish features succulent chunks of tempeh in a tasty teriyaki sauce.

◆ 8 SERVINGS ◆

1 1/2 tsp. olive oil
1/8 tsp. crushed red pepper
6 cloves garlic, minced
1/2 cup sliced scallions
1 Tbsp. grated fresh gingerroot
16 ounces seasoned tempeh, cubed (see page 148)
2 medium tomatoes, diced
3 oz. fresh shiitake mushrooms, cleaned, stemmed, and sliced (if dried, soak before proceeding)
1/4 cup mirin or dry sherry
1 Tbsp. tamari
1 1/2 cups frozen peas, thawed

Heat oil and crushed pepper in large saucepan over medium-high heat for 1 minute. Add the next 3 ingredients; stir for 2 minutes. Add tempeh to pan. Sauté mixture 5 minutes, stirring frequently. Add the next 4 ingredients. Cook 5 minutes. Add peas, then lower heat. Simmer 5 minutes or until ready to serve.

NUTRITION ANALYSIS
(PER SERVING)

Protein 16 gm., Carbohydrate 22 gm., Fiber 4 gm., Fat 4 gm., Cholesterol 0, Calcium 19 mg., Sodium 327 mg.

Calories 183
From protein: 34%; From carbohydrate: 46%; From fat: 20%

Tempting Triple Layer Casserole

This hearty dish is very appealing and reheats well.

◆ 12 SERVINGS ◆

2 cups red lentils, rinsed
4 cups chicken-flavored vegetable broth
1 3/4 cups beef-flavored vegetable broth
1 cup soy grits
1 Tbsp. tamari
14.5-oz. can peeled and diced tomatoes
1/2 tsp. granulated garlic
1 Tbsp. olive oil
1/4 tsp. crushed red pepper
1 cup chopped onion
4 cloves garlic, minced
5 medium unpeeled russet potatoes, sliced thin
1/2 cup white wine
3/4 cup chicken-flavored vegetable broth, boiling
1 Tbsp. dried basil
1 medium tomato, sliced into 1/4-inch wedges

Preheat oven to 350°. Place lentils and chicken-flavored broth in a 5-quart saucepan. Bring to a boil. Reduce heat, and simmer for 12 to 15 minutes, or until liquid is absorbed. Set aside. Place beef-flavored broth, soy grits, and tamari in a medium saucepan; bring to a boil. Reduce heat, and simmer until liquid is absorbed, about 10 minutes. Stir tomatoes and granulated garlic into the grits. Set aside.

Heat oil and crushed pepper in a large oven- and stovetop-safe casserole dish over medium-high heat for 1 minute. Add the onion and garlic; sauté 2 minutes. Add sliced potatoes, and sauté 5 minutes, stirring frequently, or until potatoes start to soften. Add wine, and cook for 2 minutes. Add broth. Cook 10 minutes over medium heat, allowing liquid to reduce by half. Spread the soy grits mixture over the potato mixture, and top with a layer of lentils. Arrange tomato wedges over top layer; sprinkle with basil. Cover casserole, and bake 1 hour. Let casserole stand 10 minutes before serving.

NUTRITION ANALYSIS
(PER SERVING)

Protein 19 gm., Carbohydrate 45 gm., Fiber 6 gm., Fat 2 gm., Cholesterol 0, Calcium 42 mg., Sodium 110 mg.

Calories 267
From protein: 28%; From carbohydrate: 67%; From fat: 6%

Tender Tofu With Mixed Vegetables

This dish has color, flavor, texture, and balance.

◆ 4 SERVINGS ◆

MARINADE:

1 1/4 cups beef-flavored vegetable broth, hot
1/2 cup dry sherry
2 Tbsp. tomato paste
1 Tbsp. tamari
2 Tbsp. liquid Fruitsource or honey
2 Tbsp. cider vinegar
2 Tbsp. fresh grated gingerroot
4 cloves garlic, minced
1 scallion, sliced

2 8-oz. pkgs. firm Nigari tofu, frozen, thawed, and cubed (see Techniques)
1 1/2 tsp. olive oil
2 cups sliced carrots
2 cups green beans, cut into 1-inch pieces
1/2 cup sliced scallions
4 large cloves garlic
3 oz. fresh shiitake mushrooms (if dried, soak before proceeding)
14.5-oz. can peeled and diced tomatoes

Using a wire whisk, blend together the marinade ingredients in the order listed. Immerse the prepared tofu in marinade for at least 3 hours or overnight, turning occasionally.

Warm oil over medium heat in a medium saucepan. Add carrots and green beans; sauté 3 minutes. Stir in scallions, garlic, and mushrooms. Sauté 5 minutes or until vegetables are crisp tender. Push vegetables to sides of pan and place tofu in center of pan with a slotted spoon. Cover, and cook 5 minutes or until tofu is browning. Turn tofu over and pour remaining marinade over tofu. Cook 5 minutes. Add tomatoes, and mix gently. Lower heat, and simmer 10 minutes or until ready to serve. Serve with brown rice and a crisp salad.

NUTRITION ANALYSIS
(PER SERVING)

Protein 19 gm., Carbohydrate 36 gm., Fiber 10 gm., Fat 5 gm., Cholesterol 0, Calcium 104 mg., Sodium 498 mg.

Calories 275
From protein: 28%; From carbohydrate: 54%; From fat: 18%

Tofu in Burgundy Sauce

In this delectable dish, marinated tofu is baked in a French-style burgundy sauce.

◆ 6 SERVINGS ◆

MARINADE:

1 3/4 cups burgundy
1/4 cup mellow white miso
1 Tbsp. tamari
3 Tbsp. balsamic vinegar
2 Tbsp. mirin or dry sherry
1/2 tsp. granulated garlic

3 6-oz. pkgs. Nigari tofu (firm), frozen, thawed, and cubed (see Techniques)
vegetable oil cooking spray
1/2 cup whole wheat flour
1/4 tsp. lemon pepper
1/8 tsp. salt
1/4 tsp. granulated garlic
dash cayenne
1 1/2 cups lightly steamed baby carrots

BURGUNDY SAUCE:

1 Tbsp. olive oil
6 cloves garlic, minced
3/4 cup thinly sliced shallots (3-oz. pkg.)
6-oz. pkg. cremini mushrooms, stemmed and sliced
3 Tbsp. whole wheat flour
1 1/4 cups reserved marinade
1/2 cup soymilk

Whisk together the marinade ingredients. Place the tofu in a single layer in a shallow glass pan. Pour marinade over tofu. Marinate for 30 minutes, turning occasionally. Preheat oven to 350°. Spray a 9" x 13" baking pan with cooking spray. In a small bowl, mix together the flour, lemon pepper, salt, granulated garlic, and cayenne. Gently squeeze some of the marinade from the tofu; reserve marinade. Spray a 10" frying pan with cooking spray. Lightly coat tofu chunks with flour mixture. Sauté tofu over medium-high heat, browning on all sides. Remove to 9" x 13" pan, and arrange with baby carrots; set aside.

Heat oil in a medium saucepan. Sauté garlic and shallots two minutes. Add mushrooms. Cook until mushrooms start to soften; stir in flour. Add reserved marinade. Lower heat, and simmer until sauce starts to thicken. Stir in soymilk; simmer 2 minutes. Pour over tofu and carrots, and cover with foil. Bake 25 to 30 minutes.

NUTRITION ANALYSIS (PER SERVING)

Protein 16 gm., Carbohydrate 30 gm., Fiber 6 gm., Fat 5 gm., Cholesterol 0, Calcium 38 mg., Sodium 296 mg.

Calories 267
From protein: 23%; From carbohydrate: 45%; From fat: 18%;

TVP Chicken Delight

This intensely flavorful dish is delightful served over brown rice.

◆ 6 SERVINGS ◆

1 cup chicken-flavored vegetable broth, boiling
2 cups TVP chicken chunks
1 cup sun-dried tomatoes
1 cup boiling water
1 1/2 tsp. olive oil
1/4 tsp. crushed red pepper
3 large cloves garlic, minced
1/2 cup chopped red bell peppers
3/4 cup sliced scallions
1 Tbsp. tamari
1/4 cup mirin or dry sherry

Combine broth and TVP in a medium bowl. Set aside. Cut dried tomatoes into thirds using a kitchen shears. Place in a small bowl, and cover with boiling water. Set aside. Sauté oil and crushed pepper in a large saucepan over medium-high heat for 2 minutes. Stir in the next 3 ingredients; sauté 3 minutes. Add reconstituted TVP. Cook 5 minutes. Add tomatoes and soaking water. Cover, and reduce heat to medium. Cook 10 minutes, stirring frequently. Add tamari and mirin; simmer for 10 minutes, stirring occasionally, or until ready to serve.

NUTRITION ANALYSIS
(PER SERVING)

Protein 16 gm., Carbohydrate 16 gm., Fiber 6 gm., Fat 2 gm., Cholesterol 0, Calcium 25 mg., Sodium 378 mg.

Calories 127
From protein: 44%; From carbohydrate: 45%; From fat: 11%

Vegetarian Beef Stroganoff

This version of a classic is easy to make and quite delicious. Serve with rice or noodles.

◆ 8 SERVINGS ◆

vegetable oil cooking spray
1 Tbsp. cider vinegar
1 1/2 cups soymilk lite
2 14-oz. pkg. Gimme Lean, ground beef style
1/4 cup bread crumbs
1/3 cup ketchup
1 Tbsp. Dijon mustard
1/2 tsp. granulated garlic
2 Tbsp. olive oil
3/4 cup chopped sweet onion (Texas, Vidalia, Maui)
6 cloves garlic, minced
1/4 cup whole wheat flour
1/2 cup white wine
1/4 cup dry vermouth
1/2 tsp. ground nutmeg
2/3 cup nutritional yeast
6 large fresh basil leaves, snipped

Preheat oven to 400°. Spray a baking pan with cooking spray. Add vinegar to soymilk in a small glass measuring cup; set aside. Place the next 5 ingredients in a large bowl, and mix thoroughly. Form into 3-inch balls, and place on prepared pan. Spray "meatballs" lightly with cooking spray. Bake for 10 minutes, then broil to brown tops.

Meanwhile, heat oil in a 5-quart saucepan over medium heat for 1 minute. Add onions and garlic; sauté 3 minutes. Add flour and stir for 2 minutes; then add wine, vermouth, and nutmeg. Lower heat, and gradually add soymilk, stirring frequently as it simmers. Whisk in nutritional yeast, and add snipped basil. Add cooked "meatballs" to simmering sauce. Simmer 10 minutes or until ready to serve, stirring gently.

NUTRITION ANALYSIS
(PER SERVING)

Protein 26 gm., Carbohydrate 38 gm., Fiber 3 gm., Fat 4 gm., Cholesterol 0, Calcium 13 mg., Sodium 553 mg.

Calories 289
From protein: 35%; From carbohydrate: 51%; From fat: 14%

Western Scrambler

Serve this delicious tofu scrambler with pita pockets for a delightful brunch or light supper.

◆ 6 SERVINGS ◆

2 1/2 cups lite silken tofu (extra firm), drained
14.5-oz. can diced tomatoes and jalapeños
1 1/2 tsp. olive oil
1/8 tsp. crushed red pepper
2/3 cup chopped onion
4 cloves garlic, minced
1/3 cup chopped green bell pepper
6-oz. pkg. Yves veggie Canadian bacon, diced
1/2 tsp. turmeric
1 rounded Tbsp. mellow white miso
1 1/2 Tbsp. very dry sherry
1 tsp. dried cilantro

Place tofu in a large microwave-safe bowl, and mash with a potato masher. Cover and microwave for 3 minutes. Transfer tofu to a colander to drain. Set aside. Place tomatoes in a separate strainer, and set aside to drain. In a 4-quart saucepan, heat oil and crushed pepper over medium-high heat. Add the next 3 ingredients, and sauté 2 minutes. Add diced veggie bacon. Sauté mixture an additional 5 minutes. Add well-drained tofu and tomatoes along with turmeric. Simmer 5 minutes, stirring frequently. Place miso in a small bowl. Add sherry, and blend until smooth. Stir miso into the mixture; sprinkle with cilantro. Simmer gently 1 minute. Serve with pita pockets.

NUTRITION ANALYSIS
(PER SERVING)

Protein 16 gm., Carbohydrate 8 gm., Fiber 2 gm., Fat 2 gm., Cholesterol 0, Calcium 25 mg., Sodium 672 mg.

Calories 117
From protein: 54%; From carbohydrate: 28%; From fat: 19%

Soyful Sides

In this section you will find side dishes to complement any type of entrée, all of which bring the goodness of soy to the table. Dishes that accompany the main course needn't be an afterthought; a little advance planning will ensure balance of color, texture, and flavor. Of course, choosing a side dish with an abundance of soy protein will boost the nutritional value of any meal. Plan your meals with recipes from *Soy of Cooking* for each course and you will enjoy the benefits of a high-fiber, low-fat diet, an abundance of complex carbohydrates, and all those nifty little phytochemicals.

Side dishes are chosen to complement the main entrée, without clashing with, or overshadowing the overall presentation. If you were serving an entrée with a lusty tomato sauce, you wouldn't choose a side dish drenched in brown gravy. Likewise a heavy potato dish wouldn't be a good bet to accompany Pasta Primavera. In this section you can choose creamy Garlic Mashed Potatoes to accompany Tempeh Burgers or Homestyle Veggie Loaf. Dilly Broccoli Rice is a delightfully colorful dish that would complement Tofu in Burgundy Sauce or the Vegetarian Beef Stroganoff, equally. How about a wonderful, crusty gratin, like the Florentine Penne Gratin, or the Crusted Butternut Squash Casserole? One of the succulent tofu-based breads would surely round out the meal.

Whether it's an interesting side pasta you are looking for, a soysational Creamed Spinach, or an elegant treatment like Brussels Sprouts and Chestnuts in a Savory Sauce, you will find them here. Whatever you choose, you can be assured of the wholesomeness of the ingredients, and quality of flavor, texture, and style. ◆

Acorn Squash With Tofu & Vegetables

A flavorful marinade, firm and chewy tofu, chick-peas, and vegetables make a delicious filling for acorn squash.

◆ 8 SERVINGS ◆

2 8-oz. pkg. firm Nigari tofu (frozen in cutlet form), thawed

MARINADE:

1 Tbsp. mellow barley miso

1/2 cup white wine

3 Tbsp. tomato paste

2 Tbsp. balsamic vinegar

1 tsp. granulated garlic

2 Tbsp. Dijon mustard

1 Tbsp. mild molasses

1/3 cup sliced scallions

2 acorn squash, seeded and quartered (about 2 lbs.)

Vegetable oil cooking spray

1/4 tsp. crushed red pepper

2 Tbsp. grated gingerroot

3/4 cup chopped onions

4 cloves garlic, minced

2 cups sliced baby carrots

2 cups sliced mushrooms

15-oz. can garbanzo beans, drained

1/4 cup mirin or dry sherry

1/3 cup nutritional yeast

1 Tbsp. Bragg liquid aminos

Thaw and squeeze tofu (see Techniques). Slice each tofu cutlet in fourths, and place in a shallow pan. Place miso in a small bowl. Blend wine into miso. Add the rest of the marinade ingredients, and blend well. Pour marinade over tofu. Cover and refrigerate at least an hour or overnight.

Preheat oven to 350.° Coat squash quarters lightly with cooking spray. Place squash, cut side down, in shallow baking pan in 2 inches of water. Bake 45 minutes, turning at 15-minute intervals. Spray a 4-quart stovetop- and ovensafe casserole dish with cooking spray. Add red pepper, and heat 1 minute. Add the next 4 ingredients, and sauté 5 minutes. Add mushrooms; cook 2 minutes. Add remaining ingredients; cook 3 minutes. Gently add marinated tofu, and lower heat. Simmer 5 minutes, gently turning mixture with a slotted spoon. Cover casserole and bake 30 minutes while the squash bakes. Place squash on dinner plates, cut side up, and top with filling.

NUTRITION ANALYSIS
(PER SERVING)

Protein 17 gm., Carbohydrate 80 gm., Fiber 10 gm., Fat 3 gm., Cholesterol 0, Calcium 80 mg., Sodium 193 mg.

Calories 266
From protein: 16%; From carbohydrate: 78%; From fat: 7%

Bonzo Rice Loaf

Serve this tasty and nutritious brown rice loaf with tomato sauce.

◆ 8 SERVINGS ◆

vegetable oil cooking spray
2 cups beef-flavored vegetable broth
1 cup brown rice
15-oz. can garbanzo beans, drained
1 cup soy grits
1/2 cup thinly sliced scallions
1/4 cup chopped red bell peppers
1 tsp. granulated garlic
2 Tbsp. Dijon mustard
1 Tbsp. Bragg liquid aminos
2 Tbsp. egg replacer powder
1/2 cup water
2 tsp. dried marjoram, separated
2 Tbsp. whole wheat bread crumbs

Preheat oven to 350°. Spray a loaf pan with cooking spray. Bring broth to a boil. Add rice, bring to a second boil, and simmer, covered, about 40 minutes. Set aside to cool. Place garbanzo beans in a large bowl. Partially mash the beans, leaving some whole. Add rice, and mix well. Add the next 6 ingredients, and mix well. Whisk egg replacer powder with water in a small bowl until foamy. Add egg replacer with 1 teaspoon marjoram to mixture; mix thoroughly. Spoon into prepared loaf pan. Top with remaining marjoram, and sprinkle with bread crumbs. Bake 30 to 40 minutes or until browned. Serve topped with tomato sauce.

NUTRITION ANALYSIS
(PER SERVING)

Protein 12 gm., Carbohydrate 76 gm., Fiber 6 gm., Fat 4 gm., Cholesterol 0, Calcium 16 mg., Sodium 139 mg.

Calories 230
From protein: 13%; From carbohydrate: 77%; From fat: 10%

Brussels Sprouts and Chestnuts in a Savory Sauce

This dish features the rich flavors and textures of chestnuts and pungent brussels sprouts in a luscious, creamy sauce.

◆ 6 SERVINGS ◆

2 cups shelled chestnuts, blanched and peeled
1 1/2 tsp. olive oil
1/8 tsp. crushed red pepper
1/2 cup sliced scallions
4 cloves garlic, minced
1 1/2 cups baby carrots, cut crosswise into thirds
1 1/2 pound. brussels sprouts, trimmed and halved vertically
1/4 cup mirin or dry sherry
1 Tbsp. Bragg liquid aminos
1 cup soymilk lite
1 tsp. dried parsley
1/2 tsp. granulated garlic
1/2 tsp. ground coriander
1/2 cup nutritional yeast
1 Tbsp. cornstarch
2 Tbsp. water

Prepare chestnuts (see Techniques) Cover and set aside. Heat oil and crushed pepper in a 4-quart saucepan over medium-high heat for 1 minute. Add scallions and garlic, and sauté 2 minutes. Add carrot chunks; sauté 2 minutes. Add brussels sprouts, and sauté 5 minutes or until crisp tender. Add mirin, and cook 2 minutes. Add chestnuts. Lower heat, and simmer 3 minutes. Add liquid aminos, soymilk, and next 3 ingredients; stir gently. Stir in nutritional yeast. Blend together cornstarch and water in a small bowl; stir into pan. Simmer gently 5 minutes or until ready to serve.

NUTRITION ANALYSIS
(PER SERVING)

Protein 14 gm., Carbohydrate 92 gm., Fiber 11 gm., Fat 3 gm., Cholesterol 0, Calcium 96 mg., Sodium 198 mg.

Calories 241
From protein: 12%; From carbohydrate: 81%; From fat: 6%

Cranberry Surprise

This is a lovely side dish, especially for Thanksgiving or Christmas dinner.

◆ 8 SERVINGS ◆

12-oz. pkg. fresh or frozen cranberries
1/2 cup white grape juice concentrate, thawed
1/2 cup Sucanat or brown sugar
1/2 tsp. almond extract
1 1/4 cups lite silken tofu (extra firm)
1/2 cup prune purée
1 1/2 cups canned pumpkin
1/2 tsp. ground allspice
1/2 tsp. cinnamon
1/2 cup Florida Crystals or sugar
1 tsp. vanilla extract
1 cup slivered apricots
1/4 cup apricot brandy
1/3 cup chopped pecans
nutmeg

Preheat oven to 350°. Place cranberries in a 2-quart stovetop- and oven-safe casserole over medium heat. Add juice concentrate, Sucanat, and almond extract. Cook 8 to 10 minutes, stirring frequently. Remove from heat when mixture thickens and berries begin to pop. Place tofu in food processor, and blend. Add prune and pumpkin purées. Blend until smooth. Add the next 4 ingredients, and blend until smooth. Spread pumpkin mixture evenly over cranberries. Place slivered apricots in a small saucepan with brandy. Simmer 5 minutes or until liquid is absorbed. Remove from heat, and mix with chopped pecans. Arrange apricot/pecan topping over pumpkin layer. Sprinkle with nutmeg. Bake 20 to 25 minutes or until bubbling and lightly browned.

NUTRITION ANALYSIS
(PER SERVING)

Protein 4 gm., Carbohydrate 56 gm., Fiber 4 gm., Fat 4 gm., Cholesterol 0, Calcium 36 mg., Sodium 85 mg.

Calories 244
From protein: 6%; From carbohydrate: 81%; From fat: 13%

Creamed Artichokes

Tender artichokes melt in your mouth, drenched in a luscious, creamy sauce.

◆ 4 SERVINGS ◆

1 Tbsp. olive oil
1/8 tsp. crushed red pepper
3/4 cup sliced scallions
3 cloves garlic, minced
3 Tbsp. whole wheat flour
1 1/2 cups soymilk lite
1/2 cup nutritional yeast
13 3/4-oz. can quartered artichokes
1 cup frozen white corn, thawed
1 Tbsp. dried marjoram
1 Tbsp. tamari
dash cayenne

Heat oil and crushed pepper in a medium saucepan over medium-high heat. Add scallions and garlic; sauté 3 minutes. Stir in flour and cook to a paste, 1 to 2 minutes. Add soymilk gradually, stirring over medium heat. Add nutritional yeast, stirring until smooth and thickened, about 2 minutes. Add remaining ingredients and lower heat. Simmer 8 minutes, or until ready to serve.

NUTRITION ANALYSIS
(PER SERVING)

Protein 17 gm., Carbohydrate 36 gm., Fiber 5 gm., Fat 5 gm., Cholesterol 0, Calcium 33 mg., Sodium 493 mg.

Calories 250
From protein: 26%; From carbohydrate: 56%; From fat: 18%

Creamed Peas and Pearl Onions

This simple yet elegant side dish features delicate pearl onions and sweet peas simmered in a dairy-free cream sauce.

◆ 6 SERVINGS ◆

1 1/2 cups pearl onions, blanched and peeled (see Techniques)
2 Tbsp. olive oil
1/4 cup whole wheat flour
1/4 cup dry vermouth
1 cup soymilk lite
16-oz. pkg. frozen peas, thawed
1 Tbsp. nutritional yeast
1 tsp. dried parsley
1/2 tsp. dried thyme
1 tsp. Bragg liquid aminos

Prepare onions, and set aside in a colander. Heat olive oil in a medium saucepan over medium heat. Add onions, and cook 10 minutes, stirring frequently. They will brown lightly. Add flour, and stir 2 minutes. Stir in vermouth, and then gradually add the soymilk. Add the remaining ingredients. Simmer for 10 minutes, stirring frequently. Keep warm until ready to serve.

NUTRITION ANALYSIS (PER SERVING)

Protein 7 gm., Carbohydrate 38 gm., Fiber 6 gm., Fat 5 gm., Cholesterol 0, Calcium 37 mg., Sodium 232 mg.

Calories 166
From protein: 12%; From carbohydrate: 67%; From fat: 21%

Creamed Spinach

This flavorful side dish loses nothing in its translation to dairy freedom.

◆ 6 SERVINGS ◆

10-oz. pkg. frozen spinach, thawed
1 1/2 tsp. olive oil
1/2 cup sliced scallions
1 rib celery, sliced, including tops
1/3 cup dry vermouth
1 1/4 cups lite silken tofu (firm), drained
1 cup soymilk lite
3 Tbsp. nutritional yeast
1/4 tsp. ground nutmeg
1 tsp. Bragg liquid aminos

Place thawed spinach in a colander; press out moisture. Heat oil in a medium saucepan. Sauté the scallions and celery over medium-high heat for 3 minutes. Add spinach, and sauté 5 minutes, stirring to mix. Add vermouth, and lower heat. Simmer 5 minutes. Place tofu in food processor, and blend. Add soymilk, and blend. Add spinach mixture, and pulse to mix. Add remaining ingredients. Process, but do not purée. Return to pan, and simmer until ready to serve, stirring frequently.

NUTRITION ANALYSIS
(PER SERVING)

Protein 9 gm., Carbohydrate 26 gm., Fiber 2 gm., Fat 2 gm.,
Cholesterol 0, Calcium 80 mg., Sodium 150 mg.

Calories 103
From protein: 21%; From carbohydrate: 65%; From fat: 13%

Crusted Asparagus Bake

This delightful mélange is baked in a creamed tomato sauce under a crisp crumb topping.

◆ 8 SERVINGS ◆

1 Tbsp. olive oil
1 leek, cleaned and cut into 1/4-inch slices (see Techniques)
4 cloves garlic
2 cups baby carrots, cut into thirds
1 medium zucchini, sliced (about 2 cups)
1 pound. asparagus, cut in 4-inch pieces
1/2 pound. mushrooms, sliced
1 cup white wine
2 cups chopped fresh tomatoes (about 1 large)
1 cup frozen peas, thawed
1/4 cup whole wheat flour
1 cup soymilk lite

TOPPING:

2 Tbsp. soy grits
2 Tbsp. whole wheat bread crumbs
1 Tbsp. nutritional yeast
1 tsp. dried basil
1 tsp. dried rosemary, crumbled

Preheat oven to 375°. Heat oil over medium-high heat in an oven- and stovetop-proof 3-quart casserole. Add the leeks and garlic, and sauté 3 minutes. Add carrots, and sauté 2 minutes. Add zucchini and asparagus; sauté 2 minutes. Add mushrooms, and cook 3 minutes or until vegetables are crisp-tender. Add wine, tomatoes, and peas. Lower heat to simmer, 3 minutes. Stir in flour, forming a paste. Gradually add soymilk, and stir until mixture starts to thicken.

Combine the topping ingredients in a small bowl. Sprinkle this topping over all, and place casserole in preheated oven. Bake 20 minutes or until topping is browned and casserole is bubbling.

NUTRITION ANALYSIS
(PER SERVING)

Protein 8 gm., Carbohydrate 23 gm., Fiber 4 gm., Fat 3 gm., Cholesterol 0, Calcium 54 mg., Sodium 51 mg.

Calories 145
From protein: 20%; From carbohydrate: 64%; From fat: 16%

Crusted Butternut Squash Casserole

This "gratin" is tasty, colorful, and simple to prepare.

◆ 6 SERVINGS ◆

1 Tbsp. olive oil
1/4 tsp. crushed red pepper
1 medium onion, cut into 1-inch wedges
4 large cloves garlic, minced
1 large red bell pepper, cut into 1-inch strips
8 cups peeled, cubed butternut squash* (about 3 lbs.)
1 1/2 cups halved cherry tomatoes
1/2 cup white wine

TOPPING:

1/4 cup whole wheat bread crumbs
1/4 cup soy grits
3 Tbsp. nutritional yeast
1 tsp. dried basil
1 tsp. dried rosemary, crumbled

Preheat oven to 350.° Heat olive oil and crushed pepper in a 4-quart stovetop-safe and ovenproof casserole over medium-high heat for 1 minute. Add the next 3 ingredients, and sauté 3 minutes. Add the squash and cook mixture 5 minutes. Add tomatoes and wine. Lower heat, and simmer 10 minutes. In a small bowl, mix together the topping ingredients. Sprinkle the topping over all. Bake 30 minutes.

*The easiest way to peel a butternut squash is to make several crosswise cuts with a sharp knife. Then place the squash cut side down on a cutting board, and slice the peel away from you.

NUTRITION ANALYSIS
(PER SERVING)

Protein 13 gm., Carbohydrate 50 gm., Fiber 9 gm., Fat 3 gm., Cholesterol 0, Calcium 139 mg., Sodium 19 mg.

Calories 243
From protein: 18%; From carbohydrate: 72%; From fat: 10%

Dilly Broccoli Rice

This quick and easy dish is quite dill-icious!

◆ 6 SERVINGS ◆

1 1/2 tsp. olive oil
3 cloves garlic, minced
1/3 cup sliced scallions
3 cups cooked brown rice
10-oz. pkg. frozen chopped broccoli, thawed and drained
1 cup corn (if frozen, thawed)
3/4 cup soymilk lite
2/3 cup nutritional yeast
1 tsp. dried dillweed

In a medium saucepan, heat oil over medium heat. Add garlic and scallions; sauté 3 minutes. Add rice. Cook and stir 3 minutes. Add broccoli and corn. Lower heat, and simmer, stirring occasionally. Place soymilk in a small bowl. Add nutritional yeast, 1/3 cup at a time, blending with a whisk or fork. Stir dill into soymilk mixture; add to saucepan. Simmer 5 minutes or until ready to serve.

NUTRITION ANALYSIS
(PER SERVING)

Protein 15 gm., Carbohydrate 36 gm., Fiber 4 gm., Fat 3 gm., Cholesterol 0, Calcium 39 mg., Sodium 23 mg.

Calories 224
From protein: 25%; From carbohydrate: 63%; From fat: 12%

Dirty Rice

This hearty version of a Cajun specialty is made especially delicious with tofu and Cajun-spiced stewed tomatoes.

◆ 8 SERVINGS ◆

2 tsp. olive oil
3 cloves garlic, minced
3/4 cup chopped red onion
1/4 cup green bell pepper
1 cup white rice
3 1/2 cups beef-flavored vegetable broth, separated
14.5-oz. can Cajun- (or Mexican-) style stewed tomatoes
16-oz. pkg. Ready Ground Tofu, hot and spicy
1/2 tsp. ground cumin
1/2 tsp. ground coriander
1/3 cup snipped fresh cilantro

In a 10" frying pan, heat oil over medium-high heat. Add the next 3 ingredients, and sauté 3 minutes. Stir in the rice, and sauté 2 minutes. Add 2 cups of the broth. Bring mixture to a boil, then lower heat and simmer 12 minutes or until liquid is almost absorbed. Add tomatoes and tofu, and simmer 5 minutes longer. Add the reserved broth and remaining ingredients. Simmer until liquid is absorbed and rice is tender, about 10 minutes.

NUTRITION ANALYSIS
(PER SERVING)

Protein 5 gm., Carbohydrate 24 gm., Fiber 2 gm., Fat 3 gm., Cholesterol 0, Calcium 27 mg., Sodium 263 mg.

Calories 140
From protein: 15%; From carbohydrate: 66%; From fat: 19%

Fettuccine With Sun-Dried Tomato/Basil Cream Sauce

The luscious sauce clinging to thick ribbons of pasta is so flavorful and rich tasting, you won't believe it's dairy free.

◆ 6 SERVINGS ◆

1 cup soymilk lite
1 Tbsp. cider vinegar
1/2 cup snipped sun-dried tomatoes
2/3 cup boiling water
1 1/2 Tbsp. olive oil
1/2 cup chopped onion
4 large cloves garlic, minced
1/3 cup white wheat or unbleached flour
1/4 cup dry vermouth
1 1/2 cups chicken-flavored vegetable broth
1/4 cup loosely packed snipped fresh basil leaves
1 1/4 cups lite silken tofu (firm), drained
1 tsp. tamari
1 Tbsp. nutritional yeast
16-oz. pkg. egg-free fettuccine, cooked according to package directions

Place soymilk in a small glass measuring cup. Add vinegar, and set aside. Immerse sun-dried tomatoes in boiling water, and set aside. Heat olive oil in a large saucepan over medium-high heat. Add onions and garlic. Sauté 3 minutes or until crisp tender. Stir in flour, then add vermouth. Stir in broth with a wire whisk. Lower heat to simmer. Add sun-dried tomatoes, soaking water, and basil. Simmer, stirring frequently. Place tofu in food processor, and blend. Add soymilk, and blend until smooth. Whisk tofu mixture into the saucepan along with tamari and yeast. Continue to simmer, stirring frequently. Serve over pasta.

NUTRITION ANALYSIS
(PER SERVING)

Protein 11 gm., Carbohydrate 37 gm., Fiber 2 gm., Fat 5 gm., Cholesterol 0, Calcium 36 mg., Sodium 267 mg.

Calories 244
From protein: 18%; From carbohydrate: 62%; From fat: 20%

Florentine Penne Gratin

This delicious dish is dairy-free and true to its French roots.

◆ 6 SERVINGS ◆

1 cup snipped sun-dried tomatoes
1 cup boiling water
10-oz. pkg. frozen chopped spinach, thawed
1/2 pound. penne rigate*, cooked al dente, rinsed in cold water
1 tsp. dried basil
1/4 cup nutritional yeast

SAUCE:

1 Tbsp. olive oil
1/4 tsp. crushed red pepper
1/3 cup chopped shallots
4 cloves garlic, minced
6 oz. cremini mushrooms, sliced
3 Tbsp. whole wheat flour
2 cups soymilk lite, separated
3 Tbsp. tomato paste

TOPPING:

1/4 cup whole wheat bread crumbs
1/4 cup soy grits
3 Tbsp. nutritional yeast
1 tsp. dried basil
1 tsp. dried thyme

Preheat oven to 350.° In a small bowl, steep the snipped tomatoes in boiling water; set aside. Place spinach in a colander, and squeeze out liquid; set aside. While penne is cooking, make the sauce:

Heat oil and crushed pepper in a medium saucepan 1 minute. Stir in shallots and garlic; cook 2 minutes. Add mushrooms. Cook 3 to 4 minutes or until mushrooms are tender. Stir in flour, and cook mixture 2 minutes. Add 1/2 cup of the soymilk and the tomato paste; stir until blended. Add the remainder of the soymilk; reduce heat and simmer. Place the well-drained pasta in a shallow 3-quart baking dish. Toss with the tomatoes and soaking liquid, spinach, basil, and yeast. Add the sauce, and mix thoroughly. Combine the topping ingredients in a small bowl; sprinkle generously over all. Bake 20 minutes or until casserole is bubbly and topping is browned.

*You may use plain penne, but the ridges in rigate hold the sauce nicely.

NUTRITION ANALYSIS
(PER SERVING)

Protein 20 gm., Carbohydrate 48 gm., Fiber 4 gm., Fat 4 gm.,
Cholesterol 0, Calcium 111 mg., Sodium 333 mg.

Calories 274
From protein: 26%; From carbohydrate: 62%; From fat: 12%

Garlic Mashed Potatoes

This is a flavorful version of mashed potatoes.

◆ 8 SERVINGS ◆

6 medium russet potatoes, peeled and diced
4 cups salted water
1 Tbsp. olive oil
3 cloves garlic, minced
1/4 cup sliced scallions
2/3 cup hot soymilk lite
1/4 tsp. salt

Place diced potatoes in a medium saucepan with water. Bring to a boil, and reduce to medium-low heat. Cook potatoes (covered, with lid left slightly ajar) 20 minutes or until pierced easily with a fork, but not mushy. Drain thoroughly, and return to the saucepan. Use a potato masher to mash potatoes. When you've reached the desired consistency, set aside. Heat oil in a small frying pan over medium heat. Add garlic and scallions. Sauté 8 minutes, stirring frequently, or until cooked through and softened. Scrape scallion mixture and any remaining oil into potatoes. Add hot soymilk gradually, beating with a fork after each addition; add salt. Keep warm until ready to serve.

NUTRITION ANALYSIS
(PER SERVING)

Protein 4 gm., Carbohydrate 40 gm., Fiber 1 gm., Fat 2 gm., Cholesterol 0, Calcium 4 mg., Sodium 78 mg.

Calories 191
From protein: 8%; From carbohydrate: 82%; From fat: 9%

Indian-Spiced Potatoes and Spinach

Aromatic Indian spices lend a complex flavor that transforms potatoes and spinach into an exciting side dish.

◆ 8 SERVINGS ◆

1 Tbsp. olive oil
1 tsp. black mustard seeds
2 bay leaves
2 sticks cinnamon
1/4 tsp. crushed red pepper
3 cups coarsely chopped red onion
4 medium unpeeled Yukon Gold potatoes, cubed (about 4 cups)
1 tsp. granulated garlic
1/4 tsp. turmeric
1 tsp. ground cumin
1 tsp. ground coriander
10-oz. pkg. frozen spinach, thawed and drained
2 tsp. Bragg liquid aminos
1 cup soymilk lite

Heat oil in a 5-quart saucepan. Add mustard seeds. Cook and stir over medium heat until the seeds begin to pop. Add the bay leaves, cinnamon sticks, and crushed pepper. Stir 1 minute. Add the onions and potatoes; cook 3 minutes. Add the garlic, turmeric, cumin, and coriander. Cook 5 minutes. Add the spinach and the remaining ingredients; reduce heat. Cook over low heat for 35 minutes or until the sauce is reduced and the potatoes are tender.

NUTRITION ANALYSIS
(PER SERVING)

Protein 5 gm., Carbohydrate 61 gm., Fiber 3 gm., Fat 2 gm., Cholesterol 0, Calcium 80 mg., Sodium 103 mg.

Calories 179
From protein: 7%; From carbohydrate: 85%; From fat: 8%

Minted Orzo—"Mimi"

This is a delectably creamy dish reminiscent of Alfredo-type cream sauces. I designed it for Mimi Clark, a talented culinary instructor.

◆ 8 SERVINGS ◆

1 Tbsp. olive oil
1/3 cup chopped red onion
1 1/2 cups sliced baby carrots
1 medium zucchini, cut into julienne strips
4 large cloves garlic, minced
1 cup freshly shelled peas
1/2 cup white wine
1 1/4 cups lite silken tofu (firm), drained
3/4 cup soymilk lite
2 Tbsp. lemon juice
1 tsp. dried mint
1/4 cup nutritional yeast
1 cup orzo pasta
fresh mint leaves for garnish

Heat oil over medium-high heat in a 10" frying pan. Add onion, and sauté 1 minute. Add carrots. Cook covered, 5 minutes, stirring occasionally. Stir in zucchini, garlic, and peas; cook 3 minutes. Add wine, and cover, stirring occasionally, for 5 to 8 minutes. In a food processor, blend tofu until smooth. Add soymilk, lemon juice, mint, and yeast. Blend. Stir into pan. Reduce heat, and simmer until ready to serve.

In a small saucepan, boil 2 quarts water with a bit of salt and canola oil. Add orzo, and boil uncovered, stirring frequently, for 8 minutes. Rinse with water, and set aside. Pack cooked orzo into ramekins or custard cups. Overturn cup onto dinner plate and pour sauce over top. Garnish with sprigs of mint.

NUTRITION ANALYSIS
(PER SERVING)

Protein 10 gm., Carbohydrate 25 gm., Fiber 3 gm., Fat 3 gm., Cholesterol 0, Calcium 31 mg., Sodium 68 mg.

Calories 172
From protein: 24%; From carbohydrate: 60%; From fat: 16%

Potatoes "Marie"

This easy stovetop potato dish works equally well at brunch or dinner. The creamy, flavorful sauce is spectacular.

◆ 8 SERVINGS ◆

Vegetable oil cooking spray
1 Tbsp. olive oil
1/8 tsp. crushed red pepper
3 cloves garlic, minced
1/2 cup sliced scallions
6 cups unpeeled, thinly sliced Yukon Gold potatoes
1/4 cup mirin or dry sherry
1 cup soymilk lite
1 1/3 tsp. Bragg liquid aminos
1 Tbsp. nutritional yeast

Coat a 4-quart saucepan lightly with cooking spray. Heat oil and crushed pepper over medium-high heat for 1 minute. Add garlic and scallions; sauté 2 minutes. Add potatoes. Sauté 12 minutes, stirring frequently with a gentle lifting and turning technique so as not to break potato slices. Add mirin, and cook 5 minutes longer, stirring gently and frequently. Place soymilk in a small measuring cup. Stir in liquid aminos. Add soymilk to saucepan. Lower heat, and simmer 3 minutes. Sprinkle nutritional yeast over mixture; carefully stir to mix. Keep warm until ready to serve.

NUTRITION ANALYSIS (PER SERVING)

Protein 44 gm., Carbohydrate 52 gm., Fiber 1 gm., Fat 2 gm., Cholesterol 0, Calcium 5 mg., Sodium 51 mg.

Calories 176
From protein: 7%; From carbohydrate: 85%; From fat: 8%

Saffron Couscous

This unusual treatment for couscous is the perfect accompaniment to hearty entrées.

◆ 6 SERVINGS ◆

1/2 cup white wine
1/2 tsp. saffron threads
2 cups soymilk lite
2 cups couscous
2 tsp. Bragg liquid aminos
1 tsp. dried parsley

Place wine in a small bowl. Add saffron, and set aside for 15 minutes. In a medium saucepan, heat soymilk until almost boiling. Stir in wine mixture, and heat an additional 2 minutes. (It's OK if mixture separates.) Add couscous, aminos, and parsley. Stir to mix. Cover, and remove from heat for 5 minutes. Fluff with fork, then serve immediately.

NUTRITION ANALYSIS
(PER 3/4-CUP SERVING)

Protein 10 gm., Carbohydrate 86 gm., Fiber 0, Fat 1 gm., Cholesterol 0, Calcium 4 mg., Sodium 114 mg.

Calories 279
From protein: 10%; From carbohydrate: 88%; From fat: 2%

Savory Summer Medley

You will want to serve this colorful, flavorful side dish often.

◆ 6 SERVINGS ◆

1 Tbsp. olive oil
1/4 tsp. crushed red pepper
1 small sweet onion, chopped (about 1 cup)
5 cloves garlic, minced
1/3 cup chopped red bell pepper
1 large russet potato, unpeeled, cut into 1/4-inch slices
2 cups baby carrots, halved vertically
3 cups sliced yellow squash
1 cup dry vermouth, separated
1 bay leaf
1/4 cup mellow white miso
1 cup frozen baby peas, thawed
2 tsp. dried thyme
1 tsp. Bragg liquid aminos
1 Tbsp. nutritional yeast

Heat oil over medium-high heat in a 5-quart saucepan. Add crushed pepper and sauté 1 minute. Add the next 3 ingredients, and sauté 2 minutes. Add potatoes and carrots, and sauté 3 minutes. Add the squash, and continue to cook, stirring frequently, over medium-high heat until vegetables are crisp tender (about 10 minutes). Add 1/2 cup vermouth and bay leaf; cook 5 minutes. Blend the miso into the remaining 1/2 cup vermouth. Stir into the vegetables. Lower heat, then add peas. Simmer 2 minutes. Stir in remaining ingredients, and simmer 5 minutes or until ready to serve. Remove bay leaf before serving.

NUTRITION ANALYSIS
(PER 1 1/4-CUP SERVING)

Protein 6 gm., Carbohydrate 45 gm., Fiber 5 gm., Fat 3 gm., Cholesterol 0, Calcium 59 mg., Sodium 223 mg.

Calories 196
From protein: 9%; From carbohydrate: 79%; From fat: 12%

Yams 'n Cranberries

The aroma of this casserole is delightful, and the tart-sweet flavors complement a hearty meal.

◆ 8 SERVINGS ◆

3 medium yams, peeled and cubed
12-oz. pkg. fresh or frozen cranberries
1/2 cup golden raisins
1 cup soymilk lite
1/4 cup liquid Fruitsource or honey
1 cinnamon stick
3 Tbsp. brown sugar
1 tsp. ground nutmeg

Preheat oven to 350°. Place the first three ingredients in a 3 1/2-quart ovenproof casserole. Heat soymilk, Fruitsource, and cinnamon stick in the microwave for 1 minute or in a saucepan for 3 minutes. Pour over yam mixture. Sprinkle with brown sugar and nutmeg. Cover, and bake 1 1/2 hours, stirring a few times during baking.

NUTRITION ANALYSIS
(PER SERVING)

Protein 3 gm., Carbohydrate 67 gm., Fiber 2 gm., Fat 1 gm., Cholesterol 0, Calcium 19 mg., Sodium 170 mg.

Calories 280
From protein: 5%; From carbohydrate: 93%; From fat: 2%

Pizza and Pasta

Is it possible to make eggless pasta and cheeseless pizza that are as delicious as they are nutritious? How can you replace eggs and cheese in classic cream sauces and ricotta-style fillings? The answer to these and other timely questions are quite simple. It's all in the bean! The soybean is incredibly versatile as it lends itself to many forms and functions. As lite silken tofu, it is chameleon-like, able to replace eggs and dairy products artfully. When used in fillings and doughs, this low-fat ingredient becomes an invaluable ally to the health conscious cook. When soy is processed into textured vegetable protein, or TVP, it allows even the novice to create delicious meals in a timely fashion. Soymilk lite can be used anywhere cow's milk is called for, and becomes soy buttermilk with the addition of lemon juice or cider vinegar.

Create fabulous homemade pasta dishes like Pumpkin or Spinach Ravioli and Gnocci Primavera, all delectable gourmet feasts! Pizza is everyone's favorite and there's really no need to drown it in mountains of gelatinous cheese. Try my Saucy Pizza Abbondanza or Hawaiian Pizza for a delightful change of pace. You will be surprised at how easy it is to make a gourmet pizza that is dairy-free and delicious.

This collection of marvelous meals utilizes the versatility of the soybean as it offers a taste of Italy with an American accent. If it's homemade pastas or creamy sauces you are looking for without harmful fat and cholesterol, this is the place to find them. Tasty pizzas and hearty calzones that invite creativity are easy to assemble and sure to please. It's all here, and so wholesome and delicious, all because of the incredible soybean. ◆

Angel Hair in Sausage/Tomato Sauce

This nutritious and tasty recipe features Jerusalem artichoke pasta in a hearty and flavorful tomato sauce.

◆ 6 SERVINGS ◆

1 1/2 tsp. olive oil
1/8 tsp. crushed red pepper
1/2 cup chopped onion
5 cloves garlic, minced
1/3 cup chopped red bell pepper
1 cup baby carrots, cut into thirds
14-oz. pkg. Gimme Lean, sausage style
28-oz. can peeled and diced tomatoes
28-oz. can crushed tomatoes
2 6-oz. cans tomato paste
6 oz. burgundy wine (fill tomato paste can)
6 oz. water (fill tomato paste can)
1 tsp. dried basil
16-oz. pkg. Jerusalem artichoke angel hair pasta

Heat olive oil and crushed pepper in a large saucepan over medium-high heat for 1 minute. Add the next 4 ingredients. Saute 5 minutes or until crisp tender. Add vegetarian sausage. Cook 5 minutes, breaking apart with a large spoon, until sausage is browned. Add tomatoes, tomato paste, wine, and water. Lower heat, and simmer 20 minutes. Add basil during the last 5 minutes of cooking. Cook pasta according to package directions. Drain, and serve with sauce.

NUTRITION ANALYSIS
(PER SERVING)

Protein 20 gm., Carbohydrate 69 gm., Fiber 6 gm., Fat 2 gm., Cholesterol 0, Calcium 84 mg., Sodium 619 mg.

Calories 379
From protein: 22%; From carbohydrate: 74%; From fat: 4%

Broccoli Lasagna Rolls

The unique presentation and exceptional flavor of this entrée add flair to an elegant buffet.

◆ 10 SERVINGS ◆

3/4 lb. broccoli crowns, cut into 20 florets
25-oz. jar fat-free tomato sauce
28-oz. can whole plum tomatoes
14.5-oz. can Italian-style stewed tomatoes
6-oz. can tomato paste
6 oz. burgundy wine (fill tomato paste can)
4 fresh basil leaves, snipped, or 1 tsp. dried basil
1/2 tsp. granulated garlic
2 bay leaves
8-oz. pkg. lasagna noodles
3 3/4 cups lite silken tofu (extra firm), drained
1/3 cup sliced scallions
4 large cloves garlic, minced
10-oz. pkg. frozen chopped broccoli, thawed and well drained
1/2 cup nutritional yeast
1 tsp. dried thyme
1 Tbsp. Bragg liquid aminos
dried basil for garnish

Preheat oven to 350°. Bring a quart of water to a boil, and blanch broccoli for 30 seconds. Immediately plunge broccoli into ice water to stop cooking process. Set aside. Stir together the next 3 ingredients in 5-quart saucepan over low heat. Add the tomato paste and wine; stir. Add basil, garlic, and bay leaves. Simmer until ready to assemble casserole. Cook lasagna noodles according to package directions. Drain noodles and rinse in cold water.

Place drained tofu in a large bowl, and mash with potato masher. Add all remaining ingredients except basil, one at a time, stirring after each addition. Drain and rinse noodles. Cover bottom of a 9" x 13" pan with prepared sauce. Remove the bay leaves. Spread about 1/2 cup of filling along the center of a each noodle, then roll the noodles up. Tuck a broccoli floret in both open ends of each roll, and place in the pan, 2 across and 5 down. The rolls should lay side by side with the florets facing outward. Top with sauce, and sprinkle with dried basil. Cover loosely with foil. Bake 30 minutes, then remove foil and bake another 15 minutes.

NUTRITION ANALYSIS (PER SERVING)

Protein 17 gm., Carbohydrate 62 gm., Fiber 5 gm., Fat 2 gm., Cholesterol 0, Calcium 66 mg., Sodium 440 mg.

Calories 181
From protein: 20%; From carbohydrate: 75%; From fat: 5%

Chunky-Sauced Pasta

Serve this hearty sauce over interesting pasta shapes like wagon wheels or tri-colored twists. The rich flavor will cling to every bite.

◆ 6 SERVINGS ◆

1 1/2 tsp. olive oil
1/8 tsp. crushed red pepper
5 cloves garlic, minced
1 cup chopped onions
1/4 cup chopped green bell pepper
2 cups coarsely grated zucchini
1 1/2 cups white wine
28-oz. can plum tomatoes
6-oz. can tomato paste
25-oz. jar fat-free tomato sauce
1 cup ground beef-style TVP granules, dry
1 Tbsp. beef-flavored vegetable powder
1 small can (2 1/4 oz. dry wt.) sliced black olives, drained
8 large basil leaves
1 lb. pasta, any variety, cooked according to package directions

Heat crushed pepper in oil in a medium saucepan over medium heat for 2 minutes. Add the next 4 ingredients, and sauté 5 minutes. Add wine, and cook 3 minutes. Add the next 3 ingredients, and reduce heat to simmer. Cook for 10 minutes, stirring occasionally. Stir in the TVP and remaining ingredients except pasta. Continue to simmer for 20 minutes or until ready to serve over cooked pasta.

NUTRITION ANALYSIS
(PER SERVING)

Protein 16 gm., Carbohydrate 55 gm., Fiber 8 gm., Fat 3 gm., Cholesterol 0, Calcium 48 mg., Sodium 597 mg.

Calories 300
From protein: 20%; From carbohydrate: 70%; From fat: 9%

Creamed Pasta With Vegetables

This colorful dish features a spicy cream sauce, delicate leeks, fresh spinach, and green beans complemented with your pasta of choice.

◆ 6 SERVINGS ◆

- 1 Tbsp. olive oil
- 1/4 tsp. crushed red pepper
- 1 leek, well rinsed, cut into 1/4-inch slices (see Techniques)
- 5 cloves garlic, minced
- 1 lb. green beans, cut into 1-inch pieces (2 cups)
- 1 cup white wine
- 1 1/4 cups lite silken tofu (firm), drained
- 1 1/2 cups soymilk lite
- 1 Tbsp. Bragg liquid aminos
- 2 Tbsp. mellow white miso
- 3 Tbsp. nutritional yeast
- 2 Tbsp. whole wheat flour
- 1/2 lb. pasta (penne, large elbows, etc.)
- 1 bunch fresh spinach, well rinsed

Heat olive oil and crushed pepper in a large saucepan over medium-high heat for 1 minute. Add leeks, garlic, and green beans. Sauté 5 minutes. Add wine, and reduce heat; simmer 10 minutes. Place tofu in food processor, and blend. Add soymilk and next 4 ingredients. Pulse to mix, then blend until smooth. Fold into green bean mixture; simmer. Cook pasta according to package directions. Three minutes before pasta is finished, add spinach to the cooking water. Drain pasta and spinach in a colander. Remove green bean/cream sauce mixture from heat, and fold in pasta/spinach mixture. Serve immediately.

NUTRITION ANALYSIS
(PER SERVING)

Protein 14 gm., Carbohydrate 82 gm., Fiber 6 gm., Fat 4 gm., Cholesterol 0, Calcium 124 mg., Sodium 311 mg.

Calories 239
From protein: 13%; From carbohydrate: 78%; From fat: 9%

Curried Ragu

This sumptuous dish features spinach pasta, zucchini, and garbanzo beans in a heavenly, curry-laced cream sauce.

◆ 6 SERVINGS ◆

1 1/2 tsp. olive oil
1/2 cup chopped shallots
1 jalapeño pepper, with seeds, chopped (remove seeds to reduce heat)
5 cloves garlic, minced
1 medium zucchini, cut in julienne strips
15-oz. can low-sodium garbanzo beans, drained
28-oz. can tomatoes, peeled and diced
1 1/4 cups lite silken tofu (firm), drained
1/3 cup white wine
1/4 cup soymilk lite
2 Tbsp. lemon juice
1 tsp. ground coriander
1 tsp. ground cumin
1/2 tsp. turmeric
2 Tbsp. Bragg liquid aminos
1/4 tsp. cinnamon
1/2 tsp. granulated garlic
Cayenne pepper to taste
1 Tbsp. cornstarch
2 Tbsp. cold water
1 lb. spinach penne (or other spinach pasta)

Heat oil over medium-high heat in a 5-quart saucepan. Add the next 3 ingredients, and sauté 3 minutes. Add zucchini and garbanzo beans, and cook for 5 minutes. Add tomatoes. Cover and cook over low heat for 5 minutes. Place tofu in food processor; blend. Add wine, soymilk, and lemon juice; blend. Add the next 7 ingredients, and blend until smooth. Remove saucepan from heat. Use a wire whisk to blend in tofu mixture gradually. Return saucepan to heat, and simmer. Blend cornstarch and water in a small bowl. Add to sauce. Simmer sauce, stirring frequently, while cooking pasta.

NUTRITION ANALYSIS
(PER SERVING)

Protein 17 gm., Carbohydrate 151 gm., Fiber 6 gm., Fat 3 gm., Cholesterol 0, Calcium 36 mg., Sodium 560 mg.

Calories 260
From protein: 9%; From carbohydrate: 87%; From fat: 3%

Hawaiian Pizza

Vegetarian Canadian bacon and pineapple rings set the stage for this gourmet pizza.

◆ 16-INCH PIZZA ◆

vegetable oil cooking spray
1 recipe Prolific Pizza Dough (see page 195)

TOPPING:

25-oz. jar fat-free tomato sauce
6-oz. pkg. Yves veggie Canadian bacon, sliced in half
20-oz. can pineapple rings, drained
8 large fresh basil leaves, snipped

Preheat oven to 425°. Lightly spray a 16" heavy gauge pizza pan with cooking spray. Roll prepared pizza dough into a large circle 1/2-inch larger than pan. Place dough on pan, patting into place and folding overlap into a lip around the edge. Spread with tomato sauce. Arrange Canadian bacon and pineapple rings in an attractive pattern. Garnish with snipped basil. Set aside for 20 minutes, then place in preheated oven. Bake 20 minutes, or until topping and the crust are lightly browned.

NUTRITION ANALYSIS
(PER 2-SLICE SERVING)

Protein 14 gm., Carbohydrate 51 gm., Fiber 5 gm., Fat 1 gm., Cholesterol 0, Calcium 19 mg., Sodium 621 mg.

Calories 262
From protein: 21%; From carbohydrate: 75%; From fat: 4%

Hearty Elbow Macaroni Casserole

This homey casserole is easy and delicious.

◆ 12 SERVINGS ◆

vegetable oil cooking spray
1 1/2 cups beef-flavored vegetable broth, boiling
2 cups TVP, ground beef style
16-oz. pkg. large elbow macaroni
2 Tbsp. olive oil
1/2 cup chopped onion
1/4 cup whole wheat flour
2 cups soymilk lite
2/3 cup nutritional yeast
1 tsp. dried marjoram
1 tsp. tamari
1 tsp. granulated garlic
14.5-oz. can Italian-style tomatoes, peeled and diced

Preheat oven to 350°. Spray a 9" x 13" baking pan with cooking spray. Add boiling broth to TVP in a medium bowl. Stir, and set aside. Cook macaroni according to package directions. Rinse in cold water. Set aside, and rinse again in cold water from time to time. Heat oil in a medium saucepan over medium-high heat. Add onion, and sauté 3 minutes or until crisp tender. Stir in flour, and cook mixture 2 minutes over medium heat. Add soymilk gradually, stirring constantly. Whisk in yeast, 1/3 cup at a time. Add marjoram, tamari, and granulated garlic, then lower heat. Simmer 5 minutes, stirring occasionally. Add tomatoes to reconstituted TVP. Mix well. Place half the macaroni and all the TVP mixture in the prepared pan. Mix together using a large spoon. Top with remaining macaroni, and stir just to mix. Pour "cheese" sauce over all, and cover loosely with foil. Bake 30 minutes. Serve hot.

NUTRITION ANALYSIS
(PER SERVING)

Protein 17 gm., Carbohydrate 35 gm., Fiber 4 gm., Fat 4 gm.,
Cholesterol 0, Calcium 18 mg., Sodium 117 mg.

Calories 230
From protein: 27%; From carbohydrate: 59%; From fat: 14%

Mostaccioli in Creamy Mushroom Sauce

This rich-tasting dish is flavorful and satisfying.

◆ 6 SERVINGS ◆

1 1/2 Tbsp. olive oil
1/8 tsp. crushed red pepper
4 cloves garlic
1 cup sweet onion (Maui, Texas, or Vidalia)
1 cup chopped carrots
1/2 lb. mushroom caps, quartered
1/4 cup whole wheat flour
1/4 cup mirin or dry sherry
2 cups beef-flavored vegetable broth, boiling
1 1/4 cups lite silken tofu (firm), drained
1 cup soymilk lite
1 Tbsp. tamari
1/4 cup nutritional yeast
1 lb. mostaccioli, cooked according to package directions

In a large stovetop-safe serving dish, heat oil and crushed pepper over medium-high heat for 1 minute. Add the next 3 ingredients, and sauté 3 minutes. Add mushrooms, and sauté 5 minutes. Add flour, and stir 1 minute. Add mirin, and stir 2 minutes. Add hot broth; stir to blend. Reduce heat and simmer 5 minutes, stirring frequently. Place tofu in food processor, and blend. Add soymilk, tamari, and yeast; blend until smooth. Add tofu mixture to pan ingredients, using a whisk to blend smoothly. Simmer mixture while preparing pasta. Remove pan from heat, and add drained pasta to sauce. Toss to blend.

NUTRITION ANALYSIS
(PER SERVING)

Protein 14 gm., Carbohydrate 40 gm., Fiber 3 gm., Fat 5 gm., Cholesterol 0, Calcium 25 mg., Sodium 257 mg.

Calories 258
From protein: 21%; From carbohydrate: 60%; From fat: 18%

Mushroom Broccoli Calzones

These delicious turnovers are hearty and colorful with a delightful sherry-laced filling.

◆ 6 CALZONES ◆

1 recipe Prolific Pizza Dough (see page 195)
1 1/2 tsp. olive oil
1/4 tsp. crushed red pepper
1 cup sliced scallions
4 cloves garlic, minced
1/4 cup chopped green bell pepper
6 oz. cremini mushrooms, sliced
4 cups broccoli florets
1/4 cup very dry sherry
1 Tbsp. tamari
1 tsp. dried thyme
1 Tbsp. cornstarch
2 Tbsp. water
vegetable oil cooking spray
cornmeal

While pizza dough is rising, make filling.

Heat oil and crushed pepper in a medium saucepan for 2 minutes. Add scallions, garlic, and green pepper; sauté 3 minutes. Add mushrooms, and cook 3 minutes. Add broccoli, and cook 3 minutes. Add sherry, tamari, and thyme. Blend cornstarch and water in a small bowl; stir into mixture.

Preheat oven to 400°. Spray a baking pan with cooking spray. Dust lightly with cornmeal. Divide dough into 6 equal portions. Work with one portion at a time; keep remaining dough covered with a clean towel. Roll each portion into a ball between palms of hands. Pat dough gently, and roll into a circle. Place filling on one side of the circle, then fold dough over the filling. Press the crescent closed with a fork. Place on prepared baking pan and bake 15 to 20 minutes, until lightly browned.

NUTRITION ANALYSIS (PER SERVING)

Protein 12 gm., Carbohydrate 59 gm., Fiber 8 gm., Fat 3 gm., Cholesterol 0, Calcium 68 mg., Sodium 500 mg.

Calories 306
From protein: 15%; From carbohydrate: 75%; From fat: 10%

Penne Cacciatore

This delicious TVP variation on chicken cacciatore reheats well.

◆ 6 SERVINGS ◆

1 1/2 cups chicken-flavored vegetable broth, boiling (separated)

2 1/2 cups TVP, chicken chunk style

1 1/2 tsp. olive oil

1/4 tsp. crushed red pepper

3/4 cup chopped onion

6 cloves garlic, minced

1/2 cup chopped green pepper

1 cup sliced carrots

1 cup zucchini, cut into julienne strips

1/3 cup white wine

28-oz. can tomatoes, peeled and diced

28-oz. can crushed Italian-style tomatoes

6-oz. can tomato paste

1 bay leaf

6 large fresh basil leaves, snipped

1 lb. penne pasta, cooked according to package directions

Pour 1 cup of the boiling broth over TVP in a medium bowl. Set aside. Heat oil and crushed pepper in a 5-quart saucepan over medium-high heat. Add the next 3 ingredients, and sauté 2 minutes. Add the carrots and zucchini; sauté 3 minutes, stirring frequently. Add reconstituted TVP. Sauté 5 minutes, stirring frequently. Add wine; cook and stir for 1 minute. Add tomatoes and tomato paste. Add reserved 1/2 cup of broth along with bay leaves and basil. Lower heat, and simmer 20 to 30 minutes, stirring occasionally. Remove bay leaf. Ladle half of the sauce over the well-drained pasta. Toss, then top with remaining sauce. Garnish with fresh whole basil leaves.

NUTRITION ANALYSIS
(PER SERVING)

Protein 25 gm., Carbohydrate 56 gm., Fiber 13 gm., Fat 3 gm., Cholesterol 0, Calcium 111 mg., Sodium 342 mg.

Calories 316
From protein: 29%; From carbohydrate: 66%; From fat: 6%

Saucy Pizza Abbondanza

Abbondanza means "abundant" or "bountiful" in Italian. I think you will agree that this delightful pizza with the generous topping qualifies.

◆ 16-INCH PIZZA ◆

vegetable oil cooking spray
1 recipe Prolific Pizza Dough (see page 195)
1 cup beef-flavored vegetable broth, boiling
1 1/4 cups TVP, ground beef style
3 large cloves garlic, minced
25-oz. jar fat-free tomato sauce
3 cups broccoli florets
3 scallions, thinly sliced
6 large fresh basil leaves, snipped

Preheat oven to 425°. Lightly spray a 16" round pizza pan with cooking spray. Add broth to TVP, and set aside. Punch down dough, and knead briefly. Roll out on a floured surface into a circle 1/2-inch larger than the pan. Place dough on pizza pan. Fold the overlap, pinching to form a lip around the edge of the pan. Lightly spray dough with cooking spray. Sprinkle with minced garlic. Top with tomato sauce, TVP, broccoli, scallions, and basil. Bake 20 minutes or until crust is golden brown (check the bottom).

NUTRITION ANALYSIS
(PER 2-SLICE SERVING)

Protein 17 gm., Carbohydrate 54 gm., Fiber 9 gm., Fat 2 gm., Cholesterol 0, Calcium 41 mg., Sodium 444 mg.

Calories 271
From protein: 23%; From carbohydrate: 72%; From fat: 5%

Prolific Pizza Dough

This pizza crust is crisp, yet tender. Making this soy boosted pizza dough is a snap when using the food processor, however if you prefer the conventional method, it works just as well. Try this crust with your favorite toppings or when making calzones (see page 192).

◆ 16-INCH PIZZA (8 SERVINGS) ◆

1 1/4 cups whole wheat flour
1 1/4 cups unbleached flour
1/3 cup soy flour
1 tsp. salt
2 1/2 tsp. yeast
1 cup warm water
1 Tbsp. liquid Fruitsource or honey
vegetable oil cooking spray

FOOD PROCESSOR METHOD

Place the first 5 ingredients in the food processor, and pulse to mix. Place the water and Fruitsource in a small measuring cup. Warm in the microwave or for 3 minutes on the stovetop. It should be warm to the touch, no more than 125° (a little warmer than your finger). Add water to the food processor. Process until the mixture forms a ball. Turn onto a floured surface, and knead about 5 minutes, adding just enough white flour to make the dough smooth and not sticky. At this point you may place the dough in a lightly oiled plastic bag and store it in the refrigerator for up to 2 days.

CONVENTIONAL METHOD

Set aside 1 cup of unbleached flour. Combine the remaining flours in a large bowl with salt and yeast. Combine water and Fruitsource, and heat to 125°. Add the liquid to the dry ingredients, and mix well, adding just enough of the reserved flour so the dough pulls away from the sides of the bowl. Turn dough out onto a floured board, and knead until smooth and elastic. Lightly spray a large bowl with cooking spray. Place the dough in the prepared bowl. Cover the bowl with a clean towel, and set it in a warm place to rest for an hour or so. Place the dough on a lightly floured surface, and knead lightly for about 2 minutes.

BOTH METHODS

Roll dough into a circle about an inch larger than the perimeter of the pan. Pat dough into the pan, and fold the overlap, pinching to form a lip around the edge of the pan. Proceed with your recipe.

NUTRITION ANALYSIS
(PER SERVING)

Protein 7 gm., Carbohydrate 37 gm., Fiber 4 gm., Fat 1 gm., Cholesterol 0, Calcium 18 mg., Sodium 271 mg.

Calories 180
From protein: 14%; From carbohydrate: 80%; From fat: 6%

Quick 'n Healthy Ravioli

Frozen, prepared ravioli and an easy-to-prepare sauce save time while adding the goodness of soy to your dinner.

◆ 6 TO 8 SERVINGS ◆

1 1/2 tsp. olive oil
1/8 tsp. crushed red pepper
1/2 cup chopped onion
4 cloves garlic, minced
1/4 cup chopped red bell pepper
2 28-oz. cans Italian-style crushed tomatoes
6-oz. can tomato paste
6 oz. white wine (fill tomato paste can)
4 fresh basil leaves, snipped
1 bay leaf
2 13-oz. pkg. frozen Soy Boy ravioli, do not thaw

In a 4-quart saucepan, heat oil and crushed pepper over medium-high heat 1 minute. Add the next 3 ingredients, and sauté 3 minutes. Add tomatoes, tomato paste, wine, and herbs. Lower heat and simmer until ready to serve. Prepare ravioli according to package directions. Drain and top with sauce.

NUTRITION ANALYSIS
(PER SERVING)

Protein 12 gm., Carbohydrate 43 gm., Fiber 3 gm., Fat 4 gm., Cholesterol 0, Calcium 128 mg., Sodium 617 mg.

Calories 252
From protein: 19%; From carbohydrate: 66%; From fat 15%

Pumpkin Ravioli Filling

The pumpkin filling encased in colorful dough makes an attractive presentation.

◆ 8 SERVINGS ◆

1/2 cup + 2 Tbsp. lite silken tofu (extra firm), drained
1 cup canned pumpkin
3 Tbsp. prune purée
1 Tbsp. liquid Fruitsource or honey
1/4 tsp. nutmeg

Prepare one recipe Tomato Basil Pasta (see page 202). Place tofu in the food processor; add pumpkin, and blend. Add remaining ingredients, and process until smooth. Roll out 2 large sheets of dough. Place rounded teaspoonfuls of filling at regular intervals on the first sheet of dough. Cover with the second sheet of dough. Use your thumbs to gently press down the spaces between the mounds of filling. Dip the rim of a 3-inch diameter glass into a small bowl of flour. Use the glass to cut circles around each ravioli. Press the edges of each circle with a fork to close. Roll dough scraps into remaining dough. Ravioli may be made up to a day ahead before cooking. Drop into gently boiling salted water, to which 1 tablespoon oil has been added. Boil 12 to 15 minutes, carefully stirring occasionally. Serve topped with tomato sauce.

NUTRITION ANALYSIS
(PER SERVING WITH SAUCE)

Protein 11 gm., Carbohydrate 53 gm., Fiber 6 gm., Fat 4 gm., Cholesterol 0, Calcium 34 mg., Sodium 427 mg.

Calories 273
From protein: 15%; From carbohydrate: 73%; From fat: 11%

Soysational Pasta Dough

This versatile pasta dough is a natural for fettuccine or for Spinach Ravioli Filling.

◆ 1 POUND ◆

1 cup lite silken tofu (extra firm), drained
1 cup semolina
1/2 tsp. salt
1/2 cup soy flour
2 Tbsp. unbleached flour
1 Tbsp. olive oil

Place tofu in food processor, and blend until smooth. Add semolina and salt, and process. Repeat with soy flour and unbleached flour. Add oil, and process. The dough may seem a little sticky. Turn dough onto a board sprinkled with unbleached flour, and knead for about 3 minutes or until dough appears elastic. Add unbleached flour sparingly, if necessary. Sprinkle with unbleached flour, and place in a plastic bag or wrap with plastic wrap. Allow dough to rest for an hour or more. Divide dough into 4 equal portions. Work with one portion at a time; keep remaining portions in the bag.

Hand-cut pasta: On a floured board, roll the dough into an oblong shape, about 7" x 16". Dough should be thin, but not translucent. (For filled pasta, roll dough to 1/16th-inch thick.) Divide sheets crosswise, and set aside to dry on wax paper in a warm place for about 30 minutes, or until dry and pliable but not brittle.

Sprinkle dough lightly with flour, and roll dough loosely, jelly-roll style. Use a sharp knife to cut according to the type of pasta desired. Remember that pasta will swell about double when cooked, so make cuts about half the diameter desired. Allow the cut pasta to dry for at least an hour by tossing it into a loose pile or laying flat on wax paper. This will prevent the pasta from sticking after it has been cut, and keep it firm after cooking.

Pasta machine (manual): Divide dough into 4 equal portions. Place one portion on a lightly floured board and return remaining portions to plastic bag. Roll dough into oval sheet. Sprinkle with flour and feed into the widest roller setting. Fold dough into thirds, and feed it through again; repeat several times at this setting. Continue to feed dough (without folding) through machine, setting the rollers one notch closer each time, until the sheet is 16" x 20" inches. Divide sheets crosswise, and set aside to dry on wax paper in a warm place for about 30 minutes, or until dry and pliable but not brittle. Sprinkle dough lightly with flour, and cut to desired shape by feeding through wide, thin, or narrow blades. Allow the cut pasta to dry for at least an hour by tossing it into a loose pile or laying flat on wax paper. This will prevent the pasta from sticking after it has been cut, and keep it firm after cooking.

Cooking homemade pasta: Cook pasta in about 6 quarts of water with 1 tablespoon oil and 1 teaspoon salt. Drop pasta into boiling water and bring to a second boil. Cook 3 to 5 minutes, stirring frequently. Drain and top with sauce.

NUTRITION ANALYSIS
(PER SERVING)

Protein 9 gm., Carbohydrate 25 gm., Fiber 2 gm., Fat 4 gm., Cholesterol 0, Calcium 21 mg., Sodium 215 mg.

Calories 176
From protein: 21%; From carbohydrate: 56%; From fat: 23%

Whole Wheat Pasta

This easy to make pasta is delicious topped with your favorite sauce.

◆ 1 POUND ◆

1 cup lite silken tofu (extra firm)
1 cup semolina
1/2 tsp. salt
1/2 cup whole wheat flour
1 Tbsp. olive oil

Place tofu in food processor and blend until smooth. Add semolina and salt, and process. Add whole wheat flour, and process again. Add oil while processing. Turn dough onto board sprinkled with semolina flour. Knead for about 3 minutes or until dough appears elastic. Sprinkle with semolina flour and place in zip lock bag or wrap with plastic wrap. Allow dough to rest for an hour or more.

Hand-cut pasta: Divide dough into 4 equal portions. Place one portion on a lightly floured board, and return remaining portions to plastic bag. Flatten the dough into an oval shape and roll the dough into an oblong sheet, about 7" x 16". Dough should be thin, but not translucent. (For filled pasta, roll dough to 1/16th-inch thick.) Divide sheets crosswise and set aside to dry on wax paper in a warm place for about 30 minutes, or until it is dry and pliable, but not brittle.

Sprinkle dough lightly with flour and roll up loosely, jelly-roll style. Use a sharp knife to cut according to the type of pasta desired. Remember that pasta will swell about double when cooked, so make cuts about half the diameter desired. Allow the cut pasta to dry by tossing into a loose pile or laying flat on wax paper in the open air for at least an hour. This will prevent the pasta from sticking after it has been cut, and keep it firm after cooking.

Pasta machine (manual): Divide dough into 4 equal portions. Place one portion on a lightly floured board, and return remaining portions to plastic bag. Flatten dough into an oval shape, sprinkle with flour, and feed it through the widest roller setting. Fold dough into thirds and feed it through again. Fold and roll dough several times at this setting. Continue to feed dough (without folding), setting rollers one notch closer together each time, until you have a sheet between 16 and 20 inches long. Cut dough crosswise and set sheets aside to dry, 30 minutes, on wax paper in a warm place. Lightly flour dough and cut to desired shape by feeding through wide, thin, or narrow blades. Allow the cut pasta to dry by tossing into a loose pile or laying flat on wax paper in the open air for at least an hour. This will prevent the pasta from sticking after it has been cut, and keep it firm after cooking.

Cooking homemade pasta: Cook pasta in about 6 quarts. of boiling water with 1 tablespoon oil and 1 teaspoon salt. Drop pasta into boiling water and bring to a second boil. Cook 3 to 5 minutes, stirring frequently. Drain and top with sauce.

NUTRITION ANALYSIS
(PER SERVING)

Protein 8 gm., Carbohydrate 28 gm., Fiber 2 gm., Fat 3 gm., Cholesterol 0, Calcium 9 mg., Sodium 214 mg.

Calories 170
From protein: 18%; From carbohydrate: 66%; From fat: 17%

Tomato Basil Pasta

This colorful pasta is delightful cut into any shape.

◆ 4 SERVINGS ◆

1/2 cup lite silken tofu, extra firm, drained
6 Tbsp. tomato paste
1 cup semolina flour
1/2 cup whole wheat flour
1 1/2 tsp. dried basil
1/2 tsp. granulated garlic
1/2 tsp. salt
1 Tbsp. olive oil
25 oz.-jar fat-free tomato sauce

Place tofu in food processor and process with tomato paste. Add the next 5 ingredients and process. Add the oil and blend until dough sticks together. Turn dough onto board sprinkled with semolina. Knead until smooth, about 3 minutes. Place the dough in a zip lock plastic bag and set aside to rest for an hour.

Hand-cut pasta: Divide dough into 4 equal portions. Place one portion on a lightly floured board, and return remaining portions to plastic bag. Flatten the dough into an oval shape and roll the dough into an oblong sheet, about 7" x 16". Dough should be thin, but not translucent. Divide sheets crosswise and set aside to dry on wax paper in a warm place for about 30 minutes, or until it is dry and pliable, but not brittle. For filled pasta, roll dough on floured board to about 1/16-inch thick. (see Pumpkin Ravioli Filling).

Sprinkle dough lightly with flour and roll up loosely, jelly-roll style. Use a sharp knife to cut according to the type of pasta desired. Remember that pasta will swell about double when cooked, so make cuts about half the diameter desired. Allow the cut pasta to dry by tossing into a loose pile or laying flat on wax paper in the open air for at least an hour. This will prevent the pasta from sticking after it has been cut, and keep it firm after cooking.

Pasta machine (manual): Divide dough into 4 equal portions. Place one portion on a lightly floured board, and return remaining portions to plastic bag. Flatten dough into an oval shape, sprinkle with flour, and feed it through the widest roller setting. Fold dough into thirds and feed it through again. Fold and roll dough through several times at this setting. Continue to feed dough (without folding), setting rollers one notch closer together each time, until you have a sheet between 16 and 20 inches long. Cut dough crosswise and set sheets aside to dry about 30 minutes on wax paper in a warm place. Lightly flour dough and cut to desired shape by feeding through wide, thin, or narrow blades. Allow the cut pasta to dry by tossing into a loose pile or laying flat on wax paper in the open air for at least an hour or overnight. This will prevent the pasta from sticking after it has been cut, and keep it firm after cooking.

Cooking homemade pasta: Cook pasta in about 6 quarts of boiling water with 1 tablespoon oil and 1 teaspoon salt. Drop pasta into boiling water and bring to a second boil. Cook 3 to 5 minutes, stirring frequently. Drain and top with sauce.

NUTRITION ANALYSIS
(PER SERVING)

Protein 13 gm., Carbohydrate 64 gm., Fiber 7 gm., Fat 4 gm.,
Cholesterol 0, Calcium 34 mg., Sodium 593 mg.

Calories 335
From protein: 15%; From carbohydrate: 73%; From fat: 12%

Spinach Ravioli Filling

This variation on a spinach-cheese filling is delicious and nutritious.

◆ 6 SERVINGS ◆

10-oz. pkg. frozen spinach, thawed
1 1/4 cups lite silken tofu (firm), drained and patted dry
1/4 cup nutritional yeast
1/2 tsp. granulated garlic
1 rounded Tbsp. mellow white miso
3 scallions, minced
8 large fresh basil leaves, snipped
1/4 tsp. nutmeg

Prepare one recipe Soysational Pasta Dough (see page 198), rolling 2 large sheets of dough slightly thicker than for cut pasta. Place spinach in a fine mesh colander, and press out as much liquid as possible using paper toweling. Mash tofu with a potato masher in a large bowl. Stir in yeast, garlic, and miso. Add spinach, and mix well. Add remaining ingredients, and mix thoroughly.

Place rounded teaspoonfuls of filling at regular intervals on the first sheet of dough. Cover with the second sheet of dough. Use your thumbs to gently press down the spaces between the mounds of filling. Dip the rim of a 3-inch diameter glass into a small bowl of flour. Use the glass to cut circles around each ravioli. Press the edges of each circle with a fork to close. Roll dough scraps into remaining dough. Ravioli may be made up to a day ahead before cooking.

Drop ravioli into gently boiling salted water, to which 1 tablespoon oil has been added. Boil 12 to 15 minutes, stirring occasionally. Serve topped with tomato sauce.

NUTRITION ANALYSIS
(PER 2-OUNCE SERVING OF FILLING ONLY)

Protein 7 gm., Carbohydrate 5 gm., Fiber 1 gm., Fat 1 gm., Cholesterol 0, Calcium 45 mg., Sodium 85 mg.

Calories 50
From protein: 49%; From carbohydrate: 38%; From fat: 13%

Tasty Tempeh Calzones

Wrap a crisp textured pizza dough around a tasty tempeh filling and you have a deliciously hearty meal.

◆ 6 CALZONES ◆

- 1 recipe Prolific Pizza Dough (see page 196)
- 1 1/2 tsp. olive oil
- 1/4 tsp. crushed red pepper
- 1 cup chopped onion
- 6 cloves garlic, minced
- 1 cup thinly sliced carrots
- 1/2 recipe Seasoned Tempeh, crumbled (see page 148)
- 1 Tbsp. tamari
- 14.5-oz. can Cajun-style tomatoes
- 1/2 cup white wine
- 1/2 tsp. granulated garlic
- 1 tsp. dried marjoram
- 1 tsp. dried basil
- 1/2 tsp. dried thyme
- vegetable oil cooking spray
- cornmeal

While pizza dough is rising, make filling:

Heat olive oil and crushed pepper for 2 minutes in a medium saucepan over medium-high heat. Add onions, garlic, and carrots; sauté 5 minutes. Add tempeh, and cook 10 minutes, stirring frequently. Stir in tamari, tomatoes, and wine. Lower heat, and simmer 5 minutes. Add garlic, marjoram, basil, and thyme, and simmer until ready to fill calzones.

Preheat oven to 400°. Spray a baking pan with cooking spray, then dust it lightly with cornmeal. Divide dough into 6 equal portions. Work with one portion at a time; keep remaining dough covered with a clean towel. Roll each portion into a ball between palms of hands. Pat dough gently, and roll into a circle. Place filling on one side of the circle, then fold dough over the filling. Press the crescent closed with a fork. Place on prepared baking pan and bake 15 to 20 minutes, until lightly browned.

NUTRITION ANALYSIS (PER CALZONE)

Protein 19 gm., Carbohydrate 55 gm., Fiber 7 gm., Fat 5 gm., Cholesterol 0, Calcium 70 mg., Sodium 632 mg.

Calories 344

From protein: 22%; From carbohydrate: 64%; From fat: 14%

Tempeh-Topped Pizza

This delightful pizza features a savory topping garnished with bell pepper strips and fresh basil.

◆ 16-INCH PIZZA ◆

1 recipe Prolific Pizza Dough (see page 195)
1 Tbsp. olive oil
1/2 cup chopped onion
3 cloves garlic, minced
1 bay leaf
1/2 recipe Seasoned Tempeh, crumbled (see page 148)
1 Tbsp. tamari
vegetable oil cooking spray
25-oz. jar fat-free tomato sauce
1/2 large bell pepper, cut into strips
1/4 cup snipped fresh basil leaves
1 Tbsp. dried basil

In a 10" frying pan, heat oil over medium heat. Add the onions, garlic, and bay leaf; sauté 3 minutes. Add the tempeh, and sauté mixture 8 minutes, stirring frequently. Add the tamari; lower heat to simmer 5 minutes. Remove bay leaf before assembling pizza.

Preheat oven to 425°. Spray a 16" pizza pan with cooking spray. Roll out prepared pizza dough to about 1/2 inch larger than pizza pan. Pat it into place on the pizza pan. Fold the overlap, pinching to form a lip around the edge of the pan. Spread with tomato sauce. Top the sauce with the tempeh mixture, and garnish with the pepper strips, arranging them in a pinwheel fashion. Top with fresh basil and dried basil. Set aside for 20 minutes. Bake for 20 minutes or until topping and the crust are lightly browned.

NUTRITION ANALYSIS
(PER 2-SLICE SERVING)

Protein 14 gm., Carbohydrate 44 gm., Fiber 5 gm., Fat 5 gm., Cholesterol 0, Calcium 26 mg., Sodium 600 mg.

Calories 264
From protein: 21%; From carbohydrate: 64%; From fat: 15%

Vegetarian Italian Sausage With Ziti

Delectable chunks of savory Italian sausage made with versatile soy make this traditional favorite into a healthful meal.

◆ 8 SERVINGS ◆

vegetable oil cooking spray
1 Tbsp. olive oil
1/4 tsp. crushed red pepper
1 small onion, chopped, about 1 cup
1/2 cup chopped green bell pepper
6 cloves garlic, minced
11.2-oz. pkg. Lean Links Italian, cut in 1/2-inch pieces (see Soyfoods Pantry)
2 28-oz. cans crushed tomatoes, Italian-style
28-oz. can diced tomatoes in juice
6-oz. can tomato paste
6 oz. water (fill tomato paste can)
1/4 cup burgundy wine
1 bay leaf
4 large basil leaves, snipped
1/2 tsp. dried basil
1/4 tsp. dried thyme
1 lb. ziti or your favorite pasta, cooked according to package directions

Spray a 5-quart saucepan with cooking spray, and add oil and crushed red pepper. Sauté over medium high heat, 2 minutes. Add the next 3 ingredients and sauté for 2 minutes. Add sliced sausage and sauté 10 minutes, stirring frequently. Add the next 7 ingredients, stirring well after each addition. Lower heat to simmer and cook sauce, covered, 25 minutes, stirring frequently. Add basil, thyme, and pasta, and simmer 10 minutes or until ready to serve.

NUTRITION ANALYSIS
(PER SERVING)

Protein 12 gm., Carbohydrate 41 gm., Fiber 5 gm., Fat 5 gm., Cholesterol 0, Calcium 104 mg., Sodium 660 mg.

Calories 251
From protein: 18%; From carbohydrate: 64%; From fat: 18%

Delectable Desserts

You can create luscious, low-fat desserts without eggs, cream, butter, or added fat. Serving delectable desserts made with wholesome soyfoods is a delicious way to incorporate their nutritional advantages into your diet. Here you will find rich-tasting, gourmet desserts that look decadent, but are low in fat and completely cholesterol- and dairy-free. Scrumptious cakes, pies, cookies, and frozen confections are guaranteed to tempt dessert lovers of all ages. These seductive sweets are easy to make using these innovative techniques and versatile ingredients.

Creamy pies and puddings are created with soymilk lite and the ever-versatile lite silken tofu. Elegant mousses and rich tasting ice creams are made both egg- and dairy-free by tapping the tremendous potential of the simple soybean. Make Marie's Incredible Chocolate Brownies or the innovative Pumpkin Fudge Brownies, and the rich taste and fabulous texture of these heavenly chocolate treats will knock your socks off. My Apricot Almond Delite is a marvelous snacking cake topped with a delicate, brandy scented "cream" that makes a perfect luncheon dessert.

This chapter will show you how to create decadent desserts with grace and style, to reduce fat considerably, eliminate cholesterol, and maximize nutrition without sacrificing flavor or texture. These memorable desserts will dazzle family and friends. Impress them you will, and the added nutritional benefit will inspire you to serve these desserts often. You don't have to abandon extravagant desserts when eating more healthfully; it's easy when you know how. ◆

Apple Almond Spice Cake

This cake makes an impression at any gathering!

◆ 16 SERVINGS ◆

vegetable oil cooking spray
1 medium Pippin or Granny Smith apple, peeled, and cut into 1/4-inch chunks
2 Tbsp. lemon juice
2 1/2 cups whole wheat pastry flour
1/3 cup soy flour
1 1/2 cups Sucanat or brown sugar
1 tsp. baking powder
1 tsp. baking soda
1/4 tsp. salt
1 tsp. cinnamon
1/2 tsp. ground ginger
1/8 tsp. ground nutmeg
1/8 tsp. ground cloves
1 1/4 cups lite silken tofu (firm), drained
1/2 cup prune purée
1/4 cup liquid Fruitsource or honey
1/2 cup soymilk lite
1 Tbsp. egg replacer powder
1/4 cup water
1/2 tsp. almond extract
1/2 tsp. vanilla extract
1/3 cup chopped almonds
1/4 cup soy grits

Preheat oven to 350°. Spray a tube pan with cooking spray. Place apple chunks in a medium bowl, and toss with lemon juice; set aside. Mix together the next 10 ingredients in a large bowl; set aside. Place tofu in food processor, and blend. Add prune purée, Fruitsource, and soymilk; pulse to mix, then blend. Whisk egg replacer powder with water in a small bowl until foamy. Add to tofu mixture along with extracts, and blend until smooth. Mix together almonds with soy grits in a small bowl; set aside. Quickly fold the tofu mixture into the dry ingredients. Fold in apple chunks and almond mixture, and pour into prepared pan. Bake 45 minutes or until tester comes out clean. Cool 20 minutes in pan, then remove to rack. Serve dusted with powdered sugar.

NUTRITION ANALYSIS
(PER SERVING)

Protein 6 gm., Carbohydrate 39 gm., Fiber 3 gm.,
Fat 3 gm., Cholesterol 0, Calcium 57 mg., Sodium 197 mg.

Calories: 196
From protein: 12%; From carbohydrate: 76%; From fat: 12%

Apple Crunch Cake

Pippin apple slices and a crunchy pecan topping make a beautiful presentation in this delicious coffee cake.

◆ 12 SERVINGS ◆

vegetable oil cooking spray
1 cup soymilk lite
2 Tbsp. lemon juice
2 cups whole wheat pastry flour
1/3 cup yellow cornmeal
1/4 cup soy flour
1 tsp. baking powder
1 tsp. baking soda
2/3 cup Sucanat or brown sugar
1/4 tsp. salt
1/2 cup unsweetened applesauce
1 Tbsp. liquid Fruitsource or honey
1 Tbsp. egg replacer powder
1/4 cup water
1 tsp. vanilla extract
1 medium Pippin apple, peeled and thinly sliced

TOPPING:

1/3 cup pecans
1/3 cup Sucanat or brown sugar
2 Tbsp. soy grits
1/2 tsp. cinnamon
1/4 tsp. ground nutmeg
2 Tbsp. frozen apple juice concentrate (do not thaw)

Preheat oven to 350.° Spray an 8" or 9" square baking pan with cooking spray. Place soymilk in a small bowl, and add lemon juice. Set aside. Mix together the next 7 ingredients in a medium bowl. Set aside. Place applesauce in a large bowl with Fruitsource; mix well. Whisk egg replacer powder with water in a small bowl until foamy. Add soymilk and vanilla; mix thoroughly. Fold dry ingredients into liquid ingredients just until mixed. Pour batter into prepared pan. Arrange apples in an overlapping pattern. Mix topping ingredients together in a small bowl. Sprinkle over apples. Bake 25 to 30 minutes or until toothpick inserted in center comes out clean.

NUTRITION ANALYSIS
(PER SERVING)

Protein 5 gm., Carbohydrate 38 gm., Fiber 3 gm., Fat 4 gm., Cholesterol 0, Calcium 58 mg., Sodium 221 mg.

Calories 195
From protein: 10%; From carbohydrate: 75%; From fat: 16%

Apricot Almond Delite

Served with rich-tasting tofu cream, this luscious cake delivers delicious chunks of brandied apricots and slivered almonds in every bite.

◆ 8 SERVINGS ◆

vegetable oil cooking spray
1/2 cup snipped apricots
1/4 cup apricot brandy
1 1/4 cups whole wheat pastry flour
1 cup Sucanat or brown sugar
1/2 tsp. baking soda
1/2 tsp. baking powder
1/2 tsp. cinnamon
1/8 tsp. salt
1/2 cup plus 2 Tbsp. lite silken tofu (firm)
1/4 cup prune purée
1/2 cup soymilk lite
1/2 tsp. almond extract
1/4 cup almond pieces

Preheat oven to 350°. Spray an 8" square pan with cooking spray. Place apricots in a small saucepan with the brandy. Cook over low heat until brandy is absorbed, about 3 minutes, stirring frequently. Set aside. In a large bowl, stir together flour with the next 5 dry ingredients. Set aside. Place tofu in the food processor, and blend. Add prune purée, and blend. Add soymilk and almond extract, and blend until smooth. Add the tofu mixture to the dry ingredients. Fold in apricots and almonds. Pour batter into prepared pan. Bake 25 minutes or until toothpick inserted into center comes out clean. Serve with Tofu Cream (next page).

NUTRITION ANALYSIS
(PER SERVING, INCLUDING TOFU TOPPING)

Protein 4 gm., Carbohydrate 36 gm., Fiber 2 gm., Fat 2 gm., Cholesterol 0, Calcium 47 mg., Sodium 153 mg.

Calories 185
From protein: 10%; From carbohydrate: 80%; From fat: 10%

Tofu Cream

Serve this topping with Apricot Almond Delite or use to stuff dates or Calimyrna figs.

◆ ABOUT 1 1/2 CUPS ◆

- 1/2 cup plus 2 Tbsp. lite silken tofu (firm), drained
- 3 Tbsp. maple syrup
- 1/4 cup orange juice
- 1 tsp. grated lemon zest
- 1 tsp. vanilla extract
- 1/4 cup fruit-sweetened apricot jam
- 1 tsp. apricot brandy

Place drained tofu in food processor; blend. Add remaining ingredients and blend until smooth.

NUTRITION ANALYSIS
(PER 3 TBSP. OF TOPPING)

Protein 1 gm., Carbohydrate 10 gm., Fiber 0, Fat 0, Cholesterol 0, Calcium 7 mg., Sodium 20 mg.

Calories 48
From protein: 12%; From carbohydrate: 83%; From fat: 5%

Apricot Snack Bars

These delicious snack bars make great lunch box stuffers.

◆ 25 SNACK BARS ◆

vegetable oil cooking spray
1 cup soymilk lite
2 Tbsp. lemon juice
3/4 cup snipped dried apricots
1/2 cup golden raisins
1/3 cup apricot brandy
2 1/2 cups whole wheat pastry flour
1/3 cup soy flour
1 tsp. baking soda
1 tsp. baking powder
1/4 tsp. salt
1 tsp. cinnamon
1/2 cup unsweetened applesauce
2/3 cup Florida Crystals or sugar
1 Tbsp. egg replacer powder
1/4 cup water
1 tsp. vanilla extract
1/4 cup walnut pieces
1/4 cup soy grits
cinnamon
nutmeg

Preheat oven to 350°. Spray a 9" x 13" baking pan with cooking spray. Place soymilk in a small glass measuring cup; add lemon juice. Set aside. Place apricots and raisins in a small saucepan with brandy. Cover and simmer, stirring frequently, 5 minutes or until liquid is absorbed. Set aside.

In a medium bowl, stir together the next 6 ingredients. Set aside. Place the applesauce in a large bowl, and cream with the Florida Crystals. Whisk the egg replacer powder and water in a small bowl until foamy. Add to the applesauce mixture along with the vanilla; blend well. Fold the applesauce mixture into the dry ingredients alternately with the soymilk. Mix just until blended. Add the brandied fruit. Mix the walnut pieces and soy grits together. Add to batter. Do not overmix. Spread batter in prepared pan. Sprinkle generously with cinnamon and nutmeg. Bake 30 minutes or until toothpick inserted in center comes out clean.

NUTRITION ANALYSIS
(PER SNACK BAR)

Protein 4 gm., Carbohydrate 20 gm., Fiber 2 gm., Fat 1 gm., Cholesterol 0, Calcium 26 mg., Sodium 94 mg.

Calories 106
From protein: 13%; From carbohydrate: 75%; From fat: 11%

Black Forest Cake

Dried cherries and walnut pieces fill this rich chocolate cake topped with a fudge glaze—outstanding!

◆ 12 SERVINGS ◆

vegetable oil cooking spray
2 cups whole wheat pastry flour
1 cup cocoa powder
1 tsp. baking soda
1 tsp. baking powder
1/2 tsp. salt
1 3/4 cups Florida Crystals or sugar
8-oz. pkg. dried cherries (about 1 3/4 cups)
1/3 cup walnut pieces
1 1/4 cups lite silken tofu (extra firm), drained
3/4 cup prune purée
1 cup strong coffee
2 tsp. vanilla extract

Preheat oven to 350.° Spray a Bundt pan with cooking spray. In a large bowl, mix together flour with the following 5 ingredients. Add cherries and walnut pieces, and set aside. Blend tofu in food processor until smooth. Add prune purée, and blend. Add coffee and vanilla, and blend. Fold tofu mixture into the dry ingredients. Turn into prepared pan, and bake for 40 minutes or until a toothpick inserted comes out clean. Cool 15 minutes in the pan, then invert onto a rack.

GLAZE

3 Tbsp. tapioca flour (or arrowroot)
1/4 cup cocoa powder
2 Tbsp. Florida Crystals or sugar
3/4 cup liquid Fruitsource or rice syrup

In a small bowl, stir together the first 3 ingredients. Heat Fruitsource in microwave 1 minute. Whisk into cocoa mixture until smooth. Drizzle onto cooled cake.

NUTRITION ANALYSIS
(PER SERVING)

Protein 8 gm., Carbohydrate 72 gm., Fiber 7 gm., Fat 4 gm., Cholesterol 0, Calcium 58 mg., Sodium 268 mg.

Calories 324
From protein: 9%; From carbohydrate: 81%; From fat: 10%

Cake Newton

This cake features a fig filling made with luscious Calimyrna figs.

◆ 20 "NEWTONS" ◆

vegetable oil cooking spray
2 cups whole wheat pastry flour
3/4 cup yellow corn meal
1/3 cup soy grits
1 tsp. baking powder
1 tsp. baking soda
1/2 tsp. salt
1/2 cup prune purée
1 cup Florida Crystals or sugar
1 Tbsp. egg replacer powder
1/4 cup water
1 tsp. vanilla extract
1 cup soymilk lite

FILLING:

8-oz. pkg. Calimyrna figs
1/4 cup frozen apple juice concentrate
1 cup golden raisins
1/2 cup date pieces
1/4 cup prune purée

Preheat oven to 350°. Spray a 9" square baking pan with cooking spray. Mix flour and the following 5 ingredients in a medium bowl. Set aside. Place prune purée in a large bowl, and cream with Florida Crystals. Whisk egg replacer powder with water in a small bowl until foamy. Whisk into the prune mixture along with the vanilla and soymilk. Fold the dry ingredients into the liquid ingredients just until mixed.

Stem figs and slice into thirds. Place sliced figs and remaining filling ingredients in a food processor; process until mixed (filling will be thick). Spoon half of the batter into the pan. Place filling over batter by pressing handfuls together, then gently placing over batter. Filling needn't form a solid covering. Top with remaining batter. Bake 45 to 50 minutes or until tester comes out clean.

NUTRITION ANALYSIS
(PER 3-OUNCE SLICE)

Protein 4 gm., Carbohydrate 43 gm., Fiber 4 gm., Fat 1 gm., Cholesterol 0, Calcium 28 mg., Sodium 153 mg.

Calories 187
From protein: 8%; From carbohydrate: 88%; From fat: 4%

Cherry Truffles

You can make these chewy fudge truffles in advance for a dinner party or just to have a very special treat on hand.

◆ ONE DOZEN TRUFFLES ◆

1 cup dried cherries
1/2 cup date pieces
1/2 cup golden raisins
1/4 cup apricot brandy
1 1/4 cups lite silken tofu (extra firm), drained
1/3 cup prune purée
1/2 cup Liquid Fruitsource or honey or rice syrup
1/3 cup cocoa powder
3 Tbsp. agar flakes
1/2 cup white grape juice concentrate, thawed
1/2 cup whole dry roasted almonds (unsalted)
3/4 cups Sunspire organic dark chocolate chips

TOPPING:

1/4 cup cocoa powder
3 Tbsp. tapioca powder or arrowroot
2 Tbsp. Florida Crystals or sugar
1/2 cup liquid Fruitsource or honey
1 tsp. vanilla extract

Place the first three ingredients in a small saucepan with the brandy. Heat over medium-low heat until the brandy is absorbed. Set aside. Place tofu in food processor, and blend until smooth. Add prune purée, and blend. Place Fruitsource in a small glass measuring cup, and heat 1 minute in the microwave. Whisk in cocoa, and blend to make a smooth syrup. Add to food processor; blend. Whisk agar flakes into juice concentrate. Add to the tofu mixture; blend. Fold tofu mixture into brandied fruit, and mix thoroughly. Add almonds. Fold in chocolate chips. Spoon into 2-inch paper cups, and place in miniature muffin tins or square pans. In a small bowl, mix together cocoa powder, tapioca powder, and Florida Crystals. Place the Fruitsource in a small glass measuring cup; microwave 30 seconds. Whisk into dry ingredients; add vanilla. Spoon topping over truffles and place the truffles in the freezer, uncovered, for at least 2 hours.

NUTRITION ANALYSIS
(PER 2-TRUFFLE SERVING)

Protein 3 gm., Carbohydrate 28 gm., Fiber 2 gm., Fat 4 gm., Cholesterol 0, Calcium 24 mg., Sodium 216 mg.

Calories 155
From protein: 7%; From carbohydrate: 69%; From fat: 24%

Chocolate Almond Fruitcake

A thick fudge glaze accents this festive chocolate cake. Rich with crunchy almonds and brandied fruit, this luscious cake is a welcome finale.

◆ 24 SERVINGS ◆

vegetable oil cooking spray
2 Tbsp. lemon juice
1 1/4 cups soymilk lite
1 cup snipped apricots
1/2 cup golden raisins
1/2 cup apricot brandy
2 1/2 cups whole wheat pastry flour
1/2 cup soy grits
1/4 tsp. salt
1 tsp. cinnamon
1/2 cup unbleached flour
1 cup Wonderslim cocoa
1 1/4 cups lite silken tofu (extra firm), drained
2/3 cup prune purée
1 Tbsp. egg replacer powder
1/4 cup water
1 tsp. vanilla extract
1/2 tsp. almond extract
1/2 cup almond pieces

Preheat oven to 350°. Spray a 9" x 13" baking pan with cooking spray. In a small bowl, add lemon juice to soymilk, and set aside. Combine apricots, raisins, and brandy in a small saucepan. Simmer fruit 3 to 5 minutes, stirring often, until liquid is absorbed; set aside. Mix the next 6 ingredients in a medium bowl; set aside. Place tofu in a food processor and blend. Add prune purée and blend until smooth. In a small bowl, whisk egg replacer with water; add to tofu mixture along with vanilla, soymilk, and almond extract. Fold tofu mixture into dry ingredients. Fold in fruit and almond pieces, just until mixed. Pour into prepared pan. Bake 40 minutes or until toothpick inserted in center comes out clean. Cool completely in pan, and top with Cinnamon Almond Fudge Glaze (recipe and nutrition analysis follow).

Cinnamon Almond Fudge Glaze

Serve this topping with Chocolate Almond Fruitcake.

3 Tbsp. tapioca flour or arrowroot
1/3 cup Wonderslim cocoa
1/2 cup liquid Fruitsource or honey
1 tsp. cinnamon
1 tsp. vanilla extract
1/2 tsp. almond extract

In a small bowl, stir together tapioca flour and cocoa; set aside. Heat Fruitsource 40 seconds in microwave or simmer in saucepan 2 minutes. Whisk hot Fruitsource into cocoa mixture until smooth; whisk in remaining ingredients. Drizzle onto cooled cake.

NUTRITION ANALYSIS
(PER SERVING OF CAKE WITH GLAZE TOPPING)

Protein 6 gm., Carbohydrate 33 gm., Fiber 4 gm., Fat 3 gm., Cholesterol 0, Calcium 22 mg., Sodium 50 mg.

Calories 189
From protein: 14%; From carbohydrate: 72%; From fat: 14%

Chocolate Chip Cranberry Bliss

Dust this luscious cake with powdered sugar or drizzle with Fudgy Chocolate Glaze (page 228).

◆ 16 SERVINGS ◆

vegetable oil cooking spray
1 cup soymilk lite
2 Tbsp. lemon juice
3 cups whole wheat pastry flour
1/4 cup yellow cornmeal
1 tsp. baking soda
1 tsp. baking powder
1/4 tsp. salt
1 tsp. cinnamon
1/2 cup Sunspire organic dark chocolate chips
1/2 cup dried cranberries
1 1/4 cups lite silken tofu (extra firm), drained
1/4 cup unsweetened applesauce
1/4 cup liquid Fruitsource or honey
1 Tbsp. egg replacer powder
1/4 cup water
1 1/2 cups Florida Crystals or sugar
1 tsp. vanilla extract
1/2 tsp. almond extract
1/3 cup almond pieces
1/4 cup soy grits

Preheat oven to 350°. Spray a tube pan with cooking spray. Place soymilk in a small glass measuring cup; add lemon juice. Set aside. Mix together the next 8 ingredients in a large bowl. Set aside. Place tofu in food processor; blend until smooth. Add applesauce and Fruitsource; pulse to mix, then blend. Whisk egg replacer powder with water in a small bowl until foamy. Add to tofu mixture; blend. Add Florida Crystals and extracts, and blend. Fold the liquid ingredients into the dry just until mixed. Mix almond pieces and soy grits in a small bowl. Fold into batter. Do not overbeat. Pour batter into prepared pan. Bake 45 to 50 minutes or until toothpick inserted in center comes out clean. Cool 20 minutes in pan, then remove to rack to finish cooling.

NUTRITION ANALYSIS
(PER SERVING)

Protein 7 gm., Carbohydrate 43 gm., Fiber 4 gm., Fat 5 gm., Cholesterol 0, Calcium 40 mg., Sodium 163 mg.

Calories 232
From protein:12%; From carbohydrate: 70%; From fat:19%

Chocolate Ice Cream

Make this delectable frozen dessert in advance; it's quite rich tasting and very easy to assemble.

◆ 8 SERVINGS ◆

- 1 1/4 cups lite silken tofu (extra firm), drained
- 2 frozen bananas (peel and break into 2-inch pieces before freezing)
- 1/3 cup cocoa powder
- 1/2 cup liquid Fruitsource or honey
- 1 cup white grape juice concentrate, thawed
- 2 rounded Tbsp. agar flakes

Place tofu in food processor, and blend. Add frozen bananas, and blend until smooth. Place cocoa in a small bowl. Warm Fruitsource in a small glass measuring cup for 50 seconds in microwave. Whisk Fruitsource into cocoa to make a smooth syrup. Add syrup to tofu, and blend. Stir agar into juice concentrate. Add to food processor; blend until smooth. Pour mixture into a covered container, and place in the freezer at least 4 hours or overnight.

Remove from freezer. Let stand 15 minutes, then place frozen chunks in food processor. Blend, then return to freezer for at least 2 hours. Serve with Fudgy Chocolate Glaze (page 228).

NUTRITION ANALYSIS
(PER 1/2-CUP SERVING)

Protein 4 gm., Carbohydrate 36 gm., Fiber 2 gm., Fat 1 gm., Cholesterol 0, Calcium 12 mg., Sodium 40 mg.

Calories 159
From protein: 9%; From carbohydrate: 85%; From fat: 6%

Chocolate Chip Cookies

These delicious cookies are moist and bursting with flavor. My son Justin thinks they are terrific!

◆ MORE THAN 7 DOZEN COOKIES ◆

vegetable oil cooking spray
2 1/2 cups whole wheat pastry flour
1/2 cup yellow cornmeal
1 1/2 cups Sucanat or brown sugar
1 tsp. baking soda
1 tsp. baking powder
1 tsp. cinnamon
1/4 tsp. salt
1 1/4 cups lite silken tofu (extra firm), drained
1/3 cup liquid Fruitsource or honey
2 Tbsp. egg replacer powder
1/3 cup water
1/2 cup soymilk lite
1 Tbsp. vanilla extract
1 cup Sunspire organic dark chocolate chips
3/4 cup golden raisins

Preheat oven to 350°. Spray baking sheets with cooking spray. Mix together flour and the following 6 dry ingredients in a large bowl. Set aside. Blend tofu in a food processor. Add Fruitsource. Pulse, then process to blend. Whisk egg replacer powder with water in a small bowl until foamy. Add to the tofu mixture along with soymilk and vanilla. Blend until smooth. Fold the tofu mixture into the dry ingredients. Mix thoroughly. Fold chocolate chips and raisins into cookie batter. Drop by rounded tablespoons onto prepared cookie sheets. Bake 10 minutes or until lightly browned. Cool 1 minute on tray and finish cooling on racks.

NUTRITION ANALYSIS
(PER 2-COOKIE SERVING)

Protein 2 gm., Carbohydrate 19 gm., Fiber 1 gm., Fat 2 gm., Cholesterol 0, Calcium 21 mg., Sodium 85 mg.

Calories 97
From protein: 8%; From carbohydrate: 75%; From fat: 17%

Cranberry Almond Cake

Top off your holiday meal with this moist and marvelous cranberry treat.

◆ 16 SERVINGS ◆

vegetable oil cooking spray
3 cups unbleached flour
3/4 cup yellow cornmeal
1 1/2 tsp. baking soda
2 tsp. baking powder
1/2 tsp. salt
1/3 cup Sucanat or brown sugar
1/3 cup almond pieces
1 1/4 cups lite silken tofu (extra firm), drained
1/2 cup unsweetened applesauce
1 cup soymilk lite
2 cups Florida Crystals or sugar
1 Tbsp. grated orange zest
1 tsp. vanilla extract
1/2 tsp. almond extract
1 cup chopped fresh cranberries

Preheat oven to 350°. Spray a tube pan with cooking spray; lightly flour the pan. In a large bowl, mix together the flour with the following 6 ingredients. Set aside. Place tofu in food processor, and blend. Add the remaining cake ingredients, except cranberries, to the food processor. Blend until smooth. Gently fold tofu mixture into the dry ingredients. Add cranberries. Pour batter into prepared tube pan. Bake 45 minutes or until lightly browned and a toothpick inserted in center comes out clean. Cool 20 minutes in pan and remove to rack to finish cooling.

TOPPING

4 cups cranberries, fresh or frozen
1 1/2 cups orange juice
1 1/2 cups Sucanat or brown sugar
1 tsp. orange blossom water
1 Tbsp. grated orange zest

In a medium saucepan, cook cranberries and orange juice for 15 minutes or until the cranberries begin to loose their shape and thicken. Add remaining ingredients, and simmer 5 minutes. Chill. Topping may be made a day or two in advance.

NUTRITION ANALYSIS (PER SERVING)

Protein 5 gm., Carbohydrate 61 gm., Fiber 3 gm., Fat 2 gm., Cholesterol 0, Calcium 79 mg., Sodium 290 mg.

Calories 282
From protein: 7%; From carbohydrate: 86%; From fat: 7%

Cranberry Oatmeal Cookies

These are great oatmeal cookies, with all the flavor and texture you expect and none of the excess fat or calories. Dried cranberries add a special touch!

◆ 5 1/2 DOZEN COOKIES ◆

vegetable oil cooking spray
2 1/2 cups whole wheat pastry flour
2 cups rolled oats
1 1/2 cups Sucanat or brown sugar
1 tsp. baking soda
1 tsp. baking powder
1 tsp. cinnamon
1/2 tsp. salt
1 1/4 cups lite silken tofu, drained
1/3 cup liquid Fruitsource or honey
1 Tbsp. egg replacer powder
1/4 cup water
1 Tbsp. vanilla extract
1/4 cup soymilk lite
1 Tbsp. canola oil
1 cup dried cranberries
1/3 cup soy grits

Preheat oven to 350°. Spray cookie sheets with cooking spray. Mix together flour with the following 6 ingredients in a large bowl. Set aside. Place tofu in food processor, and blend. Add Fruitsource. Pulse, then blend. Whisk egg replacer with water in a small bowl until foamy. Add to tofu mixture along with vanilla, soymilk, and oil. Blend until smooth. Fold the liquid ingredients into the dry. Add cranberries and soy grits. Mix thoroughly. Drop by rounded tablespoons onto cookie sheets. Bake 10 minutes or until lightly browned. Cool 1 minute on pan, then finish cooling on racks.

NUTRITION ANALYSIS
(PER 2-COOKIE SERVING)

Protein 3 gm., Carbohydrate 21 gm., Fiber 2 gm., Fat 1 gm., Cholesterol 0, Calcium 24 mg., Sodium 107 mg.

Calories 104
From protein: 11%; From carbohydrate: 79%; From fat: 10%

East Indian Spice Cake

This unique and delicious dessert is served with a delightful cream topping.

◆ 12 SERVINGS ◆

vegetable oil cooking spray
3/4 cup soymilk lite
1 Tbsp. lemon juice
1 cup whole wheat pastry flour
1 cup yellow cornmeal
1 cup Sucanat or brown sugar
1 tsp. baking powder
1 1/2 tsp. cinnamon
3/4 tsp. ground cardamom
1/2 tsp. ground ginger
1/4 tsp. ground nutmeg
1/8 tsp. ground cloves
1/4 tsp. salt
1/2 cup lite silken tofu (firm), drained
1/3 cup prune purée
1/3 cup mild molasses
cinnamon
nutmeg

Preheat oven to 350°. Spray an 8" square or round pan with cooking spray. Combine soymilk and lemon juice in small glass measuring cup; set aside. In a large bowl, mix together the next 10 ingredients. Set aside. Place 1/2 cup tofu in food processor, and blend; reserve the remaining tofu. Add prune purée, and blend. Add soymilk and molasses; blend until smooth. Fold tofu mixture into dry ingredients. Pour into prepared pan. Sprinkle with cinnamon and nutmeg. Bake 25 to 30 minutes or until toothpick inserted in center comes out clean.

MOLASSES CREAM TOPPING

3/4 cup lite silken tofu
1/2 cup Veganrella cream cheese (or low-fat cream cheese)
2 Tbsp. mild molasses
1/4 cup Florida Crystals or sugar
1 tsp. vanilla extract

Place tofu in food processor, and blend. Add cream cheese, and blend. Add remaining ingredients, and blend until smooth. Refrigerate until ready to serve.

NUTRITION ANALYSIS (PER SERVING)

Protein 4 gm., Carbohydrate 47 gm., Fiber 2 gm., Fat 3 gm., Cholesterol 0, Calcium 77 mg., Sodium 171 mg.

Calories 227
From protein: 8%; From carbohydrate: 81%; From fat: 11%

Frozen Fudge Cheesecake

Completely dairy-free, this luscious frozen ice cream pie is outstanding!

◆ 16 SERVINGS ◆

NO-BAKE PIE CRUST:

6 1/4-oz. pkg. Health Valley fat-free apple spice cookies

1/2 cup wheat germ

1/4 cup date pieces

1/4 cup frozen apple juice concentrate, thawed

FILLING:

2 1/2 cups lite silken tofu (extra firm), drained

8-oz. pkg. Veganrella or low-fat cream cheese

1/3 cup prune purée

1 cup liquid Fruitsource or honey

1/2 cup cocoa powder

1 Tbsp. vanilla extract

Place cookies in a food processor, and pulse to make crumbs. Add wheat germ, and process to mix. Add date pieces, and process to make a loose crumb. Pour juice concentrate through feed tube; mix thoroughly. Press mixture into a deep dish pie plate to form crust. Refrigerate.

Place tofu in a food processor, and blend until smooth. Add cream cheese, and process. Add prune purée, and process again. Heat Fruitsource in a small saucepan (over low heat for about 3 minutes) or in the microwave (on high for 90 seconds). Remove from heat, and whisk in cocoa powder to make a smooth syrup. Add syrup to tofu mixture along with vanilla. Process thoroughly. Pour into prepared pie crust. If there's any filling left over, pour into freezer pop containers for great fudgesicles! Freeze for at least 4 hours or overnight to give the tofu time to absorb all of the rich flavor.

NUTRITION ANALYSIS
(PER SERVING)

Protein 5 gm., Carbohydrate 32 gm., Fiber 3 gm., Fat 4 gm., Cholesterol 0, Calcium 7 mg., Sodium 100 mg.

Calories 175
From protein: 10%; From carbohydrate: 70%; From fat: 20%

Fudgy Chocolate Walnut Ring

Completely caffeine free, this luscious glazed chocolate cake is lovely garnished with fresh strawberries.

◆ 16 SERVINGS ◆

vegetable oil cooking spray
1 cup soymilk lite
2 Tbsp. lemon juice
2 1/2 cups whole wheat pastry flour
1 3/4 cups Wonderslim Cocoa (see page 28)
1 tsp. baking soda
1 tsp. baking powder
1 tsp. cinnamon
1/4 tsp. salt
1 1/4 cups. pkg. lite silken tofu, firm
1/2 cup unsweetened applesauce
1/4 cup liquid Fruitsource
1 1/2 cups Florida Crystals or sugar
2 tsp. vanilla extract
1 Tbsp. egg replacer
1/4 cup water
1/2 cup walnut pieces*
1/4 cup soy grits (see page 20)

Preheat oven to 350°. Spray a tube pan with cooking spray. Place soymilk in a small bowl or measuring cup; add lemon juice. Set aside. Mix the next 6 ingredients in a large bowl. Set aside. Place tofu in food processor and blend until smooth. Add the next 4 ingredients and pulse to mix, then blend. Whisk egg replacer powder and water in a small bowl until foamy. Add to tofu mixture along with soymilk, and blend thoroughly. Fold liquid ingredients into dry ingredients, just until mixed. Mix together nuts and soy grits; add to batter. Do not overbeat. Pour batter into prepared pan and bake 50 minutes or until tester comes out clean. Cool in pan 20 minutes, then cool completely on rack. Glaze with Fudgy Chocolate Glaze (recipe follows).

*Also delicious with almond pieces. Just add 1/2 teaspoon of almond extract, in addition to the vanilla extract, to the glaze ingredients.

NUTRITION ANALYSIS
(PER SERVING, INCLUDING GLAZE)

Protein 9 gm., Carbohydrate 44 gm., Fiber 3 gm., Fat 4 gm., Cholesterol 0, Calcium 46 mg., Sodium 267 mg.

Calories 238
From protein: 14%; From carbohydrate: 71%; From fat: 15%

Fudgy Chocolate Glaze

This is a quick and easy glaze with a rich chocolate flavor.

3 Tbsp. tapioca flour or arrowroot
1/3 cup Wonderslim cocoa
1/2 cup liquid Fruitsource
1 tsp. vanilla extract

Mix together tapioca flour and cocoa in a small bowl. Set aside. Heat Fruitsource in microwave 40 seconds or until hot (or in saucepan for a minute or so over low heat). Pour hot Fruitsource into cocoa mixture, whisking as you go. Whisk until a smooth syrup is formed and add extract. Cool slightly and drizzle over cooled cake. Refrigerate glazed cake until ready to serve.

Ginger-Spiced Fruit and Nut Bars

Aromatic and flavorful, these cookie bars are chock full of goodness.

◆ 25 COOKIE BARS ◆

vegetable oil cooking spray
1 cup snipped dried apricots
1/3 cup water
1 1/2 cups whole wheat pastry flour
1/4 cup soy flour
1/4 cup yellow cornmeal
1 tsp. baking soda
1 tsp. baking powder
1/4 tsp. salt
1 tsp. cinnamon
1/2 tsp. ground ginger
1/4 tsp. ground allspice
1/4 tsp. ground nutmeg
1/8 tsp. ground cloves
1/3 cup unsweetened applesauce
2 Tbsp. liquid Fruitsource or honey
1 cup Florida Crystals or sugar
1 Tbsp. egg replacer powder
1/4 cup water
1/4 cup soymilk lite
2 tsp. vanilla extract
1 Tbsp grated fresh gingerroot
1 Tbsp. grated lemon zest
3/4 cup dried blueberries
1/3 cup cashew pieces
1/4 cup soy grits

Preheat oven to 350°. Spray a 9" x 13" pan with cooking spray. Place apricots in a small saucepan with water, and bring to a boil. Reduce heat and simmer for 5 minutes, or until all liquid is absorbed. Set aside. Mix together the next 11 ingredients in a medium bowl; set aside. Place applesauce in a large bowl, and mix thoroughly with Fruitsource. Cream applesauce mixture with Florida Crystals. Whisk egg replacer with water in a small bowl until foamy. Whisk into applesauce mixture, then add soymilk, vanilla, gingerroot, and lemon zest. Fold dry ingredients into liquid. Add apricots, blueberries, cashews, and soy grits. Pour batter into prepared pan. Bake 25 minutes or until lightly browned and tester comes out clean.

NUTRITION ANALYSIS
(PER COOKIE BAR)

Protein 2 gm., Carbohydrate 20 gm., Fiber 1 gm., Fat 1 gm., Cholesterol 0, Calcium 21 mg., Sodium 89 mg.

Calories 101
From protein: 9%; From carbohydrate: 78%; From fat: 13%

Glazed Apple Custard Pie

Rich-tasting custard topped with fresh cinnamon-glazed apples makes a lovely presentation in this delightful pie.

◆ 8 SERVINGS ◆

CRUST

6.25-oz. box Health Valley fat-free apple spice cookies
1/2 cup wheat germ
1/4 cup date pieces
1/4 cup frozen apple juice concentrate

Place cookies in food processor, and process to crumb. Add wheat germ, and pulse to mix. Add date pieces, and blend. Add juice concentrate, and process until mixed thoroughly. Press into a deep dish pie plate. Freeze until ready to fill.

FILLING

2 1/2 cups lite silken tofu, drained and patted dry
1/4 tsp. cinnamon
1 Tbsp. vanilla extract
1 cup soymilk lite, separated
3/4 cup frozen apple juice concentrate
2 1/2 Tbsp. agar flakes
1/2 cup maple syrup
vegetable oil cooking spray
3 cups Granny Smith or Pippin apples, peeled and sliced
1 Tbsp. lemon juice

Blend tofu in food processor until smooth. Add cinnamon and vanilla. Set aside. Heat 3/4 cup of soymilk with juice concentrate in a medium saucepan. Whisk agar flakes into remaining 1/4 cup soymilk. Add to saucepan, whisking constantly over medium-low heat. When showing signs of thickening, add to tofu mixture, and blend. Add maple syrup, and mix thoroughly. Pour into pie shell. Spray a 10" frying pan with cooking spray. Cook and carefully stir apple slices over medium heat for 3 minutes. Add lemon juice. When apples are crisp-tender (about 5 to 8 minutes) remove pan from heat, and set aside.

GLAZE

1/2 cup frozen apple juice concentrate, thawed
1/4 tsp. cinnamon
1 1/2 tsp. cornstarch

Combine all glaze ingredients in a medium saucepan over low heat. Whisk constantly for 5 to 8 minutes, or until glaze thickens. Arrange apple slices in a circular pattern over custard, and pour glaze over all. Refrigerate for at least 4 hours or overnight.

NUTRITION ANALYSIS (PER SERVING)

Protein 9 gm., Carbohydrate 70 gm., Fiber 5 gm., Fat 2 gm., Cholesterol 0, Calcium 37 mg., Sodium 135 mg.

Calories 322
From protein: 11%; From carbohydrate: 83%; From fat: 6%

Glazed Chocolate Carrot Cake

Accented by a fudgy chocolate glaze, this cake is fantastic!

◆ 12 SERVINGS ◆

vegetable oil cooking spray
1 cup soymilk lite
2 Tbsp. lemon juice
2 1/2 cups whole wheat pastry flour
1 tsp. baking soda
1 tsp. baking powder
1/2 tsp. salt
1/2 cup unbleached flour
1/2 cup cocoa powder
2 cups Sucanat or brown sugar
1 1/4 cups lite silken tofu (firm), drained
1/2 cup prune purée
2 tsp. vanilla extract
2 cups grated carrots

Preheat oven to 350°. Spray a tube pan with cooking spray. Place soymilk in a small glass measuring cup, and add lemon juice. Stir together whole wheat flour and the next 3 ingredients in a large bowl. Sift the unbleached flour and cocoa into the flour mixture. Add Sucanat. Stir together, then set aside. Place tofu in food processor; blend. Add prune purée, and process. Add vanilla and half of the soymilk; blend. Fold the tofu mixture into the dry ingredients alternately with the remaining soymilk. Pour batter into the prepared pan. Bake for 50 minutes or until toothpick inserted in center comes out clean. Cool 20 minutes in pan; then remove to rack to finish cooling.

GLAZE

3 Tbsp. tapioca flour or arrowroot
1/3 cup liquid Fruitsource or honey
1/4 cup cocoa powder

Place flour in a medium bowl. Set aside. Heat Fruitsource in microwave 20 seconds or in saucepan until hot. Whisk into flour until smooth. Gradually whisk in cocoa until smooth. Let sit 5 minutes. Spoon over cooled cake.

NUTRITION ANALYSIS (PER SERVING)

Protein 7 gm., Carbohydrate 65 gm., Fiber 6 gm., Fat 2 gm., Cholesterol 0, Calcium 73 mg., Sodium 329 mg.

Calories 291
From protein: 10%; From carbohydrate:85%; From fat: 5%

Marie's Incredible Chocolate Brownies

My daughter Kyra's favorite, these outrageous brownies will disappear as fast as you make them.

◆ 30 BROWNIES ◆

- vegetable oil cooking spray
- 2 Tbsp. lemon juice
- 1 1/2 cups soymilk lite
- 2 cups unbleached flour
- 2 tsp. baking soda
- 2 tsp. baking powder
- 2 cups Wonderslim cocoa powder
- 1/2 tsp. salt
- 3 cups Sucanat or brown sugar
- 1 1/4 cups lite silken tofu (firm or extra firm), drained
- 1 3/4 cup prune purée
- 1 Tbsp. vanilla extract
- 1/2 cup walnut pieces

Preheat oven to 350°. Spray a 9" x 13" baking pan with cooking spray. In a glass measuring cup, add lemon juice to soymilk; set aside. In a large bowl, stir together the next 6 ingredients. Set aside. Purée the tofu in a food processor or blender until smooth. Add prune purée, and blend. Add one cup of the soymilk along with the vanilla extract; blend. Add the tofu mixture to the dry ingredients alternately with the reserved 1/2 cup of soymilk; mix thoroughly. Fold in walnut pieces. Pour batter into prepared pan. Bake 40 to 45 minutes.

NUTRITION ANALYSIS
(PER SERVING)

Protein 2 gm., Carbohydrate 30 gm., Fiber 1 gm., Fat 2 gm., Cholesterol 0, Calcium 42 mg., Sodium 204 mg.

Calories 141
From protein: 6%; From carbohydrate: 82%; From fat: 12%

Lemon Blueberry Delite

Sweet dried blueberries are suspended in a lovely lemon cake with a luscious blueberry topping–superb!

◆ 12 SERVINGS ◆

vegetable oil cooking spray
1 cup soymilk lite
2 Tbsp. lemon juice
3 cups unbleached flour
1 1/2 tsp. baking soda
1 tsp. baking powder
1/2 tsp. salt
1 1/4 cups lite silken tofu (firm), drained
1/2 cup unsweetened applesauce
3 Tbsp. lemon juice
1 Tbsp. grated lemon zest
1/4 tsp. lemon extract
1 tsp. vanilla extract
1 1/2 cups Florida Crystals or sugar
2/3 cup dried blueberries

Preheat oven to 350°. Spray a tube pan with cooking spray. Place soymilk in a small glass measuring cup; add lemon juice, and set aside. Sift flour with the next 3 ingredients in a large bowl. Set aside. Place tofu in food processor, and blend. Add the next 5 ingredients, and process. Add Florida Crystals, and blend until smooth. Fold tofu mixture into the dry ingredients alternately with the soymilk, just until mixed. Fold in blueberries, being careful not to overmix. Bake 45 to 50 minutes or until a toothpick inserted comes out clean. Cool 20 minutes in the pan, then remove onto a rack to complete cooling. Serve with Lemon Blueberry Delite Topping (recipe follows).

NUTRITION ANALYSIS
(PER SERVING, INCLUDING TOPPING)

Protein 6 gm., Carbohydrate 62 gm., Fiber 2 gm., Fat 1 gm., Cholesterol 0, Calcium 40 mg., Sodium 314 mg.

Calories 278
From protein: 8%; From carbohydrate: 89%; From fat: 3%

Lemon Blueberry Delite Topping

◆ 3 CUPS ◆

6-oz. pkg. fresh blueberries (1 1/2 cups)
1 cup white grape juice concentrate, thawed
1/2 cup Florida Crystals or sugar
1/4 tsp. lemon extract
1 tsp. grated lemon zest
2 Tbsp. cornstarch
3 Tbsp. cold water

Rinse blueberries. Place berries and juice concentrate in a medium saucepan over medium heat. Bring to a boil, then add the next 3 ingredients. Cook for 10 minutes or until berries soften and the mixture is dark. Combine the cornstarch and water in a small bowl. Add to the blueberries. Reduce heat, and simmer for 10 to 12 minutes or until sauce is thickened. Refrigerate until ready to use. Spoon over a slice of Lemon Blueberry Delite cake or any dessert that would be complemented by blueberries.

NUTRITION ANALYSIS
(PER 2-OZ. SERVING)

Protein 0, Carbohydrate 16 gm., Fiber 1 gm., Fat 0, Cholesterol 0, Calcium 4 mg., Sodium 3 mg.

Calories 61
From protein: 2%; From carbohydrate: 96%; From fat: 2%

Middle Eastern "Honey" Cake

This delicious cake fills the house with the heady aroma of roses.

◆ 24 SERVINGS ◆

vegetable oil cooking spray
3 cups unbleached flour
1 1/2 tsp. baking powder
1 tsp. baking soda
1 tsp. cinnamon
1/2 tsp. salt
1 1/2 cups Sucanat or brown sugar
1 1/4 cups lite silken tofu (extra firm), drained
1 cup prune purée
3/4 cup liquid Fruitsource or honey
1 Tbsp. grated orange zest
2 tsp. rose water
1/3 cup soymilk lite
1/2 cup walnut pieces

Preheat oven to 350°. Spray a 9" x 13" pan with cooking spray. Combine flour with the next 5 ingredients in a large bowl. Place tofu in food processor; blend until smooth. Add prune purée, and blend. Add Fruitsource, orange zest, and rose water; blend. Add tofu mixture to dry ingredients alternately with the soymilk. Fold in walnuts. Pour into prepared pan. Bake 45 minutes or until toothpick inserted in the center comes out clean.

NUTRITION ANALYSIS
(PER SERVING)

Protein 3 gm., Carbohydrate 34 gm., Fiber 1 gm., Fat 2 gm., Cholesterol 0, Calcium 37 mg., Sodium 163 mg.

Calories 162
From protein: 7%; From carbohydrate: 82%; From fat: 10%

Mocha Mousse Magic

This smooth, rich-tasting dessert mousse is elegant.

◆ 12 SERVINGS ◆

2 1/2 cups lite silken tofu (firm), drained

8-oz. pkg. Veganrella cream cheese or low-fat cream cheese

2 frozen bananas

3/4 cup liquid Fruitsource or honey

1/3 cup cocoa powder

1 Tbsp. vanilla extract

1/2 cup cold soymilk lite

2 Tbsp. agar flakes

1/2 cup Florida Crystals or sugar

1/2 cup strong coffee (cold)

1/3 cup Sunspire Crystal dark chocolate chips (optional)

Place drained tofu in food processor; blend. Add cream cheese, and blend. Break frozen bananas into 3-inch chunks, and add to blended tofu. Pulse to break up chunks, then blend. Heat Fruitsource in microwave for 45 seconds or in a saucepan for 2 minutes over low heat. Place cocoa in a small bowl. Whisk in hot Fruitsource and vanilla. Add syrup to tofu mixture, and blend. Place soymilk in a small microwave-safe bowl or saucepan. Stir in agar, and heat mixture just to the boiling point. Add to tofu mixture along with Florida Crystals and coffee. Add chocolate chips, and pulse just to mix. Pour mousse into a covered container, and freeze overnight.

When ready to serve, use a knife to cut chunks out of frozen mixture. Remove only what you will be serving, and return remainder to freezer. Place chunks in food processor, and pulse, then process to blend to a mousse-like consistency. Serve immediately. Garnish with fresh mint leaves if desired.

NUTRITION ANALYSIS
(PER SERVING)

Protein 5 gm., Carbohydrate 27 gm., Fiber 1 gm., Fat 5 gm., Cholesterol 0, Calcium 5 mg., Sodium 108 mg.

Calories 166
From protein: 10%; From carbohydrate: 63%; From fat: 27%

Orange Blossom Pecan Cake

The scent of orange blossoms fills the house while this cake bakes. Dust with powdered sugar and garnish with edible flowers for a very special presentation.

◆ 12 SERVINGS ◆

- vegetable oil cooking spray
- 2 cups whole wheat pastry flour
- 1/3 cup soy flour
- 1/2 cup yellow cornmeal
- 1 tsp. baking soda
- 1 tsp. baking powder
- 1 tsp. cinnamon
- 1/4 tsp. salt
- 1 1/2 cups Sucanat or brown sugar
- 1 1/4 cups lite silken tofu (firm), drained
- 1/2 cup unsweetened applesauce
- 1/3 cup liquid Fruitsource or honey
- 1/2 cup orange juice (preferably fresh squeezed)
- 2 tsp. orange zest
- 1 tsp. orange blossom water
- 1 tsp. vanilla extract
- 1 Tbsp. egg replacer powder
- 1/4 cup water
- 1/4 cup soymilk lite
- 1/3 cup pecan pieces
- 1/4 cup soy grits

Preheat oven to 350° Spray a tube pan with cooking spray. Mix flour with the next 7 ingredients in a large bowl. Set aside. Place tofu in food processor, and blend. Add applesauce and Fruitsource. Pulse to mix, then blend. Add the next 4 ingredients, and process. Whisk egg replacer with water in a small bowl. Add to tofu mixture. Fold the liquid ingredients into dry alternately with soymilk. Mix pecan pieces with soy grits, and fold quickly into batter. Pour into prepared pan. Bake 45 minutes or until tester comes out clean. Cool in pan 20 minutes; remove to rack to finish cooling. Dust with powdered sugar before serving.

NUTRITION ANALYSIS
(PER SERVING)

Protein 7 gm., Carbohydrate 47 gm., Fiber 4 gm., Fat 4 gm., Cholesterol 0, Calcium 66 mg., Sodium 251 mg.

Calories 245
From protein: 11%; From carbohydrate: 74%; From fat: 15%

Peach Ice Dream

You'll love the brandied peaches and creamy texture of this dairy-free confection.

◆ 8 SERVINGS ◆

16-oz. pkg. frozen peaches
1/4 cup peach brandy
1 1/4 cups lite silken tofu (firm), drained
1 cup apple juice concentrate, thawed
2 rounded Tbsp. agar flakes
1/2 tsp. almond extract
1/2 cup maple syrup

Heat peaches in a medium saucepan over medium heat. When thawed, add brandy, and continue to cook over low heat until liquid is absorbed. Blend tofu in food processor. Add peaches to tofu, and blend. Whisk agar flakes into juice concentrate. Add to tofu mixture. Add almond extract and maple syrup, and blend. Pour into a covered container, and freeze at least 4 hours or overnight.

Remove from freezer, and let sit 15 minutes. Place frozen chunks in food processor, and blend until smooth. Return to freezer for 4 hours or overnight. Serve garnished with mint leaves.

NUTRITION ANALYSIS
(PER 5 1/4-OUNCE SERVING)

Protein 3 gm., Carbohydrate 28 gm., Fiber 1 gm., Fat 1 gm., Cholesterol 0, Calcium 19 mg., Sodium 46 mg.

Calories 142
From protein: 9%; From carbohydrate: 79%; From fat: 4%

Pumpkin Cranberry Ring

Cranberries add a piquant sweetness to this moist pumpkin cake.

◆ 12 SERVINGS ◆

vegetable oil cooking spray
2 cups whole wheat pastry flour
1/2 cup soy flour
1 1/2 cups Sucanat or brown sugar
1 tsp. baking powder
1 tsp. baking soda
1 tsp. cinnamon
1 tsp. ground ginger
1/2 tsp. ground nutmeg
1/4 tsp. ground cloves
1/2 tsp. salt
1 1/4 cups lite silken tofu (extra firm), drained
1/2 cup prune purée
1 cup canned pumpkin
1/4 cup liquid Fruitsource or honey
1 tsp. vanilla extract
1 Tbsp. egg replacer powder
1/4 cup water
3/4 cup soymilk lite
1 cup dried cranberries

Preheat oven to 350.° Spray a tube pan with cooking spray. Mix together the first 10 ingredients in a medium bowl. Place tofu in food processor, and blend. Add prune purée and pumpkin; blend. Add Fruitsource and vanilla; pulse to mix, then blend. Whisk egg replacer and water in a small bowl until foamy. Add to tofu mixture along with soymilk, and blend until smooth. Fold liquid ingredients into dry, just until mixed. Fold in cranberries. Bake 50 minutes or until toothpick inserted comes out clean. Cool 20 minutes in pan; remove to rack to finish cooling. Dust with powdered sugar.

NUTRITION ANALYSIS
(PER SERVING)

Protein 6 gm., Carbohydrate 56 gm., Fiber 4 gm., Fat 2 gm., Cholesterol 0, Calcium 73 mg., Sodium 309 mg.

Calories 255
From protein: 10%; From carbohydrate: 85%; From fat: 6%

Pumpkin Fudge Brownies

Pumpkin brownies with chocolate fudge swirls deliver exceptional flavor, texture, and nutrition.

◆ 30 BROWNIES ◆

vegetable oil cooking spray
1 cup soymilk lite
2 Tbsp. lemon juice
2 1/2 cups unbleached flour
1/2 cup oat bran
1 tsp. baking soda
1 tsp. baking powder
1/2 tsp. salt
1 tsp. cinnamon
1/4 tsp. ground nutmeg
1 tsp. ground ginger
1/8 tsp. ground cloves
2 cups Sucanat or brown sugar
1 1/4 cups lite silken tofu (extra firm), drained
2/3 cup prune purée
2/3 cup canned pumpkin
2 tsp. vanilla extract, separated
1/4 cup boiling water
1/4 cup cocoa powder
1 Tbsp. liquid Fruitsource or honey

Preheat oven to 350°. Spray a 9" x 13" baking pan with cooking spray. Place soymilk in a glass measuring cup. Add lemon juice, and set aside. In a large bowl, stir together the next 10 ingredients, and set aside. Place tofu in food processor and blend. Add prune purée and pumpkin; process. Add soymilk and 1 teaspoon of vanilla. Blend until smooth. Fold the tofu mixture into the dry ingredients. Remove 1 1/2 cups of the batter to a medium bowl. Whisk together boiling water and cocoa. Blend the remaining teaspoon of vanilla along with Fruitsource into the cocoa mixture. Fold cocoa mixture into the 1 1/2 cups of reserved batter.

Spread two-thirds of the pumpkin batter on the bottom of the prepared pan. Spoon dollops of the fudge batter on top, leaving spaces between dollops. Spoon dollops of the remaining pumpkin batter in an alternating fudge-pumpkin pattern. Run a butter knife through the batters to form a swirling marble pattern. Bake 30 minutes. Cool and cut into squares.

NUTRITION ANALYSIS
(PER SERVING)

Protein 2 gm., Carbohydrate 24 gm., Fiber 1 gm., Fat 1 gm., Cholesterol 0, Calcium 28 mg., Sodium 130 mg.

Calories 106
From protein: 9%; From carbohydrate: 87%; From fat: 4%

Spiced Fruitcake

This special party cake is topped with a creamy vanilla icing and filled with brandied apricots, date pieces, and chopped walnuts.

◆ 16 SERVINGS ◆

vegetable oil cooking spray
1 cup apricots, snipped
1/2 cup apricot brandy
1 cup soymilk lite
2 Tbsp. lemon juice
3 cups whole wheat pastry flour
1/2 cup wheat germ
1 tsp. baking soda
1 tsp. baking powder
1/4 tsp. salt
2 tsp. cinnamon
1/4 tsp. ground nutmeg
1 /14 cups lite silken tofu (firm), drained
2 cups brown sugar
2 tsp. vanilla extract
1/2 cup unsweetened applesauce
1/2 cup prune purée
1/2 cup date pieces
1/3 cup chopped pecans

Preheat oven to 350°. Spray a 9" x 13" pan with cooking spray. Place the apricots in a small saucepan, stir in brandy, and bring to a low boil over medium heat. Reduce heat, and simmer until brandy is absorbed (about 5 minutes). Pour soymilk into a glass measuring cup, and add lemon juice. Set aside. Stir together the next 7 ingredients in a large bowl. Set aside. Blend the tofu in a food processor until smooth. Add soymilk, brown sugar, vanilla, applesauce, and prune purée. Blend. Fold the tofu mixture into the dry ingredients. Fold the brandied apricots into the batter, along with dates and pecans. Pour into the prepared pan. Bake for 35 minutes or until a toothpick inserted in the center comes out clean. Cool in pan and top with Creamy Vanilla Icing (recipe follows).

NUTRITION ANALYSIS
(PER SERVING—WITH ICING)

Protein 7 gm., Carbohydrate 60 gm., Fiber 5 gm., Fat 3 gm., Cholesterol 0, Calcium 47 mg., Sodium 156 mg.

Calories 295
From protein: 10%; From carbohydrate: 81%; From fat: 9%

Creamy Vanilla Icing

This rich tasting frosting has a cream cheese frosting consistency, and is very attractive garnished with fruit.

◆ 2 3/4 CUPS ◆

- 1/2 cup frozen apple juice concentrate
- 3 Tbsp. agar flakes
- 1 1/4 cups lite silken tofu (firm or extra firm), drained
- 1 tsp. grated lemon zest
- 1 Tbsp. lemon juice
- 1 tsp. vanilla extract
- 1/3 cup liquid Fruitsource or honey

Place juice concentrate in a small saucepan; add agar flakes, and bring to a low boil over medium heat, stirring until dissolved. Lower heat and simmer, stirring frequently, until thickened, about 5 minutes. Place tofu in food processor, and blend until smooth. Add lemon zest, lemon juice, vanilla, and Fruitsource. Process until smooth, scraping down once or twice. Add thickened juice concentrate, and blend until smooth. Frost cake, and decorate with sliced strawberries, saving a berry with greens intact for the center.

NUTRITION ANALYSIS
(PER SERVING—ICING ONLY)

Protein 1 gm., Carbohydrate 8 gm., Fiber 0, Fat 0,
Cholesterol 0, Calcium 3 mg., Sodium 20 mg.

Calories 295
From protein: 14%; From carbohydrate: 80%; From fat: 6%

Resource Guide

Flours, grains, and natural foods products—
Arrowhead Mills
Box 2059
Hereford, TX 79045
(806) 364-0730

EnerG® egg replacer, tapioca flour, and allergy free products—
EnerG Foods, Inc.
500 First Ave. South
P.O. Box 84487
Seattle, WA 98124-5787
(800) 331-5222

Fruitsource natural sweetener and fat replacer—
Fruitsource
1803 Mission St., Ste. 404
Santa Cruz, CA 95060
(408) 464-9891

TVP in styles that include beef and chicken, ground, chunks, and strips; also a variety of natural food products, all available by catalog—
Harvest Direct
505 West Depot Ave.
Knoxville, TN 37917
(800) 835-2867

Soya Granules (soy grits)—
Fearn Natural Foods
3015 West Vera Ave
Milwaukee, WI 53209
(414) 352-3333

Dairy free products, including Rice Dream, original and vanilla rice milk—
Imagine Foods
350 Cambridge Ave., Ste. 350
Palo Alto, CA 94306
(800) 333-6339

Flour, tools, equipment, and books—
The Baker's Catalog
King Arthur Flour
P.O. Box 876
Norwich, VT 05055-0876
(800) 827-6836

Variety of soy-based products, including tempeh, deli slices, and Gimme Lean—
Lightlife Foods, Inc.
P.O. Box 870
Greenfield, MA 01302
(800) 274-6001

Bragg Liquid Aminos—
Live Food Products
P.O. Box 7
Santa Barbara, CA 93102
(805) 968-1028

TVP granules, chunks, and flakes, and organic granules and 1/2-inch chunks—
The Mail Order Catalogue
Box 180
Summertown, TN 38483
(800) 695-2241

Mori Nu Silken Tofu Lite—
Morinaga Nutritional Foods, Inc.
2050 West 190th St., Ste. 110
Torrance, CA 90504
(310) 787-0200

Tofu-based dressings and Nayonaise—
Nasoya Foods, Inc.
Loeminster, MA 01453
(800) 229-TOFU

Florida Crystals, less-refined cane sugar products—
The Natural Source
2200 Front St.
Melbourne, FL 32901
(800) 784-2721

Soy Boy Ravioli and Not Dogs—
Northern Soy, Inc.
545 West Ave.
Rochester, NY 14611-2424
(716) 235-8970

Sucanat unrefined cane sugar—
Sucanat North America Corp.
26 Clinton Drive, #117
Hollis, NH 03049
(603) 595-2922

The Soy Deli, reduced-fat soyfoods made with organic soybeans—
Quong Hop & Co.
161 Beacon St.
S. San Francisco, CA 94080
(415) 761-2002

Veganrella cream cheese alternative—
Sharon's Finest
P.O. Box 5020
Santa Rosa, CA 95402
(707) 576-7050

Variety of salad dressings made with soy—
Simply Delicious, Inc.
8411 Hwy. NC 86 North
Cedar Grove, NC 27231
(919) 732-5294

Prune purée products—
Sokol and Co.
5315 Dansher Rd.
Countryside, IL 60525
(708) 482-8250

Confections, including organic dark chocolate chips—
Sunspire
2114 Adams Ave.
San Leandro, CA 94577
(510) 569-9731

Variety of soy products, including Ready Ground Tofu and Savory Tofu—
Tree of Life
1750 Tree Blvd.
P.O. Box 410
St. Augustine, FL 32085-0410
(904) 825-2009

Variety of natural deli and tofu products—
Wildwood Natural Foods
135 Bolinas Rd.
Fairfax, CA 94930
(800) 499-TOFU (8638)

Variety of natural and organic foods, including Soymilk Lite—
Westbrae Natural Foods
1065 Walnut
Carson, CA 90746
(800) SOYMILK

Yves Canadian veggie bacon, veggie burgers, etc.—
Yves Veggie Cuisine
1138 East Georgia Street
Vancouver, BC V6A 2A8 Canada
(604) 251-1345

Recommended Reading

Barnard, Neal. *The Power of Your Plate.* Summertown, TN: The Book Publishing Company, 1990.

Barnard, Neal. *Food for Life.* New York: Harmony Books, 1993.

Barnard, Neal. *Eat Right Live Longer.* New York: Harmony Books, 1995.

Messina, Mark and Messina, Virginia. *The Simple Soybean and Your Health.* New York: Avery Publishing Group, 1994.

Messina, Virginia and Messina, Mark. *The Vegetarian Way.* New York: Crown Books, 1996.

McDougall, John. *The McDougall Program.* New York: Plume Books, 1991.

McDougall, John and McDougall, Mary. *The New McDougall Cookbook.* New York: Dutton, 1993.

McDougall, John. *The McDougall Program for a Healthy Heart.* New York: Dutton, 1996.

Ornish, Dean. *Dr. Dean Ornish's Program for Reversing Heart Disease.* New York: Random House, 1990.

Ornish, Dean. *Eat More, Weigh Less.* New York: HarperCollins, 1993.

Ornish, Dean. *Everyday Cooking with Dr. Dean Ornish.* New York: HarperCollins, 1996.

Robbins, John. *Diet For A New America.* Walpole, NH: Stillpoint Publishing, 1987.

Robbins, John. *May All Be Fed.* New York: William Morrow and Co., 1992.

Shurtleff, William and Aoyagi, Akiko. *The Book of Tofu.* New York: Ballantine Books, 1979.

Shurtleff, William and Aoyagi, Akiko. *The Book of Miso.* New York: Ballantine Books, 1981.

Bibliography

Akizuki, Tatsuichiro. (translated by Herman Aihara): *Macrobiotic Monthly* 1968; 8(5):6-12.

Akizuki, Tatsuichiro. *Physical Constitution and Food: The Way to Health.* Tokyo: Kurei Shuppan-bu, 1980.

Akizuki, Tatsuichiro: How we survived Nagasaki. *East West Journal* 1980; Dec.: 10, 12-13.

Anderson, J.J.; Ambrose, W.W.; Garner, S.C.: Orally dosed genestein from soy and prevention of canellous bone loss in two ovariectomized rat models. *Journal of Nutrition* 1995; 125(3S):799S.

Anderson, James W.; Johnstone Bryan M.; Cook-Newell, Margaret E.: Meta-analysis of soy protein intake on serum lipids. *New England Journal of Medicine* 1995; 333(5): 276-82. March supplement.

Anthony, M.S.; Clarkson, T.B.; Weddle, D.L.; Wolfe, M.S.: Effects of soy protein phytoestrogens on cardiovascular risk factors in rhesus monkeys. *Journal of Nutrition* 1995;125(3S): 803S-04S. March supplement.

Barnard, Neal. *Food for Life.* New York: Harmony Books, 1993.

Barnard, Neal. *Eat Right Live Longer.* New York: Harmony Books, 1995.

Barnard, Neal: Hormone replacement increases cancer risk. *Good Medicine* 1995; 4(3):14-15.

Barnes, Stephan: Effect of genestein on in vitro and in vivo models on cancer. *Journal of Nutrition* 1995; 125(3S):771S-76S. March supplement.

Barnes, Stephan; Peterson, Greg, T: Biochemical targets of the isoflavone genistein in tumor cell lines. *Proceedings of the Society for Experimental Biology and Medicine* 1995; 208(1):103-08.

Campbell, Colin: The latest from the China diet and health study. *Good Medicine* 1995; 3(3):10-14.

Constantinou, A.; Huberman, E.: Genistein as an inducer of tumor cell differentiation: possible mechinisms for action. *Proceedings of the Society for Experimental Biology and Medicine* 1995; 208(1):109-15.

Fotsis, T.; Pepper, M; Aldercreutz, H; Hase, T.; Montesano, R.; Schweigerer, L.: Genistein, a dietary ingested isoflavanoid, inhibits cell proliferation and in vitro angiogenesis and angiogenic diseases. *Journal of Nutrition* 1995; 125(3S): 800S. March supplement.

Giovannucci, E.; et al.: Intake of carotenoids and retinol in relation to risk of prostate cancer. *Journal of the National Cancer Institute* 1995; 87:1767-76.

Hartwell, Jonathon L.: Plants used against cancer: a survey. *Lloydia* 1967-1971; 30(4):379-46; 31(2):71-170; 32(1):79-107; 32(2):153-205; 32(3):247-96; 33(1):97-194; 33(3):288-392.

Herman, Aldercreutz, T; Goldin, B.R.; Gorbach, S.L.; et al.: Soybean phytoestrogens intake and cancer risk. *Journal of Nutrition* 1995; 125(3S):757S-770S. March supplement.

Kennedy, Ann R.: The evidence for soybean products as cancer preventive agents. *Journal of Nutrition* 1995; 125(3S):733S-43S. March supplement.

McDougall, John; Litzau, K; Haver, E; Saunders, V; Spiller, G.: Rapid reduction of serum cholesterol and blood pressure by a twelve day, very low fat, strictly vegetarian diet. *Journal of the American College of Nutrition* 1995; 14:491-96.

Messina, Mark; Messina, Virginia; Setchell, Kenneth R. *The Simple Soybean and Your Health.* Garden City Park, NY: Avery Publishing Group, Inc., 1994.

Messina M.; Erdman Jr., J., eds: First international symposium on the role of soy in preventing and treating chronic disease. *Journal of Nutrition* .1994; 125(3S):677S-808S. March supplement.

Messina, M.: Putting protein in perspective. *The Soy Connection* (United Soybean Board). 1994; 2(1):1-2.

Messina, M.: Fiber, soyfoods, and health. *The Soy Connection* (United Soybean Board). 1995; 3(2):1-2.

Messina, M.; Messina, V.: Soybeans linked to health benefits. *Vegetarian Voice* 1995; 20(4):10-11.

Mindell, Earl. *Earl Mindell's Food as Medicine.* New York: Simon & Schuster (A Fireside Book), 1994.

Mindell, Earl. *Earl Mindell's Soy Miracle.* New York: Simon & Schuster (A Fireside Book), 1995.

Molteni, Agostino; Brizio-Molteni, L.; Persky. V. In vitro hormonal effects of soybean isoflavones. *Journal of Nutrition 1*995; 125(3S):751S-770S. March supplement.

Northrup, Christiane. *Heal Your Symptoms Naturally.* Potomoc, MD: Phillips Publishing Inc., 1995.

Northrup, Christiane: Should you switch to a natural estrogen? *Health Wisdom For Women* 1995; 2(10):1-3.

Ornish, Dean. *Dr. Dean Ornish's Program For Reversing Heart Disease.* New York: Random House, 1990.

Ornish, Dean. *Eat More, Weigh Less.* New York: Harper Collins, 1993.

Peterson, Greg: Evaluation of the biochemical targets of genistein in tumor cells. *Journal of Nutrition* 1995; 125(3S):790S-97S. March supplement.

Petrakis, N.; Wiencke, J.; Coward, L.; Kirk, M.; Barnes, S.: A clinical trial of the chemoprotective effect of a soy beverage on women at high risk for breast cancer. *Journal of Nutrition* 1995; 125(3S):800S. March supplement.

Setchell, K.D.R.; Borriello, S.P.; Hulme, P; et al.: Nonsteroidal estrogens of dietary origin; possible roles in hormone dependent disease. *American Journal of Clinical Nutrition* 1984; 40(3):569-78.

Slavin, Joanne, L.: Health benefits of soy fiber. *The Soy Connection* (United Soybean Board) 1995; 3(2)1-4.

Steele, Vernon E., ; Pereira, M.A.; Sigman, C.C.; Kelloff, G.J.: Cancer chemoprevention agent development strategies for genistein. *Journal of Nutrition* 1995; 125(3S):713S-16S. March supplement.

Tufts University Diet and Nutrition Newsletter. Scientists spotlight phytoestrogens for better health. 1995; 12(2):3-6.

Urban, D. Grizzie, W.E.; Coward, L.; Kirk, M.; Barnes, S.: A clinical trial of the chemopreventive effect of soy beverage on men at high risk for prostate cancer. *Journal of Nutrition* 1995; 125(3S):800S.

Wei, Huachen; Ronald, Cai, Quiyin; Barnes, S; Wang, Y.: Antioxidant and antipromotional effects of the soybean isoflavone genistein. *Proceedings of the Society for Experimental Biology and Medicine* 1995; S208(1):124-30.

Zava, David T.: The phytoestrogen paradox. *The Soy Connection* (United Soybean board) 1994; 3(1):1, 4.

Index